D1301702

This Book
Donated By

Books by Yolande Donlan
Sand in My Mink

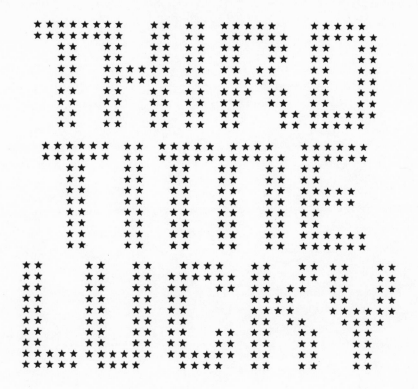

THIRD TIME LUCKY?

by Yolande Donlan

The Dial Press / James Wade
1976 New York

Manufactured in the United States of America

First printing

Library of Congress Cataloging in Publication Data

Donlan, Yolande, 1920–
  Third time lucky.

  1. Donlan, Yolande, 1920– I. Title.
PN2287.D52A32   792'.028'0924 [B]   75-45161
ISBN 0-8037-7780-9

For Val, Dorothy Casey, and George Greenfield,
without whose encouragement
there would be one less book in the world

THIRD
TIME
LUCKY

Daddy's Hollywood funeral was fabulous, stupendous, gigantic, and typical of the not-so-Golden Era. My "Loved One" lay in state with rose-painted cheeks like Mary Pickford in an open wooden coffin.

According to *Variety* he was James Donlan, a forty-nine-year-old dead film actor. And he was having a funeral service at Pierce Brothers' Mortuary, Hollywood, California. But, according to me standing there, he was in a coffin too small for his head. Or, perhaps, being an actor, his head was too big for his coffin. Whatever the problem, his head was up at one end as if to take one last look at the audience.

It wasn't a bad house either, for Hollywood, June 1938. Sprinkled between the chorus girls, agents, and film directors were a collection of Harold Lloyds, Clark Gables, Gary Coopers, James Gleasons, various Barrymores, and other people he'd worked with. The stars who were busy making movies sent wreathes—including Dracula, who acted under the name of Bela Lugosi. In fact, there were so many flowers it looked like a funeral parlor. Bob Hope sent some too, or else his agent Louis Shurr did it for him. Who knows?

I had graduated not long before from the Immaculate Heart Convent and was now dancing around Bob Hope in a stage operetta called *Roberta*. He wasn't the film Bob Hope yet, but about to be. In those days he was a stage star and always seemed kind and pleasant to us dancers. It was nice of him, or whoever it was, to send flowers to the funeral of a chorus girl's father whom he didn't know.

Now, where were we? Oh, yes, that damn funeral. The show must go on. That's what Daddy used to say and also that I was to follow in his footsteps in the trouper's tradition and become a star actor—I mean actress. But now Daddy's big trap was shut forever, I thought. I stood there, stared at him, and felt nothing. I was yet to learn that true grief is not unlike a stone. The Catholic priest who had never met James Donlan alive was babbling on about him dead. The priest didn't mention that his Catholic Church had refused to have a funeral mass said in it because James Donlan, while still alive, had lapsed and was therefore in a state of mortal sin. The last time I had seen my old man he was full of booze and in no state to commit any sin, mortal or venial, except to roar at me like the MGM lion.

He had come to see me in my first job as a chorus girl in the stage revival of the operetta *New Moon*, directed by its author, the legendary Sigmund Romberg. After the show we had stopped at a bar restaurant where Daddy, dear Daddy, drank huge whiskies and I ate huge steaks.

"My God, you even eat like a chorus girl," he bellowed. "They're always hungry. I've told you before, once a chorus girl always a chorus girl. With the Donlan talent you should be acting!"

The Donlan talent that was sitting opposite me was bleary-eyed, bloated, and poached. His swollen hands clutched the whisky and the water chaser. He always sipped his whisky as if it were medicine, grimacing with every swallow and afterward letting out a gasping cough. Maybe it was the water that caused this. It was the only time he ever swallowed water. He agreed implicitly with W. C. Fields who said, "Water? I could never touch water—fish fuck in it." Well, that wasn't my old man's problem now. So, while the dogmatic priest ranted on about life and death, I slipped my prayerbook and rosary on to Daddy's now dealcoholized chest. His need for these Hereafter props looked more immediate than mine.

When the funeral was over the audience returned to their Beverly Hills mansions. My mother, the widow who had divorced him years before, and I followed the luxurious black hearse in a luxurious black limousine to the Calvary Cemetery in Los Angeles. With great dignity the chauffeur drove us past the iron gates and down the well-kept roads, through acres and acres of lawns covered with statues and headstones and mausoleums. At the end of the winding road was a patch of ground with no headstones, no nothing. It was called the Paupers' Graveyard. James Donlan, dead film actor, was lowered into Grave 9, Lot 535 and covered with massive wreaths of flowers sent by donors from Hollywood's Golden Era. His final exit had been paid for by the Screen Actors Benevolent Fund. He died broke, buried by the charity to which he had contributed during his more lucrative years. It was the same charity for which Frank Sinatra was to give the first of his farewell concerts exactly thirty-three Junes later—1971.

On that June evening in 1938 I went back to work dancing around Bob Hope. I had to. It was dough. Mr. Hope made funny wisecracks and I paid attention and watched him so that I could learn how to do it. I was Daddy now.

I made my first professional appearance stark naked in a Los Angeles nightclub in the roaring twenties. It was New Year's Eve. I was three years old and my French mother, Thérèse, a frustrated opera singer, was singing in the club and as I couldn't be left alone she took me along. As the midnight bells rang out, an unemployed, bent actor hobbled across the stage as Old Father Time and I came on as chirping Baby New Year. Bare, except for a ribbon across my chest saying "Happy New Year," I found it most embarrassing. It was long before the days of frontal nudity.

Mother's theatrical ambition had always led her into trouble. That's how she found my father. He was a successful actor-manager of the Permanent Players in Winnipeg, and Mother, who had been training her voice and belonged to the amateur theater society, called on him for an interview. He took one look at this tiny, French brunette and hired her for a small role.

Within a week she was playing the leads. Within six months they were married and left the small town of Winnipeg for the big town of New York. It was here he found he couldn't stop her singing and she couldn't stop his drinking. So she flounced out on him to sing on her own and, lo and behold, she found she was pregnant. Back Mother went to his drinking, she stopped singing, and that's where I came in. I was born between bouts. They fought up and down the east coast while he appeared in plays and she looked after the baby. When they read that Hollywood film companies were now paying huge sums to movie actors they fought their way across the States to the west coast.

Hollywood in the twenties was Rudolph Valentino breaking ladies' hearts and box office records, the natives dancing the torrid tango, Douglas Fairbanks and Goldilocks Pickford king and queening it around the world. Chaplin was walking his penguin way into posterity and Harold Lloyd was hanging from skyscraper clocks. Prohibition was brewing the gangsters who brewed the illegal booze that made all the natives throw up and pass out. Property speculators were buying up blocks of barren desert, the San Fernando Valley was still a valley and there were less than eight hundred people living in Beverly Hills. We were not among them. Our first home was in Hollywood on Sunset Boulevard, in one of those bungalow courts where rootless film people lived. It was the forerunner to the Garden of Allah bungalow estate where the stars cavorted with the starlets and John Barrymore was forever falling into the swimming pool fully clothed.

As soon as we'd settled into the bungalow court my French grandmother, Leopoldine Mollot, sailed over from Paris to join us. Daddy wasn't at all pleased about this. She couldn't speak English and he couldn't speak French. Whenever my mother and she talked in French he thought they were conspiring against him and flew into a blind rage.

"Get that skinny old frog back to her snails!" he would bellow.

At that time Daddy wasn't getting much work in either films or theater and Mother kept saying he was a lazy bum, sitting on his behind rolling cigarettes all day and drinking all night. Then Mother started singing again. Every day she sat at the piano and practiced her scales, which made our dog howl and often brought an answering chorus from neighboring *chiens*. Daddy didn't say much—just, "Chri-i-i-st!"

On the last-straw day, Mother was singing the "La Habanera" aria from *Carmen*. She had taken the Spanish shawl off the piano and draped it around her. She was in the middle of high C when Daddy crept over and banged the lid on her fingers. She let out an almighty howl and the match was on. Shouting and screaming, in and out of the kitchen, bedroom, and bathroom, Mother started packing her things and my things while Grandmother scuttled past them and out the front door. When Mother had packed she grabbed my right arm and we started out after Grandmother. Daddy grabbed my left arm, pulling me back into the hall and said she wasn't taking the baby with her. To prove his point Daddy took out a gun and waved it in our direction. This was the first time I remember seeing the famous Donlan gun. It was a heavy black revolver which he kept fully loaded as an antidote for burglars. As we had nothing to burgle he used it on us to keep in practice. Over the years I was to see it flourished every so often to clinch an argument. It certainly clinched this one. Mother dropped my arm and disappeared from the bungalow. Grandma disappeared too because Daddy, convinced she had plotted against him in French, went to the authorities and had her deported. She had come in as a tourist and had outstayed her visa and welcome.

The rest of that year was a blur of traumatic happenings. Daddy got a starring role in a play called *The Barker* to open in San Francisco, and Mother managed to find a job as an usherette at Grauman's Egyptian Theater, a less famous but no less flamboyant sibling of Grauman's Chinese Theater with its legendary front sidewalk. Daddy decided that before he left he would try to get Mother back. I was delighted. He thought it would be a nice surprise if we met her at Grauman's after her work.

I remember it was raining that night as we sped along Hollywood Boulevard and came to a stop outside the theater. The twinkling lights in the shops on either side of its large courtyard reflected in the wet cement and the theater itself looked like some giant stage set for an overembellished *Aida*.

Just before we pulled up, Daddy had warned me not to put my arms out of the window or let Mother hug me until he said it was okay. He was afraid she might grab my arm and kidnap me. It wasn't long before I saw her coming out of the theater. Daddy leaned across and wound down the window.

"Call her," he said, nudging me.

I did. After a moment of surprise she hurried forward with a happy cry and reached through the window to give me a kiss. I shook my head "no" and backed away. Puzzled, she tried again and Daddy pulled out his gun.

"Leave her alone and get in the car," he said. "We both want you back," he added incongruously.

Mother let out a frightened gasp, turned on her little high heels, and ran back into the theater. Daddy sighed and returned the gun to his pocket.

"Well, you can't say I didn't try," he said as we drove off. I sat there trembling. Even at that age I could see you can't get a dame with a gun.

8
☆

Daddy sent me ahead of him to San Francisco, alone on the overnight sleeper. He told me not to worry and I'd be met at the other end by his sister Adelaide. I remember the dollar he gave me to tip the colored porter; the excitement of watching the Pacific Ocean whiz by as I undressed in my berth; waking at dawn, finding the dining car all by myself and ordering a breakfast of waffles, maple syrup, and "little pig" sausages before arriving in San Francisco with my clothes on backward.

I stood in the vast terminal staring wide-eyed as the swirling tide of people flowed around me. I wondered which of them was Aunt Adelaide. A few minutes later she smiled her way through to greet me. She was five feet tall, round and comforting like a baked potato, and destined to become a memorable part of my early life in Hollywood.

Daddy Donlan arrived later with a flurry of staccato orders and the next thing I knew I was at the Geary Theater making my professional stage debut in his play. I had to walk on in one scene carrying a balloon and say two words, "How much?" For this I received twenty dollars a week. I remember the notes being counted out into my hand, but I don't remember what I did with them. Mother always said I was probably mugged by my father outside the stage door.

We shared a twin-bedded room in a hotel near the theater and after the show I was put to bed while my old man went out carousing all night. It didn't seem fair, because children's carousing hours are in the morning and that was just when he wanted to sleep. I used to lie awake grumbling quietly to myself while he snored and snorted until noon. Then, if he didn't have a howling hangover, we rode on a cable car to the Fisherman's Wharf district and ate fresh prawns or steamed clams before moving on to the Golden Gate Park for a swing and a slide.

The San Francisco "happening" I recall most vividly was the day Daddy promised me I was going to see Mother again. He had arranged a meeting at his sister's apartment in a final attempt to patch things up. I was thrilled, just as I'd been before the ill-fated try outside the Egyptian Theater.

We stood expectantly by the window awaiting her arrival. But when she climbed out of the taxi she was flanked by two plainclothes detectives.

"Shit!" said Daddy as he scooped me up and fled out the back entrance.

It wasn't until we were back in Hollywood for Christmas that I was allowed to see my mother again. Daddy had asked me what I wanted most for a present.

"Mother," I told him.

For a moment his face was blank, then he nodded slowly. The season must have mellowed him because a few days later he even let me move in with her.

She was now sharing an apartment with her sister Gabrielle, a concert pianist who was between tours. They festooned the place with toys, ornaments, food, and Christmas trinkets. None of which meant anything to me. I kept dreaming that Daddy would come down the chimney dressed as Santa Claus with a gun in his hand.

Mother's sister told her that whenever she left the apartment the baby went into her cupboard and kissed Mother's clothes. I was terrified she would disappear again and her clothes comforted me in the same way that a puppy is comforted by its mistress's scarf.

Life with Mother turned out to be almost as confusing as life with Father. After sister Gabrielle went back to her piano-playing tour, Mother and I moved in and out of a series of apartments, sharing them with a series of other usherettes with little girls and escapading husbands. All the usherettes were beauties who had come to Hollywood to seek fame in the movies and they were pursued by handsome young doormen who had come for the same reason. As a result there were spasmodic clashes in the night between the disorderly husbands and the handsome young doormen. We little girls kept our ears glued to the door listening to the beautiful people enacting scenes that might have come straight from the movie magazines.

Daddy didn't participate in these scuffles; he had simmered down considerably. He had also broken his arm by falling down the backstage stairs of Los Angeles's Biltmore Theater while playing in *The Front Page*. He was being looked after by Aunty Adelaide and her husband Jack who had moved into his Los Angeles apartment. Unfortunately, his arm stayed broken for longer than any arm has ever stayed broken because his doctor was a fellow lush. Every time they went out on a binge the doctor reset his arm and it grew in the wrong direction.

Eventually Mother found a bungalow apartment where we lived on our own and I started going to kindergarten. She would take me there in the morning with my lunch box of honey and peanut butter sandwiches and in the afternoon she would slip out of Grauman's Egyptian to hurry me home for a lamb chop supper. At my request I had the same meal every day; I didn't want any more changes in my life.

On weekends and holidays, while Mother blinked her flashlight, I sat in the Egyptian Theater watching Douglas Fairbanks in *The Thief of Bagdad* for month after month of its run. During the fourth month I fell in love with him and sent him my autographed photo. He sent me his in return.

But on weeknights, when mother was working, I had to stay home in bed. Alone in the bungalow I often felt frightened. Sometimes in the dark spooky moments I would clamber up onto a chair and telephone Aunt Adelaide. Aunty would always sneak over and keep me company. I would get dressed and we'd walk around the corner to the soda fountain for a chocolate ice cream soda.

In her youth Aunty had been, in turn, a Christian Science practitioner, a spiritualist medium, a fortune-teller by tea leaves, palms, cards, or crystal balls, and an illegal bookie. I would sit sucking my soda while she told me her plans for combining all these talents by forming a new Hollywood religion. After all, she figured, the evangelist Aimee Semple McPherson was making a fortune and she didn't even take bets on horses.

By the time Mother returned I was back in bed and Aunty had gone. One night there was no reply from Aunty's number so I decided to find the soda fountain by myself. Without remembering to get dressed. When Mother came home from the Egyptian Theater she found her five-year-old daughter roaming the streets in her nightgown. That did it. Within a few weeks this tug-of-love child was packed up and bundled off to live in the Sacred Heart Convent in the back streets of downtown Los Angeles.

It was an order of Dominican nuns who ran this junior concentration camp. Every morning at five o'clock a tall Teutonic nun clanged a great cowbell in our ears as she whisked back and forth along the rows of beds in our chilly dormitory. Up we jumped and filled our washing bowls with cold water, washed, dressed, made our beds, and were herded into the dank chapel to attend mass before our porridge breakfast. Not many mornings went by without one or two of the little girls fainting during mass. I was never so lucky.

All of this drill was supposed to be done in silence. One day I asked a girl to pass the salt—before grace was said—and for penance was promptly locked in the coal cellar for the rest of the afternoon. But that wasn't as terrifying as the night I wet the bed. It was around eleven in the evening when, with my wet sheet under my arm, I knocked on the Hun nun's door. Her angry, boiled red face poked out at me from under her cotton nightcap.

"I'm sorry, Sister, I've wet my bed," I said meekly.

Without a word she put on her brown wool dressing gown, tied the cord angrily and marched me to the bathroom.

"Put it in there," she ordered pointing to the bathtub. I did. "Now wash it, you dirty little girl." And with that she stomped back into her room. The sheet seemed enormous and I had never washed anything before. I filled the tub with water, climbed into it, and swirled the sheet around me. When Sister Simon Legree returned she squeezed the water out of the sheet, marched me back down the passage, and put me in the linen cupboard.

"This will teach you never to wet the bed again," she said and locked me in the pitch black cupboard for the night.

What it taught me was not to go to sleep at night in case I wet the bed. Night after night I lay awake for hours watching the rows of other little girls sleeping soundly and wondered why they didn't feel as awful as I did. Eventually I would quietly cry myself to sleep with a bottomless yearning for my singing mother and gun-toting daddy.

It was Aunt Adelaide who finally sprung me from this convent. I had pleaded with both Mother and Father to let me out of there. But Mother had to work and said she couldn't cope with a daughter who was a streetwalker. And Daddy's broken arm had incapacitated him from everything except drinking. So I concentrated all my efforts of persuasion on Aunty. Particularly as she was my most frequent visitor. Every Sunday she arrived in her best navy blue suit, veiled straw hat, and white gloves. Although she was very stout she managed to look neat and stylish. Her voice was gentle and warm and her manners impeccable. She always greeted me with, "How's my sweet Child of God?" and I would rush into her comforting arms.

On the day of the surprise springing Aunty arrived at the convent parlor a bit late. Her face was slightly flushed, her hat was slightly askew, and she walked with a careful roll. I rushed up and threw my arms around her welcome corpulence, but this time when she kissed me I noticed she didn't smell like Aunty anymore. She smelled just like Daddy, and Daddy usually smelled like a whisky sour.

12
☆

"All right, Child of God," she said, "I'm taking you out of this shithouse."

It was then I realized Aunty was drunk. When this angelic ball of avoirdupois had been guzzling her language became less genteel. She grabbed my hand as two white-habited nuns floated by.

"Come and get your things before I tangle with these holy witches!"

Elated, I started up the stairs to the dormitory with Aunty weaving close behind. While I collected my belongings Aunty sat on my bed, opened her handbag, and produced a small bottle. The label stated it was Virginia Dare wine tonic.

Aunty stated: "My heart tonic. The doctor says to take a sip whenever I'm upset."

Having revitalized her heart, she was suddenly very keen to find the Hun nun and give her hell. But I was afraid that if any of the nuns noticed her condition I wouldn't be allowed out with her. Somehow I managed to persuade her to skip away silently. We taxied to the furnished duplex apartment in Los Angeles that she shared with my father and with her current husband, Jack.

In spite of her baked potato shape and occasional lapses into the bottle, Aunty had plenty of sex appeal. Before she was fifty she had had three husbands and thirteen lovers. Uncle Jack, the only husband I knew, was of Italian descent. From an indiscriminate New York background he had a deze-dem-and-doze accent, and a childish sense of humor. My father always referred to him as "Useless" because he didn't have any real occupation. But Daddy was a bit unfair as Useless often bought cars with Daddy's money and drove people around in them, mostly on guided tours of the stars' homes. When Daddy was broke Uncle Jack would sell the car and drive a taxi.

Uncle Jack's other occupation, which suited me, was driving to the Venice Beach amusement pier. There, while I wandered through the haunted house concession scaring myself, he stood outside the entrance watching the wind machines blow the ladies' skirts up. He hooted and howled with

13
☆

delight while the girls squealed and pulled at their skirts. About this, Daddy said Useless was a silly old fool. And this was the only point on which he and his sister Adelaide agreed.

When little Child of God and sloshed Aunty completed the great convent escape, Daddy was waiting for us in the apartment. He was cold sober with his arm still in a sling. He took one look at Aunty's condition and his face puffed out and turned puce.

"Jesus, Mary, and Joseph!" he exploded. "Don't tell me you've been to the convent in that condition!"

Aunty opened her blurred, hazel eyes in naïve innocence.

"What condition?"

"You're tanked again."

"Look who's talking."

"And on my whisky!"

"I never touched your damn whisky."

"Give me your handbag," he demanded, reaching for it with his good arm. Aunty pulled it away from him.

"Now, Jimmy," she admonished, "you mustn't get me upset. You know my heart is weak and the doctor says——"

"I know all about your heart and the doctor says!"

As a matter of fact we all knew about it because it was Aunty's last-ditch defense whenever she found herself at bay. Daddy often referred to her simply as "My-heart-and-the-doctor-says."

He made another grab at her handbag, but again she eluded him. She weaved her way to the front room window, opened it, and promptly threw the bag out into the street. Daddy took a deep breath.

"You're almost as stupid as my wife," he said scathingly.

This was one of his favorite demolishers. Whenever I did something incorrectly or messed up some mission that I'd been sent on he would berate me with, "You're plain stupid, just like your mother!"

As the two of them stood facing each other like a couple of Siamese fighting fish, the front door slammed downstairs and up came Uncle Jack, carrying the fatal handbag.

"Adelaide," he blinked, "what in God's name is your handbag doin'—" He trailed off as his brown, Italian doe eyes took in the two antagonists. With a wisdom born of experience he sized up the situation, quickly slid the bag on the dining room table, said, "So long, folks," and went right back out again, clattering down the stairs two at a time.

Aunty ran after him screaming, "Jack! Jack, come back— I've cooked your favorite stuffing——"

But her husband kept going—into the car and off. When Aunty returned, Daddy had sniffed out the Virginia Dare tonic bottle and poured its whisky contents down the sink. He always did this to Aunty when he was on the wagon and she did the same to him when she was sober. The only one who made a profit was the family bootlegger, one of our most regular visitors.

Most of the time it worked out that when Aunt Adelaide was on the bottle Daddy Donlan was sober, and vice versa. But on the occasions when both of them were bingeing it was a question of, "Stand by for blast-off." So it wasn't surprising that our other constant visitors were the police and the fire brigade.

The police usually appeared when the noise level in the Donlan ménage had risen to a vibrating crescendo. Alcohol being strictly illegal, our irate neighbors would call in the law, hoping they could put a stop to the Donlan soirées. And to get even with the niggling neighbors Aunty would sometimes send them the fire brigade in the wee small hours of the morning. I was often awakened by the clanging bells and the clatter of hoses and ladders going up, but in spite of all the noise I would soon drift back to sleep again, secure in the knowledge that at least firemen didn't lock little girls in linen cupboards.

During the morning-after-the-night-before a fireman would sometimes arrive to find out why the hell we'd called the brigade without a fire and didn't we know it was a serious offense? For a while my old man acted as Aunty's unwilling cover-up, denying all knowledge of any call or even what the man was talking about. But one day when he answered the door he found a chief inspector on the step.

Daddy surveyed him silently, then lifted his hands and eyes heavenward in despair, pointed the inspector down the hall toward Aunty's bedroom and retreated snarling into his own lion's den.

Aunty was sitting up in bed recovering from her escapade and innocently sipping her California orange juice when the inspector walked in. Utterly unperturbed she extended a regal hand to receive him.

"How nice of you to call in person," she said in her gentle queen mother voice. "Won't you sit down?"

And before he had a chance to start his investigations, she was explaining how she was suffering from a touch of "My-heart-and-the-doctor-says." This always won her sympathy and time for maneuvers. The inspector made empathetic noises and then:

"Someone placed another false alarm last night, ma'am. The neighbors say . . ." he paused to clear his throat—which was his fatal mistake. Aunty leaped into the pause with all guns firing.

"The neighbors are very naughty people," she said sweetly. "Have you seen their garage? Full of newspapers and gasoline and matches and you name the fire hazard. No one wants to see them get into trouble, inspector, but waking up and smelling fumes in the night, I mean, better safe than blown up. And your men turned out so quickly—so smart and working with such precision—I felt safe right away. You must be very proud of them, inspector."

Before he left she had him believing implicitly in her innocent hazel eyes, her Ouija board and the coming good fortune in his palm. And as a mark of gratitude for his splendid fire department she even sold him a half share in her Irish Sweepstakes ticket.

I remember one dawn, when Aunty and Daddy Donlan were both on the bottle, quarreling and chasing each other around the dining table, four policemen arrived and took up positions in each corner of the room. Daddy was standing at the far end of the table still in his overcoat and hat, a whisky bottle in one hand, his drink in the other and Aunty facing him at the opposite end. Daddy surveyed each of the policemen in turn before returning his soft-focused gaze to Aunty.

"See what you've done?" he scowled. "The boys are with us again." Then he turned back to the policemen. "All right boys, take me in. I'm ready. Here's the evidence."

He raised the whisky bottle in case they hadn't seen it. Within seconds the four policemen had joined them, sat around the table and were drinking the evidence while Aunty told them their good fortunes.

In most of these brother versus sister bouts, however, Aunty managed to win on points. She knew she could always get her own back by putting garlic in his food, which he hated, or by giving him fried rabbit and telling him it was chicken. Or, worst of all, interfering with his seductions. And of those there were many.

When he was away from the family Jimmy Donlan had a load of Irish charm, a sense of humor, and a warmth that made him great company. Because of this he was seldom at a loss for female company, be they stars, starlets, or merely girls that go bang in the night. Normally, when Daddy brought a girl friend home, we all stayed hidden, locked behind our doors. But if Aunty was on the "heart tonic" she would breeze in and join them, using her tricks as a medium to capture the girl's interest.

"I see a pale yellow aura surrounding you," she would announce mysteriously, "and its vibrations are sending me messages."

End of Daddy's seduction. And while Aunty worked on her captive audience my infuriated father was left to drink and talk to himself. One evening Daddy returned from the film studios with a particularly attractive young up-and-coming actress by the name of Carole Lombard. He was working with her in a picture called *Big News* and had been so impressed by her beauty, her sense of humor, and her bawdy jollity that he brought her home hoping to spend the evening impressing her in return.

But he reckoned without Sister Adelaide. Aunty, who was very sloshed, maneuvered herself on to the sofa next to Miss Lombard and went through her entire repertoire of colored auras, spirit messages, tea leaves, and crystal balls.

"Your future is full of romance," she predicted unsteadily. "And you will marry a tall, dark, and handsome actor." Which was a pretty safe bet in Hollywood. A few years later at Paramount studios, Carole Lombard met William Powell on the set of *Ladies' Man* and married him shortly after. Within a few more years that marriage was over and she wed another actor called Clark Gable. Maybe Aunty could have foretold this, too, if she'd lasted the evening but halfway through her prognostications, while she was reading Miss Lombard's palm, she slipped off the couch onto her bottom and passed out. Daddy was delighted.

"Thank God," he sighed with relief. "The seance is over and the medium has fallen on her prat."

As Daddy usually slept things off in the mornings, the rest of us had learned to soft-shoe around the apartment and speak in whispers. After Aunty had cooked our breakfast of French toast, jam, and coffee, Uncle Jack would drive off on his movieland tours and Aunty would peel off her dressing gown and nightdress and do her housework strip-naked.

"I don't like getting my clothes dirty," she explained. "It's easier to take a bath than do laundry."

She always found a logical explanation for her more bizarre habits. Like the fact that once a year she threw all her clothes out the back window near the rubbish bin where they lay scattered over the courtyard like emasculated scarecrows. She insisted this display made it easier for the passing tramps to select what they needed. As this sort of thing is quick to get around, it wasn't long before we suffered from tramps like other people suffer from mice. Until one day my old man returned early from the studios and exorcised them with a barrage of well-chosen words.

This annual dumping of Aunty's clothes meant she always had a wardrobe of new and fashionable outfits, and three afternoons a week she would put one of them on, pick me up at St. Vincent's—my new day school—and take me to my piano or dancing lessons. She charmed all the nuns and teachers with her gentle voice, engaging smile and manners.

It was sometimes difficult for me to reconcile this sweet queen mother lady with the Tugboat Annie who periodically staggered around our apartment.

As soon as we returned home she would help me with my piano exercises. But only if Daddy was out. He couldn't stand noise. In fact he couldn't stand any noise at all, except the noisy noise *he* made cursing the noisemakers. No one dare turn on a radio or play a record. Ringing telephones were strangled at first bleep. Even the singing birds were attacked. Daddy Donlan was always flinging open his windows, shaking his fists at the inmates of the nearest tree, shouting, "For Christ's sake, shut up, you goddam chirping buzzards!" or, "Get the hell back to Capistrano!" It was such a relief whenever he left the flat that the moment we heard the front door click all our noises broke out. Uncle Jack switched on the radio at full volume, Aunty played the piano, and I tap-danced.

For some reason the only time Daddy could tolerate my tap-dancing was when he was drunk. In fact, unlike his sister, he was always much jollier when he was drinking. If he was having a party he would sometimes ask me to do a few steps and as I clipperty-clopped he'd clap and chuckle and say, "Ah, she's a chip off the old block. Third time lucky. She'll be the star of this family."

Since the age of three he'd told me I was to be the third generation of actors, following in his illustrious footsteps. But the day he came to the dancing school's end-of-term show-off concert he was sober. Thinking I would impress him I sang and danced "Making Whoopie," rolling my eyes and trying to emulate Eddie Cantor. I should have cut my throat first. Daddy was almost apoplectic.

"What the hell d'you think you were doing?" he snorted when we got home. "The world can only take one Eddie Cantor—and not as a midget in drag!"

Daddy hated child performers and although he was ambitious for my future he kept insisting I should finish my education and lead a normal child's life. So between binges and bouts he put my hair up in rags at night and helped me with my homework. He even stopped trying to shoot Mother when she came to visit me.

By this time she had been promoted from Grauman's Egyptian Theater to Grauman's Chinese Theater, farther up Hollywood Boulevard. She now stood in the Oriental foyer collecting her tickets, dressed and madeup to look like a Chinese princess. Strategically placed among the usherettes in the dimly lit foyer were lifelike wax effigies wearing the same Oriental costumes and the customers were always glee-fully groping the usherettes to see if they were real. On my visits to the theater I enjoyed this game so much that I put on Mother's Chinese makeup and sat cross-legged in a pot of sand intended for cigarette butts.

My pleasures were as simple as Uncle Jack's, perhaps that was why I was so fond of him. Whenever I returned from a visit with my French mother, Uncle Jack would break into his version of French.

"And how is Madame Chevrolet Coupé Fromage du Breeze?" he would ask with his Brooklyn accent. Then he would make a raspberry sound and finish with, "Kiss, kid-die?"

Daddy would say, "Oh, Christ!" stamp off into his room and slam the door.

Since this seemed to be everyone's reaction to Uncle Jack's attempts at humor it came as quite a shock to me when Aunty began to complain that he was having an affair with another woman. I couldn't imagine anyone loving Uncle Jack, except me.

Aunty insisted she had seen the "other woman" in her crystal ball and in Uncle's Buick. On top of that, Venus was crossing Jupiter which upset Sagittarians and took Uncle Jack for weekend love tours in Mexico. Besides which, the queen of spades told Aunty it was an ominous sign when he started bringing her back expensive bottles of French perfume from his Mexican jaunts. Soon she was surrounded by a black aura that drove her to her spirits—the ones in the bottle. From then on when Aunty drank and fought it was with a kitchen carving knife and it was aimed at Uncle Jack. As my bed was in the corner of their room I could hear them battling up and down the hall.

Uncle would say, "Now, Adelaide, take it easy——"

And Aunty would scream, "You've been out with that woman again!"

"What woman? Please, Adelaide, be quiet and give me that goddam knife——"

"I will not give you the goddam knife! I'll cut your goddam balls off!"

Then she would make a couple of staggered lunges at him which somehow he managed to stave off. Back and forth they'd go screaming, "Stupid bitch!" and "Lying bastard!" and similar love talk. At this point Daddy Donlan would usually appear from his room in a scorching temper at all the noise. I remember him once sliding past the two combatants, striding down the hall and carrying me from my bed into his room, cursing with breathless rage.

"You two goddam nincompoops—screaming that fucking awful language in front of the C.H.I.L.D.!"

Slamming the door he paced up and down saying, "I've got to get you out of here. It's a madhouse. I've got to get you out of here!"

I said: "I hope Aunty doesn't kill Uncle Jack."

And Daddy answered: "I hope they kill each other!"

It was a regular sort of bedtime story. But none of these scenes seemed to worry me unduly at the time. I accepted them as normal family life. I knew no other. Undressing Aunty when she passed out, helping her into bed to sleep it off, leading her to the bathroom when she was sick from the bootleg gin, it was all as natural to me as playing with a doll was to other little girls. In fact I thought I was luckier because my doll was alive and warm and human and could cry real tears or laugh real chuckles and was the size of a baby elephant. Pushing my real, live doll around the apartment was like maneuvering a bag of cement.

The only time Aunty's drinking really worried me was if she drank at Daddy's Christmas Eve parties because it was her chore to escort me at six the following morning to

21
☆

Christmas Mass. I was in the choir at St. Vincent's Church and all we singers were asked to bring our family to hear us.

Daddy's celebration on Christmas Eve was the only French custom he adapted from my mother, and all of us had our respective parts to play. Aunty did the cooking, Daddy took care of the bootleggers, and I made myself generally useful and got in everybody's way. Uncle Jack, who was considered the family idiot, was the party decorator. He and I often drove through the yearly California floods with water up to his running boards to buy the ornaments. Not only did he hang baskets of mistletoe all over the ceiling as an excuse to kiss all Daddy's starlets, he also spent days constructing a miniature village under the tree.

The week before Christmas he could always be found sitting on the living room floor surrounded by hardware, building little houses with lights to go in them, cribs, stables, and mangers. I always enjoyed Uncle Jack's toy village, but Daddy didn't. Every night he'd wander dejectedly into the living room to comment on the progress.

"I see Useless is still on the floor playing with his tools," he'd complain. To me he'd say, "Your Uncle Jack is a jackass." To which Uncle Jack would reply with his jackass raspberry sound.

On my most worrisome Christmas Eve, Aunty, glowingly naked as usual except for her apron, had spent the afternoon shoving Uncle Jack's favorite Italian stuffing up the turkey's posterior. It was a mouth-watering concoction of *dolce latte* and cream cheese, parmesan, onions, garlic, chopped spinach sautéd in olive oil and bound with a dozen eggs. All Daddy's stars and starlets and even real people loved it.

During that particular Christmas Eve day I noticed Aunty wasn't her usual cheerful self. Every time she reached for the olive oil she took a swig out of the vinegar bottle next to it. Soon she became aware of my troubled stares and cutting off the turkey's crispy Pope's nose she gave it to me to chew as a distraction. Somehow it reminded me of Uncle Jack. Then she confided to her nine-year-old niece how she was worried about his "other woman." She was afraid he might leave her. Imagining Aunty without Uncle was like trying to visualize Laurel without Hardy and I told her so.

"Don't ever rely on a man," she warned me, between "vinegar" swigs. "They're all devils. Just follow your career. But for your Uncle Jack I could have been another Marie Dressler."

"Another Marie Dressler yet," scoffed Uncle Jack who had wandered in to eat his preparty plate of stuffing which she always baked separately for him. "Your Aunt Adelaide would be better off marketing her Italian spinach stuffing!"

"Another Marie Dressler," she repeated defiantly.

As Daddy had become more involved with the film world even Aunty had caught the bug, so who better to inspire her fantasies than a fat character star like the inimitable Marie Dressler who had achieved world renown in middle age. But right now, watching nude Aunty trying to reach up to the shelf for the vinegar bottle, I was inclined to agree with Uncle Jack. I was also worried about her condition for Christmas Mass in the morning.

"Aunty," I pleaded, when Uncle had left the kitchen, "please don't drink any more vinegar."

"There is no more," she answered.

"Show me no more," I insisted.

She took a last hurried gulp and showed me the empty bottle.

"You see, sweet Child of God? There is no more, no more."

But later, while she was making up for the party, Uncle found her sneaking a drink out of one of the perfume bottles he'd given her.

"I can see it's gonna be a Merry Christmas," he snorted as he clapped on his hat and coat and raced out into the Christmas Eve.

"Go! Go!" she shouted after him. "Go to your whore and tell *her* to make your goddam stuffing!"

Daddy's head popped out of his door and took in the situation.

"Christ!" he moaned and crossed himself. "How can her nibs do this to me on Christ's birthday and my party." He shook his fist at tippling Aunty. "You stupid old bag, you've fallen off the wagon and you'll soon be on your ass again. You're not getting one goddam drink out of me tonight!"

It was bad enough when this happened on his solo dates, but when he'd invited a whole lot of new studio friends it worried him even more. He'd made a big stage success in *The Front Page*—pre-broken arm—and an even bigger success in *Oh Kay!* in which he starred with Elsie Janis and a mended arm. Studio talent scouts, who had seen him in both, decided James Donlan, stage actor, was now to be James Donlan, film actor.

In fairly rapid succession he had made five pictures—*Big News, The Bishop Murder Case, Beau Bandit, Night Work,* and *Remote Control,* working with such current favorites as Basil Rathbone, Leila Hyams, Roland Young, Rod la Roque, Doris Kenyon, Robert Montgomery, and Carole Lombard. Hollywood seemed to have taken to this stocky, bluff, character actor who moved effortlessly from Irish detectives, hard-boiled editors and bankers to cowboy clowns. Sooner or later most of the casts he'd worked with turned up at our apartment and this Christmas Eve was no exception.

As my father didn't believe in merrymaking that tied people down he always gave open-house parties, so that the guests came and left when they chose. The first arrivals were Al Jolson and Fanny Brice. Daddy had dragged me to see Al Jolson when he was appearing at the Biltmore Theater in Los Angeles. In my father's opinion Jolson was the greatest entertainer of his or any other day and I was supposed to pay attention and learn. But even then I couldn't understand why a nice Jewish fellow wanted to wear a black face, fall on his knees, and sing about his mother—with white gloves on.

At the party he was wearing his white face and he didn't fall on his knees the whole time he was there. Daddy showed Mr. Jolson Uncle Jackass's Christmas village, as though he had really liked it, and Mr. Jolson said how clever and ingenious it was. I was sorry Uncle Jack had bolted out to his "other woman" and missed this praise. After all, having just made The Jazz Singer and The Singing Fool, Mr. Jolson was now even more famous than Abraham Lincoln and he might have hired Uncle Jack to decorate the sets for his new movie and then Uncle wouldn't have been Useless anymore.

Fanny Brice I loved. She came in all aglitter, looking like the million dollars she was worth. Daddy had dragged me to see her, too, as part of my theatrical education. At the time I remember liking her better than Mr. Jolson onstage. Perhaps because she looked so natural and was so funny and didn't seem to be trying so hard to please. She was just a nice Jewish lady without a black face and white gloves and was absolutely hilarious as Baby Snooks, a horrible little girl-child.

Among the rest of the guests were a bevy of glamorous blonde star ladies who popped in and out for a drink. Daddy introduced them to me as Laura la Plante, Leila Hyams, and Helen Twelvetrees. Although I'd seen Leila Hyams before on her film sets, when Daddy was acting with her, I still couldn't tell which was which. They all looked the same to me and they all wore white furs. These three ladies were really gorgeous and looked like Dolores Costello, another blonde star, who wasn't there because Daddy didn't know her. But, unfortunately, he was later to become a boozing buddy of Miss Costello's husband, John Barrymore.

So far Aunt Adelaide had behaved impeccably. She answered the door, welcomed the newcomers, and seemed blissfully unaware that her brother Jimmy kept one swivel eye charting her every movement. Mother arrived all sparkling and wearing a black monkey coat. She'd brought an armful of Christmas presents for me and a new boyfriend for herself. Little did I know he was destined to become my stepfather. He was short and stocky like my father and his name was James, too. James Ferrier. To keep from getting them mixed up Mother called the new one Jim and the old one Jimmy. Unlike my father, Jim was a dark, swarthy, outdoor type who had played football at college, watched baseball when he grew up, and voted Republican. He smoked cigars and didn't drink. After Daddy had handed him his Coca Cola and wished boyfriend Jim a Merry Christmas, Daddy Jimmy leaned down and whispered to me.

"Your mother's not going to get any jokes out of this one."

No jokes, I mused; maybe that means no cranky hangovers. But we didn't like him, Daddy and I. Somehow he didn't belong. I followed Mother around the room like a bouncing Bambi as I stroked her monkey fur.

Bebe Daniels arrived right after Mother, twinkling and laughing, lighting up the party as brightly as Uncle Jack's Christmas tree. Even though she was in the middle of shooting the strenuous musical routines of her new movie *Rio Rita* she still seemed to have more vitality than any of the others. Everyone commented on how much my beautiful mother resembled Miss Daniels. But to me the most beautiful star of all the stars in the room was my little French usherette who showed them to their seats at Grauman's Chinese Theater.

Aunty was now sitting on the couch encroaching on film director Gregory La Cava, and not on the floor on her ass as Daddy had predicted. In a strange, slightly blurred kind of Marie Dressler voice she was trying to convince Mr. La Cava that he should give her a screen test.

"It's in the cards," she confided hoarsely. "My birth sign, Leo the lion, is the exact same sign as the MGM studio lion, so naturally when the full moon appears in the New Year it means a new star is born—and that's me!"

Gregory La Cava's eyebrows arched suspiciously.

"To all of the stars who are born this Merry Christmas," he said, toasting her with his glass and trying to evade the subject.

"My brother Jimmy's not the only talent in the family," she elaborated, refusing to be sidetracked. "Grandfather Donlan was an actor, too. During the Gold Rush he owned half of downtown San Francisco, where the Geary Theater's built, until he lost it in a poker game. And our great grandmother, Bessie, sewed some of the original stars on the first American flag."

Wild as these statements may have sounded Aunty always swore to me that, "cross my heart and hope to die," they were true.

Mr. La Cava shied momentarily in front of the onslaught

and then offered to get her a drink so they could toast the whole family. "Oh, but I never drink," demurred Aunty with unflinching hazel eyes.

By the time Daddy Donlan came to La Cava's rescue she had given up trying to sell him her new Marie Dressler act and was attempting to sell him the exclusive screen rights to her Italian stuffing. Daddy gently but firmly eased her up from the couch.

"Time you two hit the hay," he said to Aunty and me. "You both have to be up early for the Christmas choir."

I obeyed, but she didn't. All night she ambled back and forth from the party room where she didn't drink to the bedroom where she did. There wasn't much sleep for me as I watched her sneaking in and out for a snifter from Uncle Jack's perfume bottle. Somehow she managed to hold herself together for Daddy's Yuletide celebrations, but she certainly fell apart for mine.

I awoke at dawn when the five o'clock alarm bell dingled. The guests had all gone, Daddy was snoring in his room, and Aunty was sitting on her bed fully dressed, half dozing with a turkey leg in one hand and her missal in the other. After washing and brushing her up I manipulated my staggering baby elephant into the taxi.

It was with great trepidation that I left her at the front entrance of St. Vincent's Church while I found my place in the choir at the side of the altar. The main altar was decked with red poinsettias, and the white-smocked altar boys were lighting the extra candles required for the solemn High Mass. Proudly we little girls and boys watched for our families to take their reserved seats in the front row pews. I could see Aunty coming down the central aisle—of all aisles—weaving with great dignity from pillar to pillar. When she reached her front pew she genuflected before the altar, made the sign of the cross, and fell flat on her face. I watched anxiously while somebody's father helped her up, politely ignoring Aunty's bomb of a fart as he sat her next to him. I saw her breathe her effusive alcoholic thanks all over him and closed my eyes.

We kids sang "Silent Night," then the bishop and two priests made an entrance wearing their finest gold vestments.

The whole congregation stood up. Except Aunty. She was slouched in her pew fast asleep, her rosary around her chubby neck and her missal on the floor. As usual she was down when she should have been up. But I was grateful she wasn't up when she should have been down. At least asleep she might be quiet for a few minutes.

Later, while the priest was reading the Epistle, I was startled to see Aunty slowly toppling onto the shoulder of the gentleman sitting next to her. I could see he was having difficulty trying to push her upright while struggling to untangle her rosary from his missal. I was even more horrified during the Consecration, which is the most sacred and silent part of the Mass. The altar bells had just tinkled thrice, the bishop was elevating the chalice, and all the congregation were on their knees with heads bowed. All was quiet. Not a creature was stirring, when Aunt Adelaide burped out a gargantuan snore which richocheted around the Gothic alcoves, through the sacristy, and over the congregation. Everyone carried on praying intently, pretending they hadn't heard it. Her sweet Child of God prayed harder than anyone that Christ would wake her up, keep her up, and shut her up.

One of Christ's followers must have got my message. A gentleman in a blue pin-striped suit picked up the collection box, which was attached to a long rod, and began plying for offerings up and down the pews. When he reached Aunty he poked her with it, shoving the box under her nose. She woke up with a start, gave him her faded queen mother smile, and fumbled a dollar into his box.

I thanked God she was awake and all was well. We kiddies began singing "Adeste Fidelis," the joyous celebration song—a sort of "Happy Birthday to Jesus." All the families beamed as they listened to us children trilling "venite adoremus" in our high-pitched angel voices. Aunty suddenly caught the jubilant spirit and joined us, belting out "venite adoremus" in her hoarse Marie Dressler baritone. The great Al Jolson himself couldn't have outshouted her. And though she should have kept her mouth shut, for once she was on her knees at the right time and in the proper place.

"*Ite missa est*," chanted the bishop.

"Deo gratias," we chanted back.

It was the end of the solemn High Mass. St. Vincent's churchbells ding-donged their medley of cheerful chimes clear across Los Angeles and over the Hollywood Hills. The sun was shining, Daddy had a job, Mother had a new boyfriend, and Aunty was awake, alive, and not on her ass on the church floor this Christmas morn.

Amen.

29
☆

By 1931 a galaxy of new stars had been discovered, but not Aunty.

A virtually unknown cricket-playing English gentleman called Boris Karloff had clumped and grunted across the screen in *Frankenstein,* and a Hungarian thespian named Bela Lugosi had just found fame nibbling ladies' necks as *Dracula.* Bing Crosby had made a crooning screen debut as one of the Three Rhythm Boys in Paul Whiteman's *King of Jazz,* but someone had yet to spot the New Marie Dressler who was still telling fortunes, placing bets, making her Italian stuffing, and looking after me.

It was two years since the Wall Street market had crashed and the banks had come tumbling down behind it. Mother had lost all her savings in a Hollywood bank and decided in the future to put her dough under the mattress as they had done in France. Will H. Hays had become Hollywood's first film censor and decreed that married couples could no longer be seen in bed together, nor with other people, nor could unmarried couples. So the film stars had started shooting each other instead. The prohibition of alcohol and gambling had begotten the gangster mobs, which begat the gangster stories, which in turn begat the gangster movies and a new star image—the tough guy—which begat a whole brood of new scrambled faces: Spencer Tracy, Humphrey Bogart, Edward G. Robinson, and James Cagney, who carried the image a step further by squashing a grapefruit in his leading lady's mush.

Daddy had lost his original stage role in the film version of *The Front Page,* which made us all sad, but appeared in *Sins of the Children* with his friend Leila Hyams, and Robert Montgomery, which made us all glad again. It was the year the original platinum blonde bombshell Jean Harlow exploded onto the screen of the Grauman's Chinese Theater and it was Mother who had shown her to her seat at the gala premiere.

"I can't understand why that pretty young girl with the sexy figure has bleached her hair so white," frowned Mother afterward, "just like a little old lady."

By now our whole family had changed partners and moved around California like a game of musical chairs. Mother moved into a Hollywood apartment with Jim Ferrier, Daddy had left me with Aunty and moved into another Hollywood apartment with a girl called Jane who was a dancer from his big stage hit *Oh Kay!,* and Uncle Jack had left Aunty to move in with "the other woman." In fact, the whole lot of them were "living in sin," which wouldn't have pleased either Mr. Will H. Hays or the nuns of St. Vincent's.

Aunty cried a great deal about Jack and I tried to comfort my baby elephant by kissing away her tears, as she had done mine on weepy occasions. It was just the two of us now and Aunty tried very hard to stay sober. We both decided she should dry out, lose some weight, and try to win Useless back again. Thus began the New Adelaide transformation scene.

She began by bleaching her hair blonde like Harlow, and with her new platinum locks we climbed on to a Greyhound bus and rode through San Jacinto Valley to the Gilman Hot Springs Health Spa where she sat in the mud and found a new boyfriend. The famous Gilman mud baths of hot, squishy slush were supposed to make you healthy, skinny, and pretty. They were arranged in a row of cubicles like a public convenience, and the clients sat in their box-shaped tubs up to their necks in muck. Aunty found her new boyfriend wallowing in the adjacent trough. I listened to their ecstatic gurgles about the benefits of their hot brown mud baths, but as a child of ten it seemed like a lot of crap to me.

In the evenings they strolled through a leafy lovers' lane of hot springs, holding hands and stopping at each healthy grotto to knock back a sulphur water. And while Aunty romanced I skipped off to the Gilman barn dance wearing a new party dress and a new pair of Cuban-heeled pumps which she had bought for my birthday. Daddy had caused an awful stink about these shoes when he saw them. He insisted the heels were too high for a young girl and that because of them I would soon become a trollop.

Standing in the barn dance sidelines on my new Cuban heels I waited hopefully to become a trollop, whatever that was, and watched the grown-ups dance by. Occasionally, a young boy my age would ask me to dance. But not often. I always felt pretty ugly with freckles, red hair, pug nose, a mouthful of protruding teeth reaching from ear to ear, and skinny toothpick legs. Everyone said I looked just like my father, who looked awful to me. I mean he looked all right for a man, but what girl wants to look like her funny-faced father when she could have looked like her beautiful mother? So I stood there trying to pull in my teeth and suck in my cheeks to look like the new star Marlene Dietrich, whom everyone was raving about and calling the new Garbo. Daddy said Marlene had been brought to Hollywood just to scare Garbo into doing lousy scripts and stop wanting to be alone.

In the daytime, while Aunty and her beau played in the mud, I went swimming in the Gilman pool and riding Western style through the San Jacinto Valley, wearing jeans and a cowboy hat. I loved galloping through the rocky streams and under the eucalyptus trees, especially since Daddy had forbidden me to have anything to do with a horse. This order came about because of a Western he was making called *The Painted Desert*. On location in Arizona he had become acquainted with a horse named Poncho whom he actively disliked. Poncho snorted all through Daddy's lines, bucked him, and wouldn't stand on the marks.

"They're treacherous beasts," he warned me later, bristling at the very recollection. "Don't ever let me catch you on a horse or near a horse. D'you understand, Yolande? Horses are out. O.U.T. Out!"

He grew to hate Poncho even more than chirruping birds; because of this horse he swore he would never make another Western. And he never did. I must say that when I first saw Poncho I thought he was fun. But then I didn't have to work with him. It was just before Aunty's refurbishing trip to Gilman's that I visited Daddy on the studio set, after his return from Arizona.

When I crept onto the sound stage the lights and camera were focused on a large, wooden ranch house, and there was Daddy Donlan standing on the porch with a gun in his hand, just like he did at home. Poncho was tied to the post at his side and in the background a tall, thin, big-eared villain in a cowboy hat was sneaking about in the cacti. Sure enough, every time Daddy spoke his lines the horse kicked up the dust, lifted its head, rattled its bit, and went, "Wheee-heee-aaah," which made the villain get the giggles and the director say, "Cut!" It took twenty-seven takes and a horse pill before Poncho buttoned his *bouche.*

While the camera and lights were moved around for the next shot, Daddy presented me to the big-eared, unknown villain in the cowboy hat.

"I'd like you to meet my daughter," he said. "Yolande, this is Clark Gable."

"Hi," said the unknown villain.

I looked up into those brown eyes under those dark bushy eyebrows under that cowboy hat, watched his dimpled cheeks pucker into that quizzical smile, and thought what a scary villain he must be. They could have lassoed me to a trading post if anyone had told me then that this gangling man would become MGM's king of Hollywood, or that my heart would be clicking like a prairie cricket the next time we met, which was several years later when we were both working at Metro on the same picture—he the star, me the extra.

But right now, on Poncho's picture, he was still a small-part actor working hard to make a go of what he said was his first real screen part. Daddy liked Mr. Gable and as we walked toward their canvas chairs he patted him across the shoulders.

"This young Gable's a fine actor," he told me. "Much better than Poncho."

Gable chuckled. "Oh, I wouldn't say that, Jimmy," he grinned. "It's just that Poncho hasn't had our stage training. All he needs is a couple of horse operas at the Met."

They both guffawed and we sat in the chairs. Someone brought them a couple of Cokes and me a chocolate-covered ice cream Eskimo Pie and the horse some cud—or whatever horses chew. Then Poncho went out for walkies and Daddy said to Gable, "Tell her about your screen test."

"Hell, she doesn't want to hear about it."

"Sure she does. Everyone should hear about it!" Daddy slapped his knee and exploded with laughter. To be honest, Mr. Gable was right, I was much more interested in following Poncho, but I listened dutifully.

Gable had been appearing at the Los Angeles Majestic Theater in a play called *The Last Mile.* He was playing Killer Mears, a role Spencer Tracy had played and it worried him taking it on as he thought Spencer Tracy had been so perfect in it. However, one night Lionel Barrymore saw his performance and promised him a screen test for the film *Bird of Paradise* which he was directing for Metro.

When the elated actor arrived at the studio they had pounced on him, curled his hair, stripped him, pushed him onto a jungle set, and made him lurk about speechless and bare-assed except for a loincloth and a flower behind his ear. Gable was desolate. So was the producer, Irving Thalberg, when he saw the test.

"You can't use him, he looks like a bat," he said succinctly, and walked out of the projection room.

"Barrymore discovered me," laughed Gable, "and Thalberg undiscovered me."

Now he was hoping this *Painted Desert* film would really get him started. *I* was hoping the horse would come back and cause a commotion again. It did. After his walkies he came in and on the way to the set dropped a load right in front of Daddy's chair.

Daddy said, "Shit!"

Gable said, "You're right," and began telling us about his own horse problems. In order to get this villain role he had lied to the producer and said he could ride. For six frenetic weeks before the film started he took secret riding lessons from a cowboy.

"I've learned to ride all right," he grinned. "But I'm so saddlesore I can hardly sit on my horse." Then he chuckled. "Lucky for me the pain in my behind gives me the angry look the director wants."

When *The Painted Desert* was finally shown, Clark Gable got his first screen review. It appeared in the Hollywood trade paper *Film Daily,* and it said: ". . . He wasn't a very good cowboy but the lady fans liked him."

On our last day at Gilman's Health Spa I had horse trouble, too. The horse and I came apart. In defiance of Daddy's orders I was galloping in a group of aspiring cowboys and cowgirls when some Kit Carson behind me suddenly whipped my horse and it ran amok. Charging under the branches of a eucalyptus tree, which was horse height but not mine, I fell off into the pebbled stream below while the rest of the cowboys and belles clobbered over me. When I hobbled into Aunty's cabin I looked a bedraggled wreck, with bleeding forehead and gory knees bursting through my torn jeans. The cuts and bruises worried us less than Daddy's reaction to my forbidden horsecapade.

"We'll tell your father you fell downstairs," plotted Aunty while the doctor bandaged the wounds. "He'll understand that, he's always doing it," she added with a certain relish.

He understood all right. "I knew it!" he bellowed, his face pink with anger. "It's those damned Cuban heels!" Then he turned on his surprised sister. "You incompetent idiot—you can't even look after the child when you're sober.

You're almost as useless as Useless!" With Daddy you could never win.

Although he visited us once a week and Useless also dropped in now and then, the place seemed empty without them. Sometimes Uncle Jack would stay overnight, but not often. Aunty's sitting in the mud with platinum bleached hair hadn't won him back and she knew that each time he left he was going back to the "other woman." Useless was in love.

Sometimes when I came back from school I would find Aunty wandering aimlessly from room to room, and I felt sad for this warm, cuddly person whose only companion seemed to be her eleven-year-old niece. Her new boyfriend, with whom she drank the waters, had turned out to be a Hot Springs holiday Romeo and was back with his family. To her credit she had stayed on the wagon but it wasn't long before she started mumbling about her heart fluttering again. So I wasn't really surprised when one day I arrived back from school to be stopped by Aunty before I could remove my jacket.

"Sweet Child of God, you know my heart—" she took a couple of short gasps as she tapped her great left bosom "—well, the doctor says I need some Virginia Dare wine tonic."

She handed me a dollar to go and fetch it from the corner drugstore and I knew we were in for trouble. There was just enough alcohol content in the tonic to get around the prohibition law and keep all the maiden aunts quiet—except mine. At least I knew she couldn't fill the empty bottle with Daddy's whisky because when he'd gone to live in sin he'd taken the bootlegger with him.

From then on it became my chore to bring her a bottle every day on my way back from St. Vincent's. But some days I forgot. Like Useless I, too, had fallen in love, with Chuck Montee, a thirteen-year-old who lived around the corner. Every day we rushed back from our respective schools to meet in the garden next to my apartment and sit under the magnolia tree, trading kisses and Baby Ruth candy bars. Chuck was a darling boy of stocky build with suntanned skin, brown eyes, and beige hair. He was also an aspiring poet and wrote lyrical love poems for me which he read aloud as we sat under our tree holding hands. It was usually during one of these once-in-a-lifetime moments that Aunty would fling open her window and shout down to us young lovers below.

"Hey, you little bastards!" she'd holler in her stewed Marie Dressler voice. "Stop smooching and get me my goddam heart tonic!"

Daddy was right, Aunty on the bottle was a real romance killer. Chuck and I would often play baseball with some Mexican kids who lived nearby and after the game our Mexican friends would collect freshly fried tacos from their homes and join us under our tree for a fiesta. We then wound up our feast by singing and dancing the Mexican hat dance which they'd taught us. Their version of this famous folk dance involved hopping in and out of the brim of a huge Mexican sombrero. As our dance heated up with much clapping of hands and shrieks it inevitably brought Aunty to her window in an exasperated alcoholic fury which reminded me of Daddy.

"You noisy little sons of bitches," she'd yell at us, "get the hell over the other side of the garden!"

We noisy little sons of bitches didn't mind because we all loved Aunty drunk or sober. She was also our favorite party organizer, at which job she was fantastic. Especially our Halloween parties when her interest in spirits and spooks came to the fore. There was one particular Halloween when she outstretched her capabilities and brought the wrath of the spirits down upon her head. Uncle Jack had agreed to come over, help with the party decorations and tidy up afterward. Early in the evening when Aunty was shaping the cakes into chocolate toads, rats, and bats, she made Uncle Jack cut faces out of pumpkins while she told him what a no-good bastard he was. He didn't like this but he persevered until he'd made the cardboard skeletons which he hung in the cupboards to scare us when we opened the doors. Having completed this job he put candles inside the pumpkins and jammed on his hat.

"I'm off to the corner movies," he announced suddenly, and before Aunty could answer he was out in the hall and grasping my arm. "Try and keep her off the booze. Be back after the shindig," he whispered and was gone.

"Movies, my ass," mumbled Aunty as she put the lit-up pumpkin faces in the windows. "He's gone to pick up another floozie."

But when the kids arrived her party spirit returned. She dressed all of us, including herself, in white sheets to look like ghosts and with her bottle tucked under her sheet she joined us in the Halloween custom of ringing neighborhood doorbells to collect candies from occupants. The neighbors never noticed that the short fat child weaving around in the background was Aunty.

After we'd haunted our way back to the apartment she fed us her toads, rats, and bats and bobbed our heads in a tub of water to catch apples with our teeth. Then she told our fortunes in her curtain Gypsy tent before sending all the little bastards home and this little bastard to bed. When I dozed off, Aunty was wandering about the candlelit flat in her sheet waiting for Uncle Jack.

Suddenly I awoke with a start. All hades had erupted. The fire engine bells were clanging and I thought Aunty had been up to her old tricks again. I was turning over to go back to sleep when to my surprise I spotted smoke wafting past my window. I shot out of bed and opened it. I could hear hoses splashing. One by one the neighbors in the opposite apartment house stuck their heads out of their windows.

"It's that silly old drunken woman again," shouted one of them. "I hope they get her this time!"

"No, look! By God, it's a real fire!"

"Somebody's car blazing like hell—down there!"

I looked down into the street below where more neighbors were standing on the wet sidewalk in their nightclothes watching helmeted firemen scurrying around with their hoses. Sure enough there was a car ablaze, flames shooting skyward almost to our first floor, a crackling inferno. It was Uncle Jack's car.

I raced into the living room. "Aunty! Uncle Jack's car is on fire!"

Aunty was sitting quietly in her Gypsy tent sipping her

wine tonic. She looked up at me hazily and stared right into my eyes. "What car?"

"Uncle Jack's. On fire. Aunty, it's a real fire!"

"Fire?"

I was exasperated. The heart tonic must have gone to her ears and made her deaf. "Didn't you hear all that noise? Uncle Jack's car is down there burning up!"

"No kidding," slurred Aunty as she tottered over to the front window to have a look. "Goodness gracious, that's one hell of a blaze!" She swayed around the room blowing out the pumpkin candles muttering, "Serves him right." Then with a giggle she added: "At least no one can blame *me* for calling the fire department."

When the blaze and the excitement had simmered down I was about to go back to bed when Uncle Jack burst into the room in a state of shock. His face was blue, his eyes were red, and he was trembling. "Jesus, Adelaide," he spluttered, "what in God's name happened to my Buick?"

Aunty looked at him and shrugged. "It got all burned up."

"Dammit, I know it got all burned up! But how did it happen?"

"How the hell should I know?" she answered evasively. "*I* didn't call the fire department."

"The one goddam time you *should* have called the fire department!"

"You're impossible," she reasoned unreasonably. "I can never do anything right."

"For God's sake, Adelaide—that Buick cost over two thousand bucks and look at it!" He strode over to the window, gazed down at the charred tangle of steel, stuffing, and springs, and nearly cried. "How am I gonna drive my clients tomorrow?"

"Serves you right," snapped Aunty. "Won't be able to drive your goddam whore around in it anymore. Damn you. Good riddance!"

"Oh, Christ," he wailed, "we're not on that again. I ain't got no more job. It's all down there—my whole life's work— burnt." He took another look at the blackened heap and his brow creased in a perplexed frown. "How could a car burn up by itself? It don't make sense." He walked over to Aunty who was leaning against the buffet table nibbling a chocolate toad. "You think maybe one of the kids? With the pumpkin candles?"

"Probably your damn whore did it when she saw your car here."

Uncle Jack shook his head in disbelief. "Naw, she wouldn't do a crazy thing like that."

"Perhaps the Holy Ghost spewed adulterous fire on it."

Uncle looked at her with sudden horror.

"Adelaide," he said quietly, trying to restrain himself. "You didn't——"

Aunty teetered to the Gypsy tent for her heart tonic and took a sip to wash down the toad. "Why not? I never did like that Buick anyway," she said haughtily.

The show was over and I climbed back into bed leaving them to argue about boring things like how to hide Aunty's arson from the fire department and the insurance company. I soon dozed off, lulled by the familiar wrangling and hoping that perhaps a little collusion might bring them together again. It didn't.

A few days later a furious Daddy Donlan burst into the flat. He told Aunt Adelaide he didn't want his child brought up by a pissed pyromaniac. Not only was she unstable and a danger to society, she deserved Useless, the charred Buick, and the jail sentence to go with it. He was going to take the child to live with him and never wanted to see her again. I could tell by the shade of ice blue in his eyes that this time he meant it. Aunty cried.

I was sad at the thought of leaving my broken baby elephant alone and vulnerable. She would have no one to look after her. No Useless, no growling brother, and now no more little bastard sweet Child of God. Of course, I could see Daddy's point. She had fallen apart to a degree beyond control. This time a charred car. Next time, perhaps, a charred child.

On the day I left, Aunty was quietly sober. We packed and hugged and sobbed. Between us there was an everlasting bond that had begun in the San Francisco station the day I had rushed into her comforting arms with my dress on backward. Chuck came over to say good-bye and we all hugged and sobbed again. He gave me a silver Mexican bracelet that he'd made in memory of our fiestas. When Daddy arrived to collect me Aunty hustled Chuck out the back entrance because she knew little boyfriends threw Daddy into the same rage as birds and horses.

As Daddy bundled me and my baggage into the taxi I looked back at her sad, chubby face in the window. But Daddy didn't. In fact he never saw his sister Adelaide again.

I was out of the fire and back into the lion's den.

When Daddy moved me into his small furnished Spanish-style apartment house on Mariposa Avenue in Hollywood, the whole family moved around again. His girl friend Jane moved back with her sister to make room for me. Uncle Jack moved to Mexico with the "other woman" to smuggle tequila. Aunty, with magical resilience, charmed her way out of an arson sentence and unexpectedly back into the arms of her first husband, an architect in San Francisco.

The only one left to be reorganized was Mother. On my occasional Sunday outings with her and boyfriend Jim we would play in the snow or swim in the sun according to the season at Lake Arrowhead or Big Bear, and she would ask me to try to wheedle Daddy into giving her a peaceful, no-shotgun divorce. But Daddy wouldn't budge. In spite of everything he was still hoping in vain that she would return one day.

"Besides," he snorted indignantly, "I can't lose her to a man who voted for Hoover!"

To give my life yet another new start he booked me into the Immaculate Heart of Mary School on Santa Monica Boulevard, just around the corner from the apartment. He bought me two new blue-and-white cotton uniforms, and as money was short and we couldn't afford the laundry I soon learned to wash and iron these by hand. The Depression had hit us, too. James Donlan hadn't made a picture since *The Painted Desert* with Poncho and Clark Gable. Although we never heard how Poncho was making out, Daddy's chum Gable was now under contract to Metro and had already made no less than eight pictures, playing opposite such MGM indestructibles as Joan Crawford and Norma Shearer, who also happened to be the wife of the man who said he looked like a bat.

In an effort to make our standard furnished apartment look more homey I took the streetcar to the five-and-dime store on Hollywood Boulevard and bought a couple of parchment lampshades and a painting of an Indian on a horse, silhouetted against an orange-colored sunset. By contrast, Mother's apartments were always beautifully furnished in the latest style. She rented them unfurnished and did them up herself to match her fantasies of a Hollywood dream world which didn't exist for any of us. Even so, she always pleaded a dollar shortage which used to make my old man laugh.

"Don't ever worry about your mother," he would chortle. "She always has ten thousand bucks rolled up in her sock!"

From the day I moved into Mariposa, Daddy took over his role of mother-father-nursemaid with great gusto. Nothing was required of me except perfection. Unaccustomed as he was to early rising, except when he was filming, he woke me at seven every morning with a glass of orange juice, drew my bath, and sent me to school with a stomachful of ham and eggs. He did the cooking and it was my job to do the shopping. It sounds simple, but shopping for victuals for the lion's den became a ritual which I could do without. Starving would have been easier. He always made the list of things required and then acted it out for me.

"I want you to get a slice of Swift's Premium ham," he'd say slowly, enunciating each word. Then with his forefinger and thumb he would indicate the thickness required. "It must be a quarter of an inch thick, you understand?"

"Yes, Daddy."

"Not half an inch thick or an eighth of an inch."

"No, Daddy."

"But a quarter of an inch."

"Yes, Daddy."

He did this routine through the whole list. When I got to the supermarket I repeated his scene to whoever would bother to listen and prayed it would come out all right. If I arrived back with the wrong make of bread or the ham was one-sixteenth of an inch out he would fix me with his icy blue eyes.

"Yolande." The word was almost a hiss. "I told you the ham must be one quarter of an inch thick. You are growing up to be as stupid as your mother. Now take it back and see if you can get it right this time."

I would plead with the butcher to try to get it perfect and tremble all the way home in case it wasn't, because each time his anger mounted. It wasn't unusual to go back three times for the same item. Eventually, I started trembling as soon as he handed me the list. One memorable Friday the thirteenth, 1933, in the supermarket, I was shaking so much I suddenly noticed all the cans were tumbling off the shelves and the glass was shattering. In panic I ran out onto Santa Monica Boulevard. Even the street was rocking from side to side like an endless ocean liner. An eerie thundering sound came from nowhere. Shop windows were breaking, buildings cracking, masonry falling. My God, I thought, it's the end of the world! Just like the nuns had told us it would be. The Day of Judgment was here. I looked into my bag of groceries to count my sins. Any second the street would open and send me crashing down into hell. I pulled out the bread. Yes, it was Langendorf's. The right make. Out came the Swift's Premium ham. Yes, I'd measured it at the butcher's with my ruler. Everything else was there. Perfect.

Someone yelled: "Hey, little girl! Get in a doorway, it's an earthquake!"

45
☆

I paid no attention. I ran back home, mid the falling debris. Elated. Excited, For once I had all the shopping right.

It wasn't until the news flashes started breaking into the radio programs to tell us there had been thirty-five shocks from Santa Barbara to San Diego that I realized I'd actually been in my first earthquake. Hundreds had been killed and thousands injured, mainly around Long Beach. And with my delayed reaction I found it all pretty scary.

"They don't know what a real earthquake's like," snorted my old man, switching off the radio and trying to calm me. "Did I ever tell you about the San Francisco one?"

He hadn't, but Aunty had. Both she and Jimmy Donlan had been in the middle of it. After that 1906 quake the whole city had caught on fire and was completely destroyed.

"No doubt," Daddy reflected caustically, "that San Francisco fire was largely aided and abetted by your damn fool aunt."

The thing Aunty remembered most about that earthquake was the fact that it had ruined their favorite playground, a string of underground opium dens that ran in a maze underneath Chinatown. She and brother Jimmy, fed up with feeding the squirrels in Golden Gate Park with the rest of the kids, had gone off exploring one day and discovered these subterranean passages by chance. From then on they spent their play days sneaking through the catacomby tunnels peering into the dens of smokers who were laid out on tiers of bunks puffing their opium pipes. It was down here that they found their favorite pet—an opium-sniffing cat who sat outside the dens permanently stoned. Feeding a stoned cat had it all over the Golden Gate Park squirrels.

The opium smokers puzzled me.

"What's the fun in lying around all day half asleep?" I remember asking her when she told me the story. "It's bad enough having to go to bed at night."

Aunty agreed. Apparently she and Jimmy had cadged a few sniffs from the cat and felt exactly the same. So they became alcoholics instead.

Hollywood eventually made the film about San Francisco's famous earthquake in which our cowboy friend Mr. Gable starred opposite Jeanette MacDonald. In it the effects department cooked up a pretty good earthquake. But there were no opium dens, no potted Chinese gentlemen, and no stoned cat. What a disappointment. They were always leaving out the best bits.

Although Daddy dismissed our Los Angeles earthquake as a big nothing, it closed our schools for a couple of weeks. After a big quake there are always a series of little afterquakes and crowd gatherings are discouraged in case of panic. In our homes all breakables were put away, standing lamps put down, and everyone adjusted to living on board a ship in a stormy sea of California palm trees. We shook back and forth in each other's homes and tried to pretend it was nothing.

The week after school had reopened I was awakened one night by the crashing sound of broken glass. My bed was shaking and the walls creaking. It was a particularly violent tremor and I was really frightened. Gingerly skirting the broken glass, I tiptoed around the horrible Indian painting, which had fallen to the floor, and crept into Daddy's room. He was snoring off a snootful of booze and had missed the whole epic. He opened one poached eye.

"What's up?"

"Me."

"Why?"

"These earthquakes scare me."

"What earthquake? Go to bed. You'll be a dunce tomorrow."

"Maybe there'll be another one. Can I come in with you?"

He mumbled something that sounded like: "Yesh and de biddle dee shleep," and was off snoring again. I climbed into the lion's lair. It smelled of stale cigarette butts, half-empty glasses of hooch, and last night's perfume, similar to a sleazy nightclub when the customers have gone. The lion roared, snorted, and hissed more alcohol fumes into the haze already hanging over his lair. He heaved and rolled, shaking the bed so that I couldn't possibly get to sleep. I got up again. The lion opened the other poached eye.

"What's up?"

"Me."

"Why, another earthquake?"

"No, you."

"Me?"

"Your snoring. I prefer the earthquake."

The year before the quake Daddy Donlan had had a long stretch without working and whenever Daddy Donlan was unemployed there was a noticeable shortage of beautiful people around to listen to his jokes. On these occasions I became his captive audience. His stories were mainly about mishaps in the theater. They were true and genuinely funny the way he told them. My school friends and I would roll on the floor in maniacal hysterics, clasping our jiggling sides. Although I listened to the stories year after year, like a dutiful wife, I was never bored. Besides which it was much better than catching hell for only reaching second place in class instead of first. Also a great improvement over the endless days of uncommunicating silence that reigned over the Mariposa apartment when he was in a black mood. At these times he sat in the kitchen in a Noël Coward dressing gown, rolling Bull Durham cigarettes over a pie-tin ashtray, doing the *Los Angeles Times* crossword puzzles.

On our evenings of communication he would suddenly turn to me and say, "Come here, my little princess." I would climb upon his knee like Sonny Boy and listen to his bedtime song of the blues. The words seldom varied. He was lonely, should never have come to Hollywood, longed to be back in the theater, the lousy booze was making him ill, he'd been a fool wasting his money on wine, women, and song, and everything would change with the next film job—if he ever got one.

When confession was over he would kiss his little princess goodnight and send her off to say her bedtime prayers for his sins. He assumed that as I was up to my emerging boobs in holy convent schools I must have a hot-line to the Holy Boss. When I did speak to the Holy Boss I reminded him that we had heard all that malarkey before. As soon as His lost sheep Donlan got another film he would think he was on the road to stardom again—Jack Oakie, Pat O'Brien, and Eugene Palette were making it, so why not James Donlan? And once more our streetcar rides would be replaced by a chauffeured limousine. Monogramed silk shirts would be ordered for him and I would be given a wad of dollars to replenish my wardrobe from Bullock's, the more expensive department store in downtown Los Angeles, instead of the nearby bargain basement at Sears and Roebuck. When there was work nothing was too good for the king of the lions and his little princess. Taxis would be sent to Gotham's delicatessen for jars of *pâté de foie gras* and caviar, beaming bootleggers would reappear with cases of hooch, and beautiful dames would arrive with open arms, legs, and hands.

I always knew when one of the latter was occupying his attention because on my return from school I would find a note from him at the apartment reception desk. It would read:

> *Frying a fish. Enclosed is ten dollars for you to see a movie and have dinner.*

I never found out why he chose this particular phrase to describe the nature of his assignation. But I was always delighted when he was "frying a fish" as it gave me an evening out with one of my school girl friends. In those days two dollars bought us a gourmet's repast, after which we little Lolitas could flirt past the handsome young doormen into the Warner Brothers Theater to see Bette Davis emoting for free. That left eight dollars which I could put in my sock like Mother, as insurance against the inevitable.

Frying a fish usually took about three hours. After all, he had to tell them a few jokes first. But he was always much jollier after his fry up. However, if he had known I'd even *looked* at a handsome young doorman, let alone flirted, the wrath of the lion would have descended on his little princess and I would have become his little budding whore. By comparison Fanny Hill would be a nun. He frightened me so much I remained a virgin until I was a hundred—well, almost. He was so concerned with my virtue he even opened my mail. Especially after my first letter from Chuck Montee. In it poor innocent Chuck had written: "Every night I lie in bed thinking of you, Yolande, and wishing you were back here." Daddy, in one of his blind rages, shook this letter in my surprised face one day when I arrived back from school.

"For Christ's sake, what were you up to while your drunken aunt was burning cars?"

"Nothing, Daddy."

"What do you mean, nothing! This Chuck says you were in bed with him," he spluttered. "A fucking eleven-year-old child?"

I looked again at the scarlet letter. I was in despair at Daddy's misinterpretation.

"Honestly, Daddy, Chuck meant living back in Los Angeles instead of Hollywood, not back in his bed. Believe me, we never fried fish—only tacos."

"Yeah? Well, see you don't. I told you before, boyfriends are out. O.U.T. Out. You'll grow up a slut and I will not have a whore in my house. Can't you understand?"

"No, Daddy, I mean, yes, Daddy." I didn't know what I meant, I was so confused. He was always having whores in the house. I thought he liked them.

He stood there solidly, his legs apart and his feet ground firmly into the floor. Then he tore my first love note, bit by bit, into tiny unpatchable pieces. As I watched him I cried inside. Chuck was out—O.U.T.—out, and I loved him with a love that was more than a love, me and my Chuck Montee. Who says kids don't fall in love? Grown-ups?

When Daddy had finished tearing my heart apart he uttered his final warning. "If I ever catch you with another boyfriend you'll go straight into an orphanage. Do you hear me?"

I heard all right, but I knew that even in Hollywood orphanages don't accept kids with two perfectly healthy parents. The frightened lion was roaring up his unreasonable tail.

"Now do your homework and come back with all A's this term!" He kissed me good night. "That's my little princess," he said, and went out and got pissed.

In 1932, toward the end of my first year with Daddy, his luck suddenly changed and at long last it seemed he, too, had grasped Hollywood's golden ring. He worked almost continuously, making and spending eight pictures in a row. Our Mariposa apartment was jumping with start-of-picture celebrations, middle-of-picture fish frying, and end-of-picture parties. His newly found chums from each cast flowed in and out of Mariposa as regularly as the tides in the Pacific.

I carried the caviar and passed the paté to people as widely assorted as Edna Mae Oliver and Bela Lugosi, ZaSu Pitts and Lupe Velez, Frank Morgan, Slim Summerville, and John Ford. Mr. Ford, who had directed my old man in a picture called *Air Mail* with Ralph Bellamy and Pat O'Brien, had made a great impression on him.

"He's the only director I've met who's got balls," was Daddy's capsuled comment.

For six frenetic months it was all happening. Then, as suddenly as it had all started, it stopped; the mad spending spree was over and we were back in the Mariposa scullery, broke. Except for my sock.

It saddened me to watch my old man relying more and more on the bootlegger's whisky and getting more and more into debt with his carousing nights on the town. With no work to occupy his mind there was more time for him to dwell on thoughts of Mother and her continuing pleas for divorce.

By now, Mother's divorce had become urgent and marriage to boyfriend Jim imperative. Not that she was pregnant again, but her French mother was threatening to leave Paris and return to live with her in California. My mother didn't want *her* mother to find her living in sin in sinful Hollywood. She wanted to marry boyfriend Jim. But that meant divorcing Daddy Jimmy.

In the Catholic Church a second marriage doesn't count unless the first partner is dead. So I didn't know what she was fussing about. There were no apparent ecclesiastical loopholes for an annulment. I was living proof of consummation. Short of shooting Daddy there was no solution. It was the first of my many religious dilemmas.

According to the nuns both murder and adultery were mortal sins. Especially if you plotted them ahead of time. Murder was only permitted in groups of holy warfare, but group sex orgies were never allowed. The price of the single fare to the Hereafter for both sins was penance on Earth, more penance after death in a dreary place called Purgatory, and if you were unlucky, an instant drop to everlasting Hell's fire. As murdering Daddy could hasten the voyage to Hell via the California gas chamber, legal civil adultery seemed the wiser choice.

When Daddy was in an approachable mood I confronted him with Mother's problem.

"Mother's fed up living in sin, Daddy. She thinks it frightens the neighbors and will worry Grandma. You're always blowing your dough, getting drunk, missing your Easter duty, and frying fish. Why don't you two lapsed Catholics get a divorce?"

He peered down at me. I could see two tiny drops of water shimmering in the corners of his puffy blue eyes. The tentative ice in them had melted. "I still love her," he said simply.

"I know you do, so do I. But Mother loves Jim now and you'll have to face it, Daddy. You're an impossible roommate."

"Yes," he agreed, "God knows I am."

"Well, then?"

His shoulders slumped. He seemed half his size. He was no longer king of the jungle. I wanted to hug my deflated lion and I did. He nodded his dejected head in assent; he was unable to say, "Tell her okay," out loud.

"Don't you ever leave me," he said. "Promise?"

"I promise."

I hoped he could eventually find someone in his own

age group who could put up with him. Still another part of me wanted to remain his number one princess.

No matter how many fish he fried, Mother was the one love in his heart until death did him part. For a lousy Catholic he kept his vows. I went to the divorce court as Mother's principal witness to swear to God under oath what a bastard he was. It was true. And yet?

The California divorce was justly granted on the grounds of mental cruelty, and Mother cut Daddy out of all her snapshots.

One night, during my routine bed-kneeling I asked the Holy Boss to please get James Donlan a new film job. In exchange for this divine favor I would attempt to get His straying sheep back into the fold. I was always making deals with the Almighty. Probably picked it up from the Hollywood agents. My first move, I decided, was to try to replace Daddy's drinking cronies with holy people.

I had barely hung up on the hotline to Heaven when the Holy Boss produced a new movie for Daddy. He was to report to RKO studios to appear in *Men of Chance* with Ricardo Cortez and Mary Astor. Within an hour of the agent's call Daddy had borrowed another two hundred dollars to pay the bootlegger and take me out for a celebration banquet. That night I thanked the Holy Boss for acting so promptly and promised to carry out my part of the bargain as quickly as possible. I might not have slept so peacefully had I known what He still had in store.

The following morning I arrived at school to find a handsome new Irish priest in attendance. His name was Father O'Sullivan, he was fresh from the Emerald Isle and had come to Hollywood to teach us kiddies our catechism and convert the souls of movieland. I was convinced God had sent him to help me rescue Daddy. How was I to know his road to Heaven would be paved with calamities?

Father O'Sullivan had the looks and command of the young Laurence Olivier combined with the sensitivity of Robert Donat. Within a short time his appearance in the pulpit of our Immaculate Heart Church doubled the takings of our hitherto unknown parish. For me, and half of Hollywood's female stars and starlets, it was love at first sight and standing room only. There were Jeanette MacDonald, Nancy Carroll, Lupe Velez, Bebe Daniels—the pews simply bristled with glamour as he leaped through the Mass with the speed and agility of today's Rudolph Nureyev, causing a sacred box-office bonanza. We did everything but queue for tickets and throw flowers at him. We couldn't wait to tell him our sins. It was boomtown in his confessional box.

Lovely stars drove all the way from exclusive Beverly Hills to seedy Santa Monica Boulevard to whisper their sexy sagas into his holy, celibate earhole. Who could compete with such glamorous sins, I thought, as I watched them pour into his confessional. The contents of Chuck's scarlet letter would send him to sleep. I decided the best way I could capture his interest would be to take him home to listen to Daddy. Surely my old man's red-hot sins would burn the whiskers out of his ears.

Between sizzling revelations The Reverend O'Sullivan, draped in his purple stole, would crawl out of his box to pace behind the last pew in the narthex, saying his daily office. On my lucky days he would take pity on this lovesick student and kiss her on the forehead. I would collapse in religious ecstasy.

Although his filmland fans were mainly female, John Barrymore frequently staggered in to attend Father O'Sullivan's performances. The Great Profile, in beachcomber clothes, always slouched in the back pew. But in spite of his condition he never carried on like Aunty—not in church, anyway. He held himself with an air of Victorian formality and even if he stumbled here and there he did it with great dignity. He was one of O'Sullivan's lost sheep and was shortly doomed to meet my lost sheep.

Not only the stars, but all the girls in our class had a crush on this gorgeous Father O'Sullivan. So did our nun teacher, Sister Marie. Every time The Reverend Glamorpuss entered our classroom Sister Marie blushed scarlet, lowered her sex-starved eyes, and hid in the cloakroom at the back of the room. Most likely on her knees scratching her hair shirt.

He strolled up and down the rows of desks giving us

God talk. Occasionally he stopped to sit on some swooning little girl's desk. There were boys in the class, too, but the Reverend Humbert-Humbert never sat on theirs. Whenever he sat on mine I quivered with excitement from head to virginal bottom and remembered all the answers in the catechism. It was the first time I got 100 percent in religion. Daddy was so pleased he asked me to bring around this genius who could get something into my dunce's head. It was the beginning of a memorable epoch!

The evening the holy priest called on us he was not alone. He had brought John Barrymore along as well. They were both profuse with their apologies.

"I hope you don't mind," said Father O'Sullivan, "but we have a dinner date later in Beverly Hills."

"Until then," said the aging Profile, "I shall hide unseen in the corner."

I was slightly worried about Mr. Barrymore. I'd heard rumors of his wild reputation which cast doubts on his holiness credentials. Daddy, however, was delighted to meet another tippler, especially one from the legitimate theater. Barrymore, although a top movie star, had served an illustrious sentence in Shakespeare and the news of his outstanding success as Hamlet had stretched from Broadway clear across the Atlantic to Stratford-upon-Avon where it even shook the British. Yes, both the British and the American actors respected the Barrymore talent, and that included my old man. The two alcoholic hams, who were sober for a minute, struck up an instant camaraderie.

At first Daddy seemed a bit uneasy with the handsome young curate in the God collar and made a beeline for the bottle. Mr. Barrymore turned to me, bowed regally, and kissed my hand.

"Enchanted to meet you, dear lady," Hamlet declaimed. "The name is Jack."

It was the first time I'd had my hand kissed. I felt like Ophelia must have felt before Hamlet drove her mad. Daddy poured out his best whisky for Barrymore who downed it with accustomed alacrity. Then he handed one to the Irish holy who swallowed it with matching speed. I could see this pleased my old man. It had broken the liturgical ice. I gurgled happily into my Coca Cola.

A few snifters later Father O'Sullivan told a couple of Irish church funnies. Daddy pulled out some of his old theater jokes. Barrymore threw in a few new ones. They were all pros from different settings. The priest, the star and the supporting actor chuckled and warmed to each other. But nobody said anything holy, except Mr. Barrymore. Every time he heard the clinking of the bottle against his glass he bowed his head.

"The Angelus!" he intoned piously.

Pretty soon they had removed their jackets and the glamorous priest unfrocked his collar. Now they all looked the same and it didn't seem like anyone was going to dine in Beverly Hills.

"Let me ask you something, Father," said Daddy, tapping O'Sullivan's knee. "Why in God's name does any man want to be a priest? My uncle was an archbishop and, God almighty, did he have a time with his chastity vows. No regular dames, no regular hours, always catching hell when he went off on a spree——"

Barrymore tapped Daddy's knee.

"I wish to hell I'd been an R.C.–J.C. salesman instead of a strolling player. At least O'Sullivan here can read his lines. Furthermore, they're all in Latin, so nobody knows if he fluffs."

Mr. Barrymore hated learning lines and was beginning to have trouble remembering them at the studios. He was fed up with dames, too. "Alimony is the most exorbitant of stud fees," was one of his more laconic statements.

The priest explained he'd been ordained by his parents to become a priest long before he was ordained. His four sisters were nuns and his eldest brother a bishop.

"It's a family trade," he smiled. Then with a tinge of nostalgia: "I was in love with an Irish girl before I took my vows."

"And you've regretted it ever since." Daddy's tone was sympathetic.

Father, James Donlan, Mother, Thérèse, daughter Yolande, in Hollywood. Taken during a lull in the fighting.

(*Above, left*) Yolande in car, Aunty Adelaide center and Mother right

(*Above, right*) Mother, Aunty, and Grand'mère, age ninety at the time

(*Left*) Yolande with "some boyfriend I must have picked up in Hollywood"

(*Below, left*) "First Communion, age seven. Mother cut someone out of the picture."

Yolande's first Hollywood photo, aged seventeen

Yolande after she moved in with Mother

(*Opposite*) Sgt. Philip Truex and author at
time of their wedding

Immaculate Heart Grammar School. "The
priest is *not* Father O'Sullivan."

Jimmy Donlan (center back) with the young Clark Gable (right) in his first speaking part in *The Painted Desert*

Daddy (center) with Harold Lloyd in *Professor Beware*, 1938

Daddy with Mae West in *Belle of the Nineties,* 1934
(PARAMOUNT PICTURES)

With Edward Everret Horton in *Design for Living*, 1933
(PARAMOUNT PICTURES)

"No. I admit it was a terrible wrench at the time," the smile again, "but I've never regretted it. I like my job."

"And now," added Barrymore, "he's the only man I know who can recite the whole of the Burghwallis Examination of Conscience."

"What the hell's that?" frowned my old man.

"It was compiled in the sixteenth century," smiled O'Sullivan. "In those days it was a preparation for confession. Jack's main interest is in the adultery section. It stimulates his waning lust. This particular examination is no longer used."

"Just as well," snorted the old Profile. "It had a list of 'have you or have you nots' to be answered before you entered the box. I assure you the questions would have kept all of us out of the box forever! Lend me your ears, Donlan. For a start: It asks your conscience 'Have you gone voluntarily into lewd company, lascivious balls or revelings?' "

"No kidding?" Daddy gurgled while he snorted his snifter.

"Would I lie in front of a man of God?"

"It's true," smiled Father O'Sullivan.

"What a lot of old balls," grunted Daddy.

"You said it, Jimmy," laughed the priest. "How can you tell what's voluntary and who's lascivious until you get to the old balls? Only our Father in Heaven knows that. Those poor sods in my job must have had one hell of a time trying to interpret that one, God bless their souls."

"God bless them," said Barrymore into his whisky.

"God bless them," said Daddy into his ditto.

"God bless them," I chirped into my coke.

We all bowed our heads and raised our glasses in memory of those poor sixteenth-century clerical sods resting in peace in never-never land. I was delighted that my holies were back onto holy land. The drunks were looking up.

"Give Jimmy the juicy examination, Jack," said Father O'Sullivan.

"Now hold on to your hat, Donlan, while I attempt to recall number two." The Barrymore brow furrowed in con-

57
☆

centration. " 'Have you showed your skin or some naked part of your body to incite others?' Now answer me that one, my sinful friend."

Daddy paused to reflect. He sipped his snifter, coughed out the fumes, and glopped down his water chaser.

"On occasion I have tried to show it," he replied "But whether or not my skin or some naked part of my body has incited anyone is questionable."

"A true Christian reply," Mr. Barrymore complimented. "On occasion even I, the reputedly Great Lover, have shared your dilemma."

"Come along, Jack," chuckled O'Sullivan. "Stop bewailing your lost opportunities and get on with it. I'm getting hungry."

"My dear Reverend Pisspot," bellowed Barrymore at the height of his dignity, "surely you know by now not to stop a Barrymore in full flow and command of his words? Replenish your holy orifice with one of those nuts."

I raced over to my idol with the nuts, genuflected before him, and passed them into his holy orifice, heart aflutter.

"Thank you, my child."

"And I thank you, too, my dear lady," said the Profile, proceeding to recall the hot bits in the ancient holy confessional book.

" 'Have you,' " he boomed at my old man, " 'deflowered a maid upon promise of marriage and not kept it?' "

Before Daddy had time to answer I assured Mr. Barrymore that my old man was innocent of that one; Mother had told me.

"A fine Christian fellow, your father," said Mr. B. "He has bred a loyal daughter, my lady."

I liked the malarkey he was handing me, but I was getting hungry too, and I wished he would now dry up. But no such luck. Actors do go on when they are on.

" 'Hast thou buggered man, woman, or beast?' " he demanded resonantly.

"Depends on the beast," joked Daddy Donlan.

Oh, bugger, bugger, bugger, I groaned inwardly.

"Or 'defrauded the prince of taxes justly imposed?' "

"Hell," sighed Daddy, "we're all in on that one."

"We damn well are," said O'Sullivan and they all laughed. I didn't. I knew the tax man only too well. He was forever on our doorstep and Daddy was forever borrowing from my sock.

In quick succession they covered the Burghwallis Examination of Conscience on fornication, adultery, incest, bestiality, sacrilege, rape, carding, and dicing. These were only a few of the ecclesiastical tidbits I was to pick up from this incredible Catholic threesome. And then, after my old man had opened up the third bottle Barrymore turned to me abruptly.

"Dear lady, forgive us for boring you with our ecumenical chatter. What may we do for our attentive little hostess?"

"Eat," I remember saying. And suddenly we were all in the kitchen. Daddy rummaged in the fridge, produced some curdled custard he'd made, and we all gathered around the kitchen table eating it out of bowls and sipping glasses of milk.

"Good for the stomach," he insisted. "Keeps the snakes out."

"It is rumored," said the priest, "that St. Patrick chased all the snakes out of Ireland. Thank God he left us our whisky."

As soon as they'd lined their stomachs they sprang from the custard and milk back into the whisky. Daddy decided they should go out on the town as his guests. The priest needed a change of routine, he urged. Why not see some of the hotspots he'd been hearing about in his confessional box? O'Sullivan demurred. He couldn't tear around Hollywood in his dog collar, it would shock the natives and shake the child. Daddy agreed he would need a new costume for the natives, but assured him the child was unshakable. He put his arm around my shoulders and gave me a warm, whisky hug.

"Nothing shakes Yolande," he chortled, making the understatement of the thirties. "She also knows how to keep her mouth shut, don't you, my little princess?"

She certainly did. To prove it his little princess nodded

59
☆

her head and buttoned her lip. Sozzled O'Sullivan succumbed. He was now too many whiskies beyond the age of reason.

The two experienced actors lost little time in disguising the reverend's garb. Daddy loaned him a blue silk shirt and his old school tie. Barrymore chose his new name.

"I christen thee Horatio Macgillicuddy."

"My God," said the new Macgillicuddy.

What to do about me? It was Friday. No school tomorrow and I didn't want to miss out on the fun. Happily, Mr. Barrymore suggested I join them. Daddy agreed.

"She usually comes out with me on weekends," he explained. "Not much she hasn't seen."

"She couldn't be in better company," pronounced the aging Profile, "than that of our friend Mr. Horatio Macgillicuddy."

Handsome Horatio grinned happily.

Elated I rushed into the bedroom to titivate my freckles. The clerical shirt and collar lay crumpled across my very own bed. How romantic. Hastily I put on my forbidden Cuban heels and some newly forbidden lipstick. I knew I was safe. The Donlan laws were always more relaxed when he was merrily soused. I had to look my grown-up wicked best for a night on the tiles with the most glamorous plastered priest in Hollywood.

With Hamlet on one arm and my secret love, Horatio, on the other I was swept off to the wicked hotspots.

I must explain that these clubs were mainly for the tourists and not normally frequented by the film colony whose early 5 A.M. calls and long working days usually sent them to bed by nine o'clock at night. Whose bed? Who knows? Not me, Daddy. Mouth shut.

The native clientele for these clubs were local businessmen, with or without wife, secretary, bird, dame, doll, or broad. Our first hotspot was the Paris Inn Supper Club in downtown Los Angeles with singing waiters everywhere. An artist in a smock and beret drifted from table to table sketching the customers. Daddy and I were sketched. Understandably, Horatio declined the offer. He was as secret as the booze in Daddy's flask, which they kept pouring into their ginger ales while the waiter closed his eyes and sang "Plaisir d'amour." Barrymore declined. The sketch, not the whisky.

Next stop was the Three Stooges Club back in Hollywood. It was a small, dimly lit nightclub where the Three Stooges, a currently popular comedy act, made us all laugh by cuffing each other around. I think it was here that I was surprised to see a fully frontal naked lady lying on her side, on one elbow, in a fishtank. This human aquarium was set into one of the walls as part of the decor and there she lay, all lit up, mid potted ferns and papier-maché rocks for the whole evening. She was advertised as The Pocket Venus. I remember wondering if perhaps this pretty little female fishlady had inspired my old man's phrase, "frying a fish."

Of the three men at our table I noticed it was Horatio Macgillicuddy who couldn't keep his eyes off The Pocket Venus. It was about this time it occurred to me that the reverend holy was getting less holy as he became more sloshed, while Daddy carried on in his normal wanton ways. My plan had gone awry. The contract between the Holy Boss in Heaven and the Immaculate Heart schoolgirl, re saving Jimmy Donlan's soul, was becoming all screwed up—like most Hollywood contracts.

The most surprising show of all was our next stop, Hollywood's most notorious den of iniquity, Jimmie's Backyard. It was a homosexual nightclub. Just off Sunset Boulevard, it was a sort of well-known secret underground place where forbidden alcohol was served by and to fairies, queens, and dykes. The term "gay" hadn't yet been invented. It was a very kinky place for those times and it was considered extremely daring to go there, even for heterosexual grown-ups with ties and shirts. I was thrilled. All the young women in the club dressed like young men and the young men like young women. Just like they do today. It was more exciting then because it was naughty. If they go on taking away all our old sins we'll soon have to get our kicks from a life of stoic mysticism. More economical, too, than forbidden Jimmie's Backyard was.

Because Daddy had been there before, we were given a

ringside table to view the drag act cabaret. It was my first homosexual nightclub and I thought it was fascinating. Especially as none of the other convent girls had even *heard* of homosexuality. Some of them had been practicing it. But they just didn't know what to call it.

The star of the show was a giant male ballerina called George. In a sparkling net tutu he looked and danced like an Alicia Markova on his great big beautiful toes. At my dancing school none of the boys in the class ever danced in toe shoes like we girls did. So this tall, muscular queen was a revelation, a Boris Karloff on points.

After his tour-de-Swan-Lake he changed into his décolleté evening gown and flounced over to our table, hovering behind Daddy's chair, hoping to meet Mr. Barrymore.

"I'd like you to meet my mother," said Daddy to all of us as he introduced George, the queen of the fairies. He called all fags mother. George joined us for drinks and Barrymore, Donlan, and Horatio Macgillicuddy toasted his agile, iron toes. George flushed with delight. I asked him if his toes still hurt like mine always did. Jingling his bracelets and waving his magenta-polished claws in my direction, he said. "But of course, dear child, my little pinkies are permanently swathed in medical gauze. Sheer torture," he giggled, "and I love every minute of it!"

But Daddy's and Barrymore's eyes were not on George. They were circling the room prospecting the lonely dames situation. It looked a pretty hopeless quest to me. The ladies they had in mind were already with male escorts, snooping like us. The single ladies were all dykes and whether in male or female garb they were only interested in other females.

As I was the only available dancing partner, Daddy foxtrotted me around the floor. They were playing our tune, Gershwin's "Someone To Watch over Me," one of the hit numbers from Daddy's old stage success *Oh Kay*. While he cased the joint for prospective females I sang my favorite part of the lyrics into his fat red ear: "He may not be the man some girls think of as handsome, but to my heart he'll carry the key. . . ."

On our second trot around he spotted a perky, elfin-type,

copper-tressed girl with an Eton crop. She was seated alone at one of the back tables and was wearing a clerical-gray man's blazer, blue shirt, and striped tie—similar to Horatio Macgillicuddy's disguise. In spite of her masculine attire she had an extremely feminine appeal which, I noticed, lit up my old man's hazy blue eyes. He rushed me back to our table, interrupting George's flamboyant discourse with Horatio and Barrymore.

"Mother George," he panted, "I've just seen a real lolla-palooza of a dame." He pointed out his lollapalooza to George and all three men peered across the murky nightclub to the distant table.

George let out a whoop. "Oh, but that's Charlie," he hooted, "She's not for the likes of you, dear Jimmy."

Horatio's handsome brows knotted into a crease of alco-holic perplexity. "Why not?" he asked. "Is Charlie a boy or a girl?"

"Oh, Charlie's a girl all right, Horatio darling. She's just taken a turn against men. Hardly puts up with me," he gig-gled. "But I adore her. Given me all her old earrings."

Determined Daddy wasn't going to be turned off. He scowled at Mother George.

"Don't give me them apples! Once a dame always a dame," he philosophized. "Ask the young lady if she'll give us the pleasure of her company for a drink."

George slithered around the crowded tables to fetch Charlie girl, and Daddy turned to Barrymore. "What the hell, we can't let female talent like hers go to waste. A couple of drinks, a few spins around the floor—who knows? What d'you say, Jack?"

Barrymore slowly lifted his profile from the drink in which it was immersed and straightened the top of his torso to its full Shakespearean height.

"Listen, craphouse Donlan," he said in measured tones, "if you wish to waste your energy trying to convert a dyke into a dame, God speed to you. As for me, I'm too old and too tired to be a missionary."

When Mother George arrived with Charlie girl all my gentlemen stood up like the gentlemen they were. Mr. B.

kissed her hand, Daddy pulled up a chair for her between him and Barrymore. George plunked himself next to Horatio to flutter his false eyelashes at the most attractive male at the table, but to no avail. All our attentions were now centered on Charlie girl who on closer viewing appeared like a young British public school girl; the tie, the shirt, the blazer, the skirt, no makeup—everything but the hat. The only unfeminine gesture was the way she held her cigarette between thumb and forefinger.

She graciously accepted the ginger ale Daddy offered but declined the nip from his flask. I liked that bit. Perhaps, I thought innocently, they could convert each other in spite of squiffy old Barrymore. What did he know? Seemed to me he was now more in love with his bottle than any dame. Perhaps with him it had been a case of too many, too easy, too soon. A bottle of booze could become an aging actor's last lover. I'd seen it happen to Daddy's boozing buddies. And I didn't want that to happen to my old man. Anyway, he was much younger than Mr. B., so there was still hope for him. I was delighted when he took Charlie girl in his arms and tripped his light fantastic with her around the floor.

She seemed to be enjoying herself. I saw her burst into a guffaw. One of the Donlan jokes. She was in her twenties, but because of her uniform and no makeup she looked almost as young as the girls at my school. After Daddy's whirl the young dyke invited me to dance. It came as no surprise as I'd spent my life dancing with other girls at my assorted Catholic schools. I must confess, however, I was a little disappointed as I'd been secretly hoping my next dance might be with the divine Horatio. Off we waltzed while she told me how fortunate I was to have such a jolly father. Hers had been torture, she said. As we danced I heard Mr. Barrymore's voice booming across the floor.

"Arise, Macgillicuddy, we shall tread the boards and pirouette together!"

Fortunately, the Rev. Horatio declined the offer. Just as he had declined Mother George's earlier invitation to tango with him. As for George, he seemed a nice guy who was just a little too ambitious. A case of, "Seek him here, seek him there, seek him in all the wrong directions." Anyway, I thought he was great on his points. I should dance so well! I liked his false eyelashes, too. They looked so natural up close. He told me he made them himself from Charlie girl's shorn tresses, that's how come the natural look. Then he showed me how he did it with a snip off the end of my hair. We had a lot in common, Mother George and I.

Suddenly Horatio announced that he required the gentlemen's powder room. Due to the great quantity of liquid he had unwittingly consumed Horatio Macgillicuddy now wished to pass some holy water. George waved his arm toward the distant men's room and then concentrated his attention on me again explaining the ins and outs of his décolleté gown about which I had expressed an interest. He had realized by now that tonight was not his night with the men at our table and was quite content to chat glamour clothes with a little girl ballet fan. I had long ago accepted my role as a last refuge for grownups when nothing else seemed to be going for them.

As George and I were chatting it up, Daddy and Charlie girl laughing it up, and Barrymore drinking it up, there was a sudden shattering noise from the men's room. All our heads snapped around in time to see Horatio burst out of the door hastily buttoning his fly. He arrived at our table in a state of breathless panic.

"My God," he exclaimed, "I was only trying to emit a pee when some hulking football player type made a pass! It was touch and go for a minute. Started hitting out with his fists. Took all my strength to get out. 'Must have thought I was exposing myself!"

"A modicum of calm, Macgillicuddy," soothed Mr. Barrymore. "And from now on learn the Eleventh Commandment: Thou shalt not get caught with private parts in public places."

"If anything sobered me up that did!" Horatio flopped back into his chair. "Haven't had to cope with one of those situations since my schooldays."

Daddy poured him another drink to quiet his nerves and everyone at our table was deeply sympathetic.

65
☆

"Men can be such boors," said the young dyke.

"The whole incident is sickmaking," shuddered Mother George. "I abhore violence. And in *our* powder room!"

"Oh, well, forget it. I'm still unscathed." Horatio reached for his glass with a trembling hand.

This last incident must have given my soaked old man an attack of the creepy-jeebies because one round of drinks later both us Donlans, Horatio, and Barrymore had bid a fond farewell to Mother George and Charlie girl and Daddy was out on Sunset Boulevard hailing a taxi.

"To the Los Angeles morgue, please," he told the driver as though it was the most natural place to end up.

"The morgue?" echoed Horatio, as Daddy hustled us into the yellow cab. "Why the morgue, you mad Irish fool?"

"A perfect place to round off an epic evening," answered Daddy. "I have to check in there to see if any of my old boozers have become stiffs yet."

Before Horatio could open his still quivering beak, Barrymore had opened his.

"The morgue it is," he agreed with happy anticipation, as the taxi sped toward L.A. "And what an ideal time to pay a call, with you in tow, Horatio. Perchance one of your last sacraments might come in handy."

The Reverend Horatio Macgillicuddy, who looked as if he was ready for beddy-byes, turned his appealing eyes to Daddy. "No. Home, James. Enough is enough. I have Mass to say in the morning. Anyway, I don't have my extreme unction oils—and I'm too oiled to use them if I did." He leaned forward and patted my hand. It felt lovely. "Besides," he added, "you can't take the child to the morgue."

"Why not?" demanded Daddy. "She's been everywhere else."

"That's for sure," Horatio had to admit. "Oh, what the hell!" With a philosophical grin he retreated back into his seat.

I was literally squeaking with excitement by the time we arrived outside the morgue, or what my old man called Stiff's Citadel.

"We have come," announced Barrymore to the somewhat surprised attendant, "to see if you have any friends of ours inside."

"Do you have any authority, sir?"

"Authority," boomed the Profile, "is something I have always had."

"Yes, sir," said the rattled attendant as he produced the official incident book. "May I have your names?"

"You may, and heed them well for they are citizens of great repute. One James Donlan and Horatio Macgillicuddy and, of course, the fair Lady Yolande."

The attendant entered us in the book not daring to ask how to spell Macgillicuddy.

"And yours, sir?"

"Barrymore."

"And the first name, sir?"

"Ethel," said Barrymore, and led us into the morgue.

It was a large, clinical room with tiled floors and walls. The corpses were stored in refrigerated filing cabinets. Any known details of the bodies were noted on labels which were tied to the corpses' toes.

Barrymore opened the first cabinet and peered down at its occupant.

"Alas, poor Yorik, I knew him——"

Daddy Donlan removed his hat and crept to the occupant's side.

"Ah, yes," he croaked, "a fellow of infinite jest."

"Where are your jibes now?" demanded Barrymore of the silent corpse. "Your gambols? Your songs?"

At this point the attendant made a move to push the corpse back, but he was stalled by the two actors who raised their resonant voices and reveled around the cabinet dueting.

"Where be your flashes of merriment that were wont to set the table on a roar? . . ."

The befuddled Horatio, who had been standing with his eyes half shut, squinted down at the marblelike cadaver and shook his head slowly.

"Bears no resemblance to poor Yorik," he slurred. "You will recall he'd reached the skull stage. . . . Bless you," he mumbled to the young stiff and as the attendant shut the drawer impatiently, Father Horatio crawled onto a slab and started to doze. Daddy turned to the prickly attendant and laid a hand on his shoulder.

"What's new in our age group, Buster?"

The man's eyes suddenly took on a new glint.

"Well—this one came in an hour ago," he said, opening another file drawer.

The two actors pulled Horatio off his slab and the three of them glided over to study the new male corpse, a man of about fifty with a pale, flabby face.

"Sudden stroke," said the attendant pointedly. "Suspected alcoholism."

Slowly the three of them straightened up. The two habitual drunks were visibly shaken.

"Home," said Daddy.

"Home," agreed Barrymore.

The attendant made no attempt to hide his sigh of relief. But before we left the cold, silent morgue the three drunketeers stopped to make a pact. In the future Father "Horatio" O'Sullivan should always accompany them on any further sprees. They'd decided it was safer to have a priest around for instant last sacrament—just in case he could catch them before rigor mortis set in.

And thus was the beginning of Father O'Sullivan's downward path which was eventually to lead him to become a most respected and venerable cardinal in San Francisco.

In spite of Father O'Sullivan's unconventional entry into our family circle, our school relationship continued as though the evening forays had never happened. If my dishy priest showed any favoritism at all it consisted of no more than allowing my girl friend, Mary Inez—whose friendship was to span the years—and me to help address envelopes in his school office.

Daddy's film with Ricardo Cortez had come to an end and so had our chauffeur-driven limousine. Mother had at last acquired her new husband and as she and Jim were now living out of sin she had planned a trip to Paris to fetch Grand'mère back to California, this time armed with the proper immigration papers.

All that term Daddy had promised me that if he got a new film I could go with her. Mother had planned her voyage by SS *California* through the Panama Canal to New York and then on to the French liner *Ile de France* across the Atlantic. What a way to spend a summer holiday. I dreamed of nothing else. In geography class, when we were asked to write a thesis on a European capital, naturally I chose Paris. I was so immersed in the famous French city that there wasn't a street, a park, a church, or a railway station with which I wasn't familiar. I could draw a map of Paris by memory.

I was aching to go with her to see the Champs-Élysées, the Arc de Triomphe through which our ancestors had marched, the Sacré Coeur where Grand'mère did her knee-bending, the Louvre where the late Grandpère had studied his painting, L'Opéra where Mother had acquired her ill-fated ambition for do-re-mi-ing, the Conservatoire de Musique where mother's sister Gabrielle had learned her arpeggios.

But when June came there was still no film. So no Paris trip. With a sinking heart I stood on the San Pedro docks with my new stepfather throwing paper streamers at Mother's departing ship. With Daddy broke again there was no vacation, no restaurants, no movies, no nothing. Not even the visiting bootleggers—they had stopped giving him credit. We spent that hot summer locked together in our claustrophobic apartment making bathtub gin. It was cheaper and easier to brew than whisky. Everything we did had to cost nothing—or almost.

I stirred his gin and he tried to improve my mind. He sent me to the local library to collect *Huckleberry Finn, The Last of the Mohicans* and *Treasure Island*—all suitable reading for a young boy like me. They were books he had relished when he was a child and he often found it difficult to reconcile himself to this female thing with whom he was cossetted. He enjoyed thumping around on one leg bellowing Long John Silver at me. How else can an unemployed actor keep in practice?

When we were both younger he had taught me to swim and dive at L.A.'s Bimini Baths, how to catch a baseball close to my belly to avoid my ever-breaking fingers (which drove him wild), and how to flick a slick marble to add to my collection.

But now I was more interested in going to my ballet classes at Ernest Belcher's Dance Academy, which was Hollywood's largest dance center. The dancing alumni of Belcher's included many well-known names, from the early screen favorites such as Mae Murray, Lina Basquette, and Ramon Navarro to the then currently popular Loretta Young.

Mr. Belcher himself taught ballet, Eduardo Cansino looked after the Spanish dancing, and Arthur Prince guided the tap classes. Mr. Belcher's pretty daughter, Marjorie, demonstrated the steps in front of us. I can still see the backs of her lean, sturdy legs as she bourréed across the enormous studio with a black mole, like a beauty spot, high on each thigh just below her frill. The boy dancers found them attractive and had difficulty concentrating on their entrechats. But the male dancer who eventually won her hand as well as her beauty-spotted legs was Gower Champion. Together they became the famous Champion dance team who starred on stage and screen throughout the country. And it was Gower who later became a director and choreographed so many New York musical hits—of which his scintillating "Hello, Dolly" number lifted that show into a world success.

Also leaping all over our classes were a galaxy of brothers and sisters called Hightowers, all of them aspiring to become ballet stars—which they did. In fact, there came a time when no American ballet company was complete without a Hightower.

And clicking her castanets through the academy corridors was Eduardo Cansino's daughter, a shy, plumpish brunette whom we all called Marguerita, until she changed her name to Rita Hayworth.

But it was Arthur Prince's tap classes that really collected the herds. There wasn't a thirties musical without its tapping cuties. 42nd Street had just shuffled an unknown tap dancer, Ruby Keeler, to stardom. It was the most popular form of dancing to reach the screen. Perhaps because it produced a lively clickety-clack for the new sound machines. Relatively quick and easy to learn, everybody on stage and screen could tap dance—and everybody did. Even newspaper mogul William Randolph Hearst summoned Arthur Prince to San Simion to coach his prótegée Marion Davies through her tap routines. I remember Arthur was thrilled to be a regular weekend guest at the Hearst castle in all that luxury—and earning thirty-five dollars a day to boot.

Among the other clogging hopefuls in Arthur's studio classes was a gangling blond boy destined to shake the film world by giving Deanna Durbin her first screen kiss, young Robert Stack. If I recall correctly, and I do, he was a better kisser than a hoofer. One of Arthur's favorites was a hard-working girl who later bounced to the top of the barrack-room pinup stars in World War II, America's secret weapon, the bubbly, blonde Betty Grable.

So there we all were, dripping through the thirties with ambitious perspiration at Ernest Belcher's exercise bars. But Daddy was dead against my ballerina ambition, so I paid for my lessons out of my sock, also for my practice dress, a yellow frill attached to a sleeveless bodice. During my first class Mr. Belcher said I had definite possibilities as a future ballerina. I was so excited that I rushed back to the apartment to spread the news without changing. There I stood in my little yellow frill with feet turned out in first position, grinning with pride from ear to ear.

Daddy Donlan took one look at his blossoming ballerina and let out a sigh of exasperation.

"Christ," he wailed, "what are you? Some kind of fairy? Who the hell goes to ballet? You'll end up flat on your keester at thirty. Then what?"

"Then I should take tap dancing too, maybe. Like Ginger Rogers and Fred Astaire. Everybody's going to *Flying Down to Rio*."

He couldn't get out of that one. Reluctantly, he agreed I could start tapping again and he would pay.

"You'll probably finish up a hoofer in the back row of the chorus," he encouraged. "Never become an actress back there. Where will that get you?"

According to him everything I did was supposed to get me some-unknown-where.

"I'll never become an actress anywhere if you don't send me to an acting school."

"Lousy drama teachers," he scathed. "If they knew anything about acting they'd be doing it."

"Well, how am I going to learn?"

"Do what I did," he snapped. "Graduate. Jump a freight

train to the east. Join a stock company and get a walk-on part. Christ, my first job was to lug a trunk onto the stage—and look at me now!"

I looked at him now—a very good actor, mostly unemployed—and I wondered how I was ever going to lug that first trunk onto the stage, let alone jump a freight.

As my interests began to move away from the apartment and us, his seemed to shrink inside it. He spent more and more of his time sitting alone at his kitchen table huddled over his pie tin spilling ashes over Scott Fitzgerald's stories in the *Saturday Evening Post*. The famous American writer and my infamous character actor had the bottle in common, as well as one daughter apiece to look after.

In my early working days I discovered that the Golden Era myth had been so well publicized by the film studios that even those who worked in them believed it. Most of the books I have read about Hollywood have been written by people who arrived there already brainwashed by the ecstatic publicity machines, machines manned by working fans writing for reading fans. And the biggest fans of all were the film producers themselves.

For those of us whose home it was, Hollywood was just a one-horse town sprinkled with men dressed as cowboys but no horses. Everybody went to sleep by midnight, except a few gangsters who hung about the corner of Hollywood Boulevard and Vine Street job hunting. During the day they were replaced by newly arrived cowboys in search of a Western.

The rest of us natives lived in our Disneyland stucco bungalows, Spanish-style apartment houses, or tumbledown wooden shacks, according to our incomes. Our busiest streets often sprouted oil wells, which was one of the other reasons people came to Hollywood. In fact, most of the inhabitants had nothing to do with filmland and wouldn't know a Gable or a Garbo if they saw one.

The stars and the film tycoons lived in Beverly Hills because it was the only bit of attractive land within fifty miles of Hollywood, with the possible exception of Pasadena where the society nobs resided. Both suburbs had rolling green hills, trees, wide avenues, and were beautiful. And expensive. But the more permanent Pasadena elite seldom mingled with the passing film trade. They were considered the more solid citizens—bankers, judges, and financiers. And their unpretentiously pretentious homes reflected this solidity in the way they seemed to squat securely into the Pasadena foothills.

The movie mob's mansions were mainly replicas of homes they had seen down South or lived in and around while in Europe. French chateaux, English Tudors, Italian villas, Spanish haciendas, and cotton-pickin' old colonial homesteads stood happily side by side behind open gardens of sprawling lawns and smiling poppies.

In my later hoofing days I remember going with some dancers to a party in one of these white Southern Comfort homesteads. I fully expected Uncle Tom to greet us at the door and shuffle us in. Instead, we were welcomed by our host, George Raft. This lean, swarthy star had the appearance of the gangsters he portrayed, but his manner was reticent and his voice soft and mellow.

"I don't know why I got this bad reputation," he protested as he showed us into his tastefully decorated drawing room. "I never done no harm to nobody. And you couldn't meet a nicer bunch of guys than my pals here."

Lounging comfortably among the early American antiquities were his squashed-faced buddies, all of them dressed in custom-made English tweed sports jackets and handmade shirts and shoes.

When we had settled into the small talk with the assorted guys and dolls, Mr. Raft slipped unobtrusively into his club chair in a quiet corner of the room to observe his soirée in relative solitary confinement. Had it been a silent film scene the group could have passed muster in the highest Washington society, let alone Pasadena. However, the ambience of the elegant surroundings was shattered by the shafts of gangsterese jargon.

"So I sez to this broad . . ."

"That ain't no broad, that's a hooker."

"What you got to squeal about, you didn't take the rap."

"Yeah, but a guy like that burns my tail."

My ears were to become attuned to this type of tough-guy patter. Later on, in the forties, when I was in Chicago looping around The Loop in the shadier bistros of that notorious city, or noshing at Lindy's in New York, it was the hoodlum talk of those towns. Frank Sinatra must have overheard the same characters as their terminology became such a part of his offstage chatter that he nursed these bygone phrases right into the seventies.

The exteriors of these Hollywood houses were always kept spruce, trimmed, and ready for the tourists and the newspaper photographers. The sightseeing bus drove the tourists through the hills every day while the conductor pointed out the stars' homes. But he was always pointing out the wrong stars in the wrong homes. It was difficult for him to keep up with their dropped options and subsequent replacements.

The Beverly Hills elite bought their minks from a cluster of small, exclusive shops off Wilshire Boulevard where they could pick up a handful of diamonds, a hot fudge sundae, and caviar at the same time. The rest of us did our bargain hunting along Hollywood Boulevard where, even in the thirties, the Hollywoodians were already doing their own thing. We ambled in and out of the cheap clothes shops, Chinese souvenir stores, Woolworth's, drugstores, hairdressing and manicure schools where nails and hair were refurbished cheaply because the refurbishers were all learners.

There was no Golden Era glamour on Hollywood Boulevard where the streetcars clanged along picking up us yokels in our come-as-you-are clothes. Whether we wore Big Chief Indian headgear, shorts, long Gypsy skirts, pajamas, or monks' robes no one turned a head. Not even at the Golden Era's own Jesus Christ Superstar, a white-bearded gent known as Peter the Hermit who appeared daily, usually wearing a shredded toga and sandals. He wandered down the Boulevard among the unfaithful mumbling, "Hollywood is Follywood—monkey see, monkey do."

The stars only visited Hollywood Boulevard to attend

their film premiers, see their lawyers, or put their footprints, handprints, or hoofprints in the cement outside Grauman's Chinese Theater. They knew they had reached their peak once they had been sunk into the forecourt.

In those days my only interest in the film business was whether or not it gave my old man a job. But luckily, thanks to the California sunshine, there were plenty of outdoor activities for broke people to enjoy. Almost everything we needed for a picnic in the Hollywood Hills or Griffith Park could be plucked from neighbors' gardens—avocados, peaches, oranges, nectarines, and grapes. We darted from tree to tree singing "The sun belongs to everyone, the best things in life are free." For free, my chum Mary Inez and I played tennis at the within-walking-distance Los Angeles Junior College and paid a meager ten cents for a swim in the pool afterward. As an added bonus the young college boys often treated us to giant milkshakes at the corner soda fountain. Daddy Donlan would have had me exorcised had he known.

Mary Inez's father had the completely opposite attitude. He encouraged us to have boyfriends, organized dances for us, and even gave us hints on how to attract the opposite sex. If he'd had a few drinks we would wheedle him into one of his sex instruction sessions. These included such memorable hints as:

A lady should never kiss anyone with her mouth shut.

She should stick her tongue out frequently to keep it supple.

A nibble is more effective than a bite.

She should never tamper with a fellow's belly-button unless he likes it.

One bit of forgettable advice he gave us was that a lady should always drink plenty of liquid before lovemaking so she could let it out afterward to prevent her getting pregnant.

It was probably this kind of thirties sex talk that led to the population explosion. The only other grown-up who mentioned the taboo subject was Aunty who once told me, "Men have this devil of a thing between their legs. It does nothing but cause trouble. So it's best to stay away from it."

Dear, unpredictable Aunty. She was not the one to heed her own advice. It had been over a year since I had seen her and I missed her homely philosophies. One day, on my way back from an illicit milkshake, I was pondering the inevitability of encountering that "devil of a thing" with my belly full of liquid when I walked smack into a surprise. Parked outside our apartment was a Model-T Ford, top heavy with goods and chattels, pots, boxes, blankets, and fishing tackle. Hanging out of the car windows waving at me were two figures who looked like Aunty Adelaide and Uncle Jack. I couldn't believe it. Was it another California mirage?

The mirage shouted, "Yolande!"

No, it was real! It was warm, huggable Aunty. My God, it was good to see her. And Uncle Jack. Just like the old days.

"Aunty!" I cried out from the depths of my lungs as I raced to greet them. "It's been too long . . . it's been forever and ever!"

Of course, to a child a year is forever. It wasn't until much later that I found out from Mother how these two vagabonds managed to be here on Mariposa Avenue in a Model-T covered wagon looking like something out of *The Grapes of Wrath.*

Uncle Jack's spree with the "other woman" hadn't survived the harsh realities of earning their keep in romantic Mexico. What with no car and no dough he found it tough trying to smuggle tequila, let alone keep a mistress, and he became Useless again. So mistress had to work as a waitress in one of the Ensenada cafes—which made for unfriendly relations between them.

It was on a moonlit night, when Useless was on his behind at a table in the cafe, the guitars were playing "La Cucaracha," and mistress was up to her armpits in enchiladas, that she threw both the enchiladas and his eternity ring slap into his Italian doe eyes. It was instant *adios, amigo.* He cried and cried, but managed to retrieve the ring. His world shattered, he wrote a let-me-come-home-all-is-forgiven letter to Aunty.

Until Aunty received this begging love letter she had been having a ball in San Francisco with her ex-first husband. Evenings at the theater, dining at the top of The St. Francis, wooing in the Japanese Gardens; rewedding bells were ringing in their ears. (He had just given her a thousand dollars to buy a trousseau and a divorce.) But the moment Aunty had her love call from Doe Eyes she secretly hopped a bus to Mexico, absconding with poor old husband Number One's dowry. This was the second time Aunty had done this to him, and it left him with a terrible stammer.

Aunty and Jack, flushed with the excitement of their reunion and her new dowry, bought themselves the second-hand Model-T Ford and raced to the Tijuana race track to celebrate. Aunty was sure that both their signs were in the right orbit to double her dowry. With Uncle Jack's race forms and her horoscopes she worked out the perfect system to beat the track. Her only handicaps were the horses and jockeys. They kept running against her horoscope and messing up her system.

It took five days of consultations with the zodiac before the Mexican track was in complete possession of the residue of her original thousand dollars. They were cleaned out. Stone broke. And would have had to sleep al fresco but for Uncle Jack's foresight. On his final trip to the tote he had a sudden lapse of faith in Aunty's signs and pocketed the last losing bet. It was not enough to live in luxury, nor even in poverty, but just enough to buy a tent, fishing tackle, a few pots, and the ingredients for his favorite spinach stuffing.

With their pieces of mobile home piled on to their Model-T they crossed the border into California just past San Diego, and Uncle Jack pitched their tent on the beach at Coronado. It was here they frolicked through their second honeymoon contemplating the wages of love. Aunty stayed in the tent with her pots while Jack went out with his fishing rod to fetch their meals. It was while he was trying to catch a mackerel that his tragedy occurred. He lost his late love's eternity ring in the sand. To top the traumatic events of the past weeks, the loss of this memento of his unrequited last-ditch romance finally broke his crumbling spirit. He rushed back into the tent in tears. Aunty thought he was upset about being useless even with his fishing.

"Never mind the mackerel," she comforted. "I've fried the last of your stuffing."

"It ain't the mackerel," he sobbed. "It's her ring! Oh, my God. My sweetheart's eternity ring. I've lost it. The only thing I had——"

Aunty was shocked into fury.

"That old whore? Your sweetheart? The only thing you had? After what I've done for you. How dare you come in here crying over that goddam whore's ring!"

Then she collapsed in front of her primus stove and cried all over his spinach. Uncle Jack let out a deep coyote howl of anguish, dashed back to the beach and wandered hysterically all over the seaside poking his rod in the sand in search of the ring.

According to Aunty's version, she was desolate at having given up the other husband and his dowry in order to watch Uncle Jack moon around in the sand all afternoon over his "other woman."

At dusk he gave up the search, crawled into the tent, and fell into an exhausted sleep. That night the whole of Southern California was deluged with one of its notorious downpours. And it washed away their tent. Mother said the heavens must have opened to pour justice on the errant couple.

And here was that lovable errant couple and I on the sidewalk outside our Mariposa apartment hugging, kissing, and chatting.

"Come in and see Daddy," I invited excitedly, hoping they were going to come back and live with us again.

"We tried to," said Uncle Jack. "He's just chucked us out."

"Why, is he frying a fish?"

☆

"No, your father's just being stubborn," said Aunty. "I asked Jimmy for a little loan to tide us over, and he wouldn't even take the chain off the door."

It seems he'd taken one look at her and shouted, "Never again! I told you before, you're out—O.U.T.—out!" and shut the door again.

Aunty's hazel eyes glistened with unshed tears as she explained how both their pockets were empty, so were their stomachs, and so was the gas tank. They were trapped for life on Mariposa Avenue. It seemed unfair that Daddy, who was always doling out to his drinking buddies, couldn't spare a few dollars for his sister. But with him there was no going back. If he put someone out of his life they were out forever. And those "someones" were also out of bounds for me as well.

The three of us stood huddled around the Ford worrying over their next move—which they couldn't make without any gas. It was the first time I had seen this couple, whom I loved, desperate and destitute. At this moment there was no one they could turn to for help—except me. All the grown-ups had given them up as irresponsible failures. I wondered what I had to offer. Not much. There were a few dollars left in my hidden sock. Just enough to move them out of sight of Daddy's wrath.

"Would five dollars help?" I asked.

"It sure as hell would," said Uncle Jack. "We could eat and buy some gas."

"Okay, I'll get it."

It felt so good to be useful for a change. Also it would be fun sneaking past the lion's lair to fetch it. My old man was huddled over his pie tin reading *Variety*. He didn't look up once as I darted in and out of the apartment.

They were both very grateful for those few dollars and while Uncle Jack hurried to fetch a pail of gas I sat in the car with Aunty.

"Damn Daddy. Why can't he ever forgive? It's enough to make us both hate him."

"Don't hate him, Yolande," she replied quietly. "I bear no grudge against your father. He's just crazy like all the

Donlans. I shall always love him as I love you, and he loves you."

When Uncle Jack had refilled the car he cranked it until it shook all over. Then he leaped up inside and they were off, spluttering down Mariposa with pots and pans clanging. I waved a last good-bye as the Model-T swayed around the corner into Santa Monica Boulevard. Then, reluctantly, I trudged back into the apartment. Daddy looked up this time and spoke very slowly and decisively.

"You are not to see them again. Do you hear me? Never."

As I grew older Daddy became stricter in his demands. Not only was I forbidden to visit Aunty and Jack, but I could no longer spend weekends at Mary Inez's house. On Saturday afternoons we had been teaching a few of the boys in our class how to dance, so we could have some partners for our parish school graduation dance. When my old man heard about our classes he was furious.

"You'll be having orgies next," he swore. "No more dancing with boys. Do you hear me? Never again."

He hated any physical sign of my growing into a woman capable of attracting men. When Mother had given me my first brassiere for my birthday it was greeted with derision.

"What a ludicrous gift for a child!"

And yet I was even more than overequipped to fill it. The beginnings of this child's periods were kept as secret as the sock. I was too embarrassed to mention such a feminine event to such an antifeminist man. The possibility of my getting married one day was never discussed. It hadn't occurred to either of us that I would do anything but work. It was all right for him to have fun with the opposite sex, but not for me. And as boys of my age group were taboo I relied more and more on the dream prince in my head, Father O'Sullivan.

On nights when my father and the dream prince decided to go out on the town together the priest would, as usual, change his church shirt and dog collar in my bedroom and get into his Horatio Macgillicuddy disguise. One evening

Daddy and the priest had gone out with a couple of beautiful converts. Knowing the two roués were away for the whole night I took the holy shirt into bed to cuddle. Like a teddy bear. Only sexier. If I was too young to enjoy the reverend's favors at least I could clasp his shirt to my budding bosom and have exciting, adolescent fantasies.

There wasn't another girl in the school who could have our idol's shirt in her bed. I fell asleep, happily humming the current song hit, "My Sin Is Loving You," to dream the most erotic dream of all for a Catholic girl—an affair with a handsome intellectual priest who was struggling to remain celibate, and beautiful weak you, struggling to retain your virginity. You are both overcome with the clash between God and Satan whispering aphrodisiacs into your soul. It's all too much. Satan wins. His flames consume your throbbing passions. The fireworks explode. It's the Fourth of July in the hay. Wow! And for free, no charge in penance. Sleeping dreams don't count, only daydreams are verboten.

Christmas 1932 saw the end of a rough year. The Depression had sunk deeper. There were 300,000 unemployed in the County of Los Angeles, including my father and Uncle Jack.

We even had collections at school for Christmas hampers for the poor, some of whom were the parents of my classmates. I remember one girl in particular, Mary Rose, whose father had been a top Hollywood portrait photographer. His studio had been shut for a year. None of the aspiring thespians could afford photos anymore and there was no other work available for him. He was one of the recipients of our Christmas hampers. Mary Rose felt so humiliated she missed school for a week afterward. I tried to tell her it was only a miracle that we weren't in line for one, too.

At the last minute Daddy's agent had found him a role in the Irene Dunne film *Back Street*. He was lucky to be working that December. Uncle Jack was considered lucky, too. He had managed to get a job driving a taxi for the Yellow Cab Company, which meant Aunty had a roof over her head. In order to keep it there she too had found work as a saleslady in a Los Angeles shop for outsize dresses. It was the one time she was grateful for her corpulence. Even with both their wages they could only afford a shabbily furnished two-room flat in downtown Los Angeles. I was able to sneak over there now and then for forbidden Sunday dinners under cover of my weekend visits to Mother.

Mother had had a rough year, too. She had overstayed her fling in Paris by three months. When she returned with Grand'mère in tow she discovered that new husband Jim had flung his fling as well. And his fling was still clinging. All was not peaceful in Mother's new honeymoon bungalow in Beverly Hills. On my weekend visits I often heard shrieks of disharmony emanating from their bedroom, reminiscent of Aunty's and Uncle Jack's nocturnal tiffs. The words were tamer but the volume and text were the same—late nights at work, mysterious phone calls, and unexplained lost weekends. Grand'mère and I kept to our respective rooms pretending we were deaf. I began to wonder if all marriages were as noisy.

However, when Mother and Jim came to us for Christmas Eve drinks they were wearing their happy faces and I assumed Jim's turbulent fling had subsided. True, his happy face bore a black eye, but I didn't know whether Mother or the fling had done it. Jim, who was now manager of the Beverly Hills Laundry, said he'd bumped it on the handle of a washing machine.

They had brought Grand'mère along, too. She was all dressed up in gray lace and although she was pushing eighty she had a new perm, makeup, and manicure; she hoped to meet her favorite star, Clark Gable. His name was one of the few things she could speak in English. Only with her French accent it came out as Clock Gobble. With every new party arrival she perked up hopefully on the edge of her chair croaking, "Gobble? Gobble?" But there was no Gobble that Christmas. In the end she had to settle for Bela Lugosi. At least he could speak French.

I have little more than a montage of memories of the Christmas Eve which was to turn into such a traumatic one for me. . . .

Mother, who seldom drank, getting ga-ga on a couple of

drinks—seated at the piano playing and singing "Jingle Bells." . . . Daddy wincing at the tipsy soprano, but unable to stop her because fellow actors Pat O'Brien and Jimmy Gleason vociferously joined her. . . . The tipsy soprano getting herself locked in the bathroom. . . . Daddy suggesting they let her stay put, and the cries of protest as nobody else could get in. . . . Grand'mère standing outside the bathroom door stamping her feet and shouting hoarsely, "Thérèse, Thérèse!" and daughter Thérèse answering with a spurt of high-pitched giggles. . . . Her final rescue by a six-foot-three actor called Slim Summerville who climbed from the kitchen window to her aid, accompanied by rousing cheers. . . .

I remember leaving Daddy to host his roomful of happy bladders and taxiing to midnight mass at the Immaculate Heart Church where my secret love, Father O'Sullivan, was celebrating to a full house. . . . I recall sitting next to my tap teacher, Arthur Prince, and inviting him and Father O'Sullivan back for Christmas drinks with Daddy and his gang.

When we arrived at the apartment door it was shut and I was surprised to find there were no sounds of celebration coming from inside. I knocked several times, but no one answered. Finally, Arthur said, "Don't you have a key?" When I admitted I had one he wondered why I didn't use it and go in.

"Maybe he's frying a fish," I said. It was the only reply I could think of.

O'Sullivan smiled and said, "Let's go in and risk it." Then he turned to Arthur and asked, "May I borrow your hat?"

As I tentatively opened the door the priest threw Arthur's hat inside. When the hat didn't come back we went in. The living room was empty. The party was over and my old man was obviously starting Christmas morn on the town.

"Never mind," I said, trying to hide my excitement at the thought of my own party with Father Horatio. "I can still fix you a drink."

I hurried off into the kitchen to find some clean glasses

and stopped dead in the doorway. Daddy was lying slumped across the table, his eyes open, pupils dilated.

"Daddy—what happened?" I cried, startled.

"Can't—breathe. . . ." he gasped, and each word seemed to be an effort.

When I rushed over to try to lift his head he choked out a groan of pain. His hands and face were clammy with sweat. By now O'Sullivan and Arthur Prince were beside me.

"Passed out?" enquired Arthur.

"Daddy never passes out."

"Can you sit up, Jimmy?" asked O'Sullivan.

"No . . . hurts. . . ."

As Father O'Sullivan moved around to feel his pulse Daddy caught sight of the priest's outfit. For the first time there was fear in his eyes.

"Last . . . rites . . . ?"

"It's not your turn yet," smiled O'Sullivan, "besides I don't have my props. You don't need me, you need a doctor."

I had to phone all over Hollywood before I could find one who wasn't out celebrating. When he finally arrived he gave my father a shot and a shock.

"You've had a heart attack, Mr. Donlan," the doctor said quietly.

Daddy looked up at him incredulously.

"Heart attack? At forty-two? With all my own hair—own teeth—iron stomach? How can my heart go?"

"I'd say it was excessive drinking," replied the doctor. "I'm afraid if you touch alcohol again you may never see fifty-two."

It was the first time any doctor had mentioned my father's drinking problem. Until now Daddy's doctors had all been fellow lushes so they avoided the subject. I was glad I had found this stranger who could give it to him straight.

"What you need now, Mr. Donlan, is complete rest for several weeks."

"Rest? How can I rest now?" Daddy pleaded. "I've got to finish a movie."

"You could also finish your life," warned the doctor.

O'Sullivan said, "Don't chance it, Jimmy."

Daddy said, "If I don't complete this role they'll have to reshoot with another actor." He turned to Arthur Prince for professional support. "You know what that means. News gets around. I'm a heart hazard. I'll never work again."

"I can only make the diagnosis," shrugged the doctor. "You'll have to make the decision."

And he did. With the help of the doctor's injections to dilate the coronary vessels he managed to pretend to romp through the rest of his part in *Back Street*. The incident was kept a secret from his agent. It also frightened him into going on the wagon. I was frightened, too, wondering how long his dry spell would last.

The following year President Roosevelt moved into the White House and we moved into our new La Paula apartment on Western Avenue. It was run more like a hotel than our other apartment blocks. There was a large lobby, reception desk with twenty-four-hour switchboard, and daily maid service, all of which made it easier for my old man to carry on his work and play life. It was also in walking distance of my new high school, the Immaculate Heart Convent on Western and Franklin avenues.

Moving for us was never a problem. Apart from our clothes all we had was Daddy's battered wardrobe trunk full of old stage makeup, unpaid bills, assorted wigs, and press cuttings; and my sackful of baseball and mitt, two-gun holster, cowboy hat and boots, toe and tap shoes, marbles, and roller skates.

To meet his extra-curricular needs, Daddy had now collected a Texas blonde named Abigail, and her five-year-old son Ricky. They were temporarily without a roof and he had offered her our new one. I think she had been jealously ejected from her own matrimonial bed into Daddy's. His three months of not drinking had gone to his head. There was barely enough room for us, let alone his two new appendages. The apartment had only one twin-bedded double room and a living room with a couch and a pull-down Murphy bed. To keep up appearances the lion slept in the other twin bed in my room and the newcomers took over the Murphy bed and the couch. Daddy referred to his new girl friend, Abigail, as his housekeeper.

She was a robust, happy-go-lucky, open-armed Texas cowgirl who had ventured to Hollywood to seek fame as a folk singer with a cowboy group, so far without success. Daddy was hoping she would bring a merry domesticity into our bachelors' existence, and she did with a vengeance. Every morning at six she sprang from her bed chirping, "Yippee!" banged the bed up into the wall, switched on her rise-and-shine cowboy program and warbled her old cowhand tunes in and out of the bathroom and into the kitchen, with little Ricky following on her heels shooting off his cap pistols.

I heard rumblings of discontent from the lion's adjacent bed and wondered how long his love in bloom would survive this riotous domesticity. Abigail stormed the kitchen flapping flapjacks, frying apple fritters for our breakfast, and baking corn bread and pineapple-upside-down-cake while we were at school. With the radio blasting her cowboy ditties to cheer her on, and flour scattered everywhere, Daddy found it tough going at his kitchen table. But he stayed off the drink.

It was during his dry period that Prohibition was repealed. I remember him grumbling into his glass of milk.

"A fine time. Just when the country goes wet I have to go dry."

Happily, he was relieved from his home life on the range by a role in a new movie, *College Humor* at Paramount studios. It was a throwback to the campus coed stories of the twenties with hip flasks, coonskin coats, and flapper cuties. The stars were Richard Arlen, Jack Oakie, Mary Carlisle, and, playing his first acting role in a feature film, a young crooner called Bing Crosby.

After the first week of shooting, Daddy came back to our Texan homestead in a grizzly mood. Abigail was frying up hominy grits and Ricky was lassoing the kitchen chairs, which didn't help.

"Damn tough week," the old man groused. He untangled the rope from his chair and made a half playful attempt to strangle Ricky with it. "The scenes are hell to play. This new Crosby kid can't act at all. Imagine signing a crooner!"

"Whatsa crooner?" asked Ricky.

"A young idiot who sings boo-boo-padoo when he can't remember his words."

"They shoulda got Gene Autry," suggested Abigail. "He sings hillbilly songs real cute."

"Hillbilly cowshit," said Daddy. "This Crosby crooner sings real cute, but he can't maneuver his wooden ass around the set during scenes. Like playing with a cigar store Indian. They've got as much chance of making him a star as I have of winning an Oscar."

Daddy never won an Oscar, but the crooner did—for *Going My Way*. And it wasn't long before Bing Crosby became Paramount's top box-office draw. My old man always blamed his misprediction on his dry period.

"Continuous sobriety always affected my better judgment."

The contrast between life in the Donlan hillbilly cowshed at La Paula and school life at the new Immaculate Heart Convent was more than striking.

Passing through the convent gates, walking up the private road through the wooded Los Felix hills toward the old Spanish-missionary style convent with its cloistered gardens was like entering another world. The bustle of Franklin Avenue was out of sight. Hollywood didn't exist. It was secluded and exclusive. So were the fees. And it was considered a privilege to study there. Most everyone else, including Lana Turner and Mickey Rooney, went to Hollywood High School, but Daddy had decided that wasn't good enough for the Donlan princess. He always had ideas above my station and his insolvency, and this was one of them.

Once he had bought my two blue silk uniforms and two white piqué summer ones with matching sweaters and coats, I was in. All he had to muster up were the monthly fees, which kept both of us busy.

Mother Superior told us we were there to become ladies, excel in academic studies, and learn self-government. Girls in the senior class with the highest grades were elected by the student body to become governing officers: president, vice-president, secretary, treasurer, and so forth. It was their responsibility to keep discipline, and surprisingly it worked.

We looked up to these girls as models of the kind of young women we aspired to become. They were refreshingly attractive, good athletes, smartly coiffed, fastidiously neat, avid scholars, and happily self-disciplined without being fuddy-duddies. Most of all they exuded a relaxed self-confidence. They were the stars of our ambitions, much more so than any of the scatty creatures on the other side of the walls in Hollywood Follywood. And although makeup, jewelry, and high-heeled shoes were forbidden, we copied their hair styles and mannerisms.

As freshmen we were now early teen-old budding women with the beginning of the secret curse, sexual stirrings, and brimming with curiosity about the opposite sex. But, alas, no boys. At that age the opinions of most parents and nuns were that boys would interfere with our academic accomplishments, were sinful objects, and would cause us to have babies if we were naughty. We were, they feared, too young for lover boyfriends and too old for playmate boyfriends.

Since there were no nearby love objects we began to get crushes on the girls in the senior classes, the president, and officers of the student body, the captains of the baseball, basketball, and volleyball teams. There were snatched kisses in the cloisters, secret love notes passed while holding hands at chapel under our dainty white veils or dancing cheek to cheek in the gymnasium hall. Most of us had crushes on some girl or other. Where else could our blossoming love longings go?

The Father, the Son, and the Holy Ghost may have been enough for our mother superior, dear Sister Eulalia, and her dedicated cronies, but they were middle-aged ladies and perhaps had forgotten what the battle of young sexual urge had been like. In any case, the nun teachers had chosen their vocation whereas we were in this sexual no-man's-land by choice of our parents. Forbidden lustful feelings had to be

89
☆

confessed in the box to the visiting priest—sadly, no longer Father O'Sullivan.

Where were we girls going? What would I become? A Charlie girl, a nun, a prostitute, a housewife, a dentist, a doctor, a physicist? Or the career girl actress I was expected to be? If so, why the heavy stress on academic accomplishment and virginity—mainly from Daddy.

"It's the girls who use their heads instead of their tails who survive," he pronounced.

Whether they used Daddy's dictum or not, most of my classmates managed to "survive" one way or another. Very few of them were attracted to the film world that surrounded us. Not even Barbara Neil, daughter of Roy William Neil who had directed Daddy in *Good Bad Girl*. While her father was directing a movie in England he sent her to the Royal Academy of Dramatic Art, hoping she would catch the acting bug. Barbara went through the motions, but the last thing in the world she wanted was to become an actress. She cast aside her golden elocution medal for a golden wedding ring.

Then there was tiny Pat Carter who looked like a miniature Maureen O'Hara. She got a schoolgirl crush on singing heartthrob Muzzy Marcellino who was appearing with a band at the Palladium Dance Hall. She was fifteen when she came back with her crush's engagement ring, sixteen when she married him, seventeen when she produced the first of her eight children. A dutiful Catholic, she managed to keep her schoolgirl figure throughout her eight productions.

And Kathryn Ward, a cheerful, likable, sporty girl who always captained our school teams. She finished up as a nun, and is still there now. There was also Juanita, who had great difficulty with her studies and was always at the bottom of the class. Juanita was a beautiful Mexican girl, a bit older than the rest of us. She and I often walked to school together smoking her forbidden cigarettes while she filled me in with the facts of life that Aunty had left out. She disappeared suddenly after her second year. When I next heard of her she had become a successful brothel keeper in Phoenix, Arizona.

As for me, I worked like hell to stay in the top five in our class of twenty-five girls. We at the convent were all being groomed for the top universities and the standards at our private school were much higher than those of Hollywood High.

Of course, Mother Superior, who taught English Lit, was hoping some of us would go to the Immaculate Heart College which was attached to our high school, a climb higher up the Hollywood Hills. We would march with these college girls on the gay May Day procession through the winding woodland paths wearing wreaths on our heads, carrying bouquets of spring flowers and singing, "Bring flowers of the rarest, bring flowers of the fairest . . ." and eventually placing them at the Grotto of Our Lady. Then we raced each other down the hill, out of the convent walls, and across the street to the corner drugstore to drink Coke and aspirin to see if it made us drunk.

At the first sight of distant hooded nuns (who had complained of our being seen smoking outside the walls in our Immaculate Heart uniforms) a warning cry would go up.

"Watch it, kids—out with the cigarettes—the hoods are coming!"

No sooner had Daddy finished *College Humor* than he was offered another part, in Paramount's screen version of Noël Coward's *Design for Living.* He was enthusiastic about this because not only was he to be directed by the sophisticated Ernst Lubitsch, but the picture also starred Fredric March, Miriam Hopkins, and Gary Cooper. Fredric March had just won the Academy Award for his role in *Doctor Jekyll and Mr. Hyde,* in which Miriam Hopkins had also scored as the trollop, Ivy.

"What a pair of experts," said Daddy, after his first day. "Of course, they're from the stage," he added as if that explained all talent.

Abigail was only interested in cowboy Gary Cooper.

"Cooper will steal the picture when he comes aridin' through on his horse."

"Noël Coward comedies don't have horses, Abigail. And if they did I wouldn't be in one."

Ricky whooped through their conversation and shot two

of his sucker-tipped arrows at the Indian picture on the wall.

"I'll be a cowboy when I grow up!" he yelled.

"*If* you grow up," snapped Daddy. He sat down and buried his nose in his script to study his lines. Abigail turned the radio on to her hillbilly singers and I could see Daddy mumbling to himself—but they weren't the words in the script.

I liked Abigail and her wholesome noisiness. It livened the apartment and also took the pressure off me. It gave Daddy Donlan another target on which to focus his irritations.

The picture had been shooting for about two weeks when Abigail had a sudden resurgence of her ambition to sing with a Western group. So while Daddy was at the studio working she started to collect singing cowboys from Hollywood and Vine and bring them back to the flat. Apart from having someone to eat her hominy grits she also had them rehearsing loud and long while she warbled. She always managed to pack them off before the old man returned.

One Friday afternoon I walked out of the school gates and found a surprise waiting for me. There was the chauffeur-driven limousine and inside was Daddy and a tall bronzed man in blue jeans and a leather jacket.

"We finished early," said Daddy. "Yolande, this is Gary Cooper."

"Howdy, Yolande," said Mr. Cooper. He had a warm, drawling voice and very blue eyes which almost disappeared when he smiled. He also had very long legs. In fact the car seemed to be full of Mr. Cooper's legs as I climbed in. It was like crawling over a bag of bones.

"Thought we'd give Abigail a little surprise," said Daddy as we drove off.

I don't know who gave whom the biggest surprise that afternoon. I recall Daddy frowning as we reached the apartment door and heard the musical cacophony coming from within. Then he opened the door, stepped into the hall, and stood transfixed. Three cowboys and Abigail were belting out "I'm an Old Cowhand." The noise coming from an accordion, guitar, and harmonica was not only electrifying, it was also off-key. So was Abigail.

When she turned around and saw us she was still singing. Her eyes opened almost as wide as her mouth, her lips were still moving, but not a sound came out. Daddy took her by the shoulders and turned her slowly and deliberately back, facing the three cowboys.

"And who are they?" he asked.

"Why, they're the 'Prairie Oysters.'"

"The who?"

"Our new singing group. We was just practicin' for our audition."

"Not here you're not," said Daddy firmly.

The three cowboys, who recognized a big Indian chief when they heard one, grabbed their instruments and scuttled out mumbling, "So long, pardner."

"Sorry about all that, Coop," said Daddy, as we started to drag the furniture back into place.

"Gee, sounded pretty good to me," answered Coop, who was obviously being polite.

"This is my housekeeper, Abigail."

"Mighty good looking housekeeper," said the tall Westerner, with a twinkle. "Glad to meet you, Abigail."

"Me, too," preened Abigail, as she went into the kitchen to fix the required drinks—a real one for Cooper and a milk for Daddy.

"It's my tough luck," sighed the old man, "I always get women who want to sing."

"Hell, women who sing have it all over women who hit," said Mr. Cooper with unexpected feeling.

In spite of his rather quiet, slow-paced image, Gary Cooper was one of the film city's faster-paced Casanovas and his tangled love life had been anything but quiet. He had clambered out of a scorching, boisterous, much-publicized romance with "It" girl Clara Bow only to plunge straight into an even wilder woo-pitching bout with Lupe Velez. In fact, Daddy told us later, right through *Design for Living* this six-foot-two-and-three-quarters-man-of-few-words had been trying to surface from three wooings at once—the old one with Lupe, a newer one with a glamorous countess, and his current assignation with a beautiful New York socialite-cum-actress called Rocky Balfe.

I sat in a corner sipping my Coke and wondering why anyone would want to strike the nice Mr. Cooper.

"I'm sure no woman is tall enough to hit you, Mr. Cooper," smiled Abigail as she handed him his drink and some freshly made popcorn.

"Well, mebbe I was on my knees at the time," he grinned, "but by golly that Lupe sure packed a mean right hook. Had a black eye for a week. Slap in the middle of a picture, too."

"Just shows you shouldn't tangle with female stars, Coop," said wise old Daddy. "Should have learned that after your troubles with Clara."

"Yup," said Coop wryly, "sure should've. She was always scratching and throwing things, too. Great girl, but she gave me a rough ride."

Abigail said, "That's 'cause she loved you, I bet."

"Could be I loved her. But hell, I'm just not strong enough to learn lines and fall off horses all day and have a boxing match all night."

"Then don't ever take a wife," said Daddy.

"Nope," said Cooper emphatically.

A few weeks later he married Rocky Balfe who had given up her ambitions to be an actress to become Mrs. Cooper. According to the gossipmongers she didn't sing or box.

Weeks later, after Daddy had finished his work on *Design for Living*, I returned home from school one evening to find him sitting quietly at his kitchen table glancing through the Hollywood trade papers. It was the quietest and tidiest kitchen I had seen since we came to La Paula. It was also the emptiest apartment. No Abigail, no Ricky, no hominy grits.

"Where is everyone?"

"Gone."

"Where?"

"Home on the range, I hope."

"More cowboys?"

Daddy shook his head, took out his bag of Bull Durham, and rolled a cigarette as though to calm himself.

Me: "What happened?"

Him: "She baked an apple pie."

Me: "But you like apple pie."

Him: "Not in my pie tin. Silly bitch knew it was an ashtray."

Although I had always thought that sooner or later Daddy's singing cowgirl would drop the final straw on the lion's tail, could I have guessed it would be his favorite pie tin?

After Abigail left, my old man moved out of my room and into the Murphy bed. He also went back on the drink again. In getting rid of the noise and achieving the freedom of his pie tin he found his liberty made him lonely. Only his bottle could make him jolly.

When he wasn't out doing the rounds of the clubs with Barrymore and The Reverend Horatio Macgillicuddy he went out on his own. And that is when the trouble started. Alone he started picking up female barflies and bringing them back to the apartment. When I awakened in the mornings I always knew if one of these was in residence as he would be snoring his alcoholic fumes back in the bed next to mine. She would be in the front room.

I met one of these girls in the hall just as I was leaving for school. She was a scrawny brunette still in her cocktail dress.

"Honey," she said, "I don't have any taxi money to get me home."

"How come?"

"He forgot. We were both pretty plastered, I guess."

"How much?"

"Only twenty dollars."

"Where do you live, San Francisco?"

"You ask your old man for it, he'll understand."

When I went in to consult the lion he was in no condition to discuss economics. He let out a grunt and waved his hungover hand toward his wallet. It was lying on the floor next to his crumpled trousers. And it was empty. I knew she had rolled him. It wasn't the first time this had happened. I took two dollars out of my sock and gave it to her.

"Two dollars is enough for your kind of taxi ride."

As I walked up Western Avenue toward the convent I saw her behind me, hopping onto the Hollywood streetcar.

The more he drank the more careless he became with his money and there were never enough movies to keep up with his debts. It was in 1934, during my second year at Immaculate Heart, that I was called into the mother superior's office. I went in wondering what I had done wrong. She told me my school fees hadn't been paid for six months and asked if I knew what had happened. I was more frustrated by his lack of responsibility than by this new problem. I told her he hadn't worked much that year, which wasn't true, and would probably make it up with his next film. If not I would have to leave and go to Hollywood High.

She said, "No, Yolande. As long as you remain a good student, and your behavior is a credit to Immaculate Heart, you can stay with us." As I left she added, "And no more smoking cigarettes in your uniform."

From that day on I struggled to stay at the top of the class and stick rigidly to the rules. I knew the fees would never be paid again.

By now most of the girls in my class had steady boyfriends who took them to the movies, and on the weekends to dances or parties. The talk at school was nothing but boys, dates, falling in and out of love, soul kisses, and who was going where over the weekend. I knew where I was going—nowhere, not if a boy was involved. Daddy Donlan was stricter than ever. I was not even allowed to bring a boyfriend home, let alone go out with one.

On a few occasions, under pretext of visiting my mother, I slipped out to a party with Mary Inez. She was extremely popular with the opposite sex and would lend me one of her cast-off boyfriends as an escort. Or her current love would get one of his buddies to come along as a blind date. The poor guys who got me as a blind date found themselves a dud. I was so shy with boys in my age group that I couldn't talk to them. If only they had been transvestites, drunken actors, or tarts it would have been far easier to communicate. As for necking, I didn't dare. The thought of Daddy Donlan's wrath was enough to shake me frigid. Yet I longed for a steady boyfriend of my own.

The battle of Daddy Donlan versus daughter's dating came to a head quite unexpectedly.

Several afternoons, on my return from school, I had run into a young actor, Frankie Darro, in the lobby of the La Paula apartments. He was usually hovering around the reception desk when I telephoned upstairs to get the all-clear sign. I'd seen him in *The Mad Genius* with John Barrymore, and *Tugboat Annie* with Marie Dressler, liked his work and liked him. We'd have a chat and I would go on up to my cage.

Eventually he asked if he could take me to a movie that night. It was Friday, the night Daddy always did his frying and sent me off for the evening, so I thought I was safe. Frankie and I agreed to meet in the lobby at seven o'clock. I was so excited; it was the first time I had been asked out on a date of my own.

When I breezed into our apartment I found Daddy in a grizzly mood. Furthermore, he wasn't wearing his seduction suit and neither were any drinks laid out. It was obvious he had no fish to fry and he had been stood up. Now I was really on the spot with keeping my date. There was no excuse I could make up for suddenly going out that night without telling a series of complicated lies. And to Jimmy Donlan lying was the most unforgivable of all sins.

I had no way of contacting Frankie. There was nothing I could do but stay in and just not show up for our meeting.

Daddy and I were having our black-mood evening meal in silence when the telephone rang. It was seven-fifteen. I leaped up a little too quickly to answer it. It was Frankie.

"Hello, Mary," I said, hoping Daddy would think I was talking to Mary Inez.

"What do you mean, 'Mary'?" said Frankie. "You'd better hurry up, we're going to miss the movie."

"I can't go with you tonight, Mary—too much homework. Maybe next week. Bye now."

I hung up shakily, praying he wouldn't call back. Daddy Donlan was standing in the hall, glowering at me.

"Who was that?"

"Mary Inez."

"You sure?"

"Yes, why?"

"What did she want?"

"Nothing. Go to the movies."

"That's all?"

"Of course."

I walked into my bedroom and quietly shut the door. Trembling I fell on my knees beside the bed. "Please God, don't let him find out. He'll kill me. . . ."

I heard him pacing the hall. Then he picked up the telephone.

"Reception, please." I held my breath. "I think someone just made a call from your desk to my apartment," he said. "Do you know who it was?"

Of course they would know. Frankie's face was only too familiar. I was sick with fear. After a pause I heard Daddy's voice again.

"Thank you, that's all I wanted to know."

He opened my door and stood quite still. His face was white with rage. The veins were standing out on his forehead and his icy blue eyes had turned to steel.

"You lied. You lied to me."

His voice had a quiet, insane fury behind it which I had never heard before. He walked toward me.

"You will never lie to me again. Do you hear me? Never."

And with that he hit me across the face with such force that I fell against the bedside table which came crashing down with its lamp and everything on it in pieces. I was stunned. He had never struck me before. But it wasn't the blow that made the impact. It was the tone of voice and his eyes that frightened me. I knew that if he'd had his gun on him he would have killed me. I was now terrified of him.

He silently walked out of the room as though nothing had happened.

I lay awake all night wondering how I could get away from him. What a pity little girls couldn't divorce their fathers, I pondered.

In the morning I was up at dawn. He was still asleep. I packed my clothes and books and left him a note. The truth this time.

Dear Daddy,

I cannot live with you any longer because you frighten me too much.

Love,
Yolande

I didn't say where I was going and I took a taxi to my mother's house in Beverly Hills, where it was also a weekend of turmoil.

Mother's marriage was on the verge of collapsing. Jim wouldn't give up his fling and Mother wouldn't take her on. The atmosphere was tense when I arrived. I didn't belong. At this inopportune moment Grand'mère's presence was bad enough without adding mine. Mother was sympathetic, but neither of us knew what to do.

There was turmoil at La Paula, too, when Daddy read my note. Father O'Sullivan told me later that my old man was in tears when he asked him to join him in trying to find me. They took a cab all over Hollywood, going to the homes of my closest girl friends. From Mary Inez they tried to find out where Aunty and Uncle Jack lived. She didn't know. He was so distraught he gave the cab driver a bad time, giving directions then changing his mind and acting like the cabby was to blame for the whole situation.

As a last resort he telephoned my mother. But I wouldn't speak to him; I was too upset. I have often wondered why he hadn't checked with Mother first. Perhaps it was because he didn't want her to know I had walked out on him.

The only other time I had heard of my old man crying was on an occasion during his broken-arm period, before he moved in with Aunty and Jack. Due to his arm he had been out of work for some time and things were tough. One evening several of the chorus girls from *Oh Kay!* came to prepare a meal for him with food they'd bought. After the meal they left without clearing the table. He thought it was strange since he was incapacitated, but when he removed the plates from the table he found a five dollar bill under each one.

His eyes still misted over every time he told the story.

He must have been in quite a state after I refused to speak to him on Mother's telephone because the following morning he sent his driver around with a letter for me. It said he was sorry for having lost his temper. It would never happen again. He would stop drinking and pay our bills.

But the last paragraph I will never forget.

You are all I have, Yolande, please don't leave me. I will disintegrate and end up in the gutter.

I went back to La Paula that night. We hugged, cried, and laughed. But somehow I knew I couldn't stay there much longer.

A few months after I had moved back to La Paula Mother and Jim's feud over his fling came to the boil and Mother did a very silly thing. She walked out on him, taking Grand'mère and the furniture, of course, but leaving a lovely home and quite a good husband. She realized her mistake when she was seventy—a bit late. By then he'd been dead for ten years.

Once again I went to the divorce court with her, this time to swear what a bastard her second husband had been. It was getting to be a habit. She soon found an unfurnished bungalow near my school, decorated it with her usual flair and at last there was room for me.

It was then that Daddy and I had a man-to-man talk about our relationship. He had just finished his first drink of the evening and was feeling merry. He was celebrating getting a new part with Edward G. Robinson and Jean Arthur in *The Whole Town's Talking*.

"Your mother just called," he said as I came in from school. "Now she's got rid of that Republican laundryman she'd like you to live with her. What do you say?"

I had been expecting this, but I didn't think it would come up so soon, or without a scene.

"Fine for me," I said after a pause, "but what happens to you? You're a mess."

"Not always."

"Your temper is getting worse."

"Yes."

"You haven't stopped drinking."

"No," he said as he poured another one.

"And our bills are still unpaid."

"Yes."

"My being here hasn't changed you at all."

"Doesn't look like it." He shook his head, took a sip of his drink, coughed, spluttered, then looked up and grinned. "Go on, move in with your mother. It'll do you good."

"You, too," I smiled and hugged him. "You'll be able to fry your fish in peace."

We both agreed I'd reached the age when I needed a woman's influence. Anything to keep me from turning into an hermaphrodite. He would pay for my keep and I agreed to visit him every day on my way back from school. It was an amicable separation.

The changes in my life with Mother were noticeable in the little things. The freedom of opening our front door without knocking first or calling up from reception; the joy of having my friends back for visits; eating regular meals with Mother and Grand'mère instead of dining alone in restaurants on fish-frying nights; and the greatest pleasure of all, having no hangups about giving my telephone number to my first steady boyfriend.

His name was Wesley and I met him at the L.A. Junior College tennis courts; he whistled at me from No. 1 court, and I whistled back. Wesley was a tall, blond, twenty-one-year-old mathematics student with sun-bronzed skin and green eyes. I thought he was gorgeous. He taught me how to play tennis, plied me with milkshakes, and took me to movies on Saturday nights.

We always had to be back home by ten o'clock and

missed the ends of quite a few movies that way. But he patiently put up with Mother's new timetable. So did I. It was great to be allowed out at all. Still I was terrified of losing him. And although he telephoned me every night, until his call came I worried and fretted that I would never hear from him again. Mother couldn't understand my anguish over such a devoted boyfriend. Perhaps it was because I was used to having those I loved disappear suddenly.

During the summer holidays before my last term at Immaculate Heart my main worry was how I was going to earn a living after graduating. I had been worrying about this since I was three, and now the problem had to be dealt with.

Not only had Daddy still neglected to pay my school fees but he had lapsed behind with the payments for my keep at Mother's, and for my dancing lessons. My only negotiable asset was my tap dancing. But aside from a brief appearance with the Belcher ballet students at the Hollywood Bowl, my professional experience was nil. I just had to start working.

I talked it over with my tap teacher, Arthur Prince, and he arranged an audition for me at Paramount studios with Leroy Prinz, who choreographed all their musicals.

Mr. Prinz was not, he warned me, the most patient of men. Apparently he'd been that way ever since he ran away from home at fifteen and joined the French Foreign Legion. He'd soon lost his patience with Algiers and joined the aviation corps in World War I. He had survived fourteen crashes and in quick succession had directed dances for the Folies Bergère, trained aviators in Mexico, flown ammunition for the Mexican rebels, air mails for the United States government, and then staged cabaret acts and musicals in New York before landing impatiently on the Paramount lot.

As I was only sixteen Arthur warned me to say I was eighteen if the subject came up. A California law required a special permit and a chaperone for youngsters under eighteen working in film studios and no one was going to bother with all that unless it was essential for the picture. I was definitely not essential for anything, especially a movie.

On the day of my interview I put on more makeup than usual, blue eye shadow, and layers of mascara to look sophisticated. I knew I would be expected to dance and was prepared with a complete dance routine that I had been rehearsing for weeks. I wasn't sure whether the dance director would have the time or the place to let me change into practice clothes, so I went on the streetcar in my tennis shorts, carrying my tap shoes, and practicing the steps in my head.

Mr. Prinz's secretary showed me into a typical dance rehearsal room with the usual mirrored wall. It was empty, which meant I was the only one to be auditioned. While she went to get the big dance director I sat on a wooden chair to put on my tap shoes and my fingers were shaking so much I kept getting the laces into tangled knots. It took forever.

When Leroy Prinz came in he had my introduction letter in his hand. He was a short, dark, middle-aged man with an air of preoccupation. It was rumored he had a silver plate in his head from one of those fourteen crashes and it gave him a fiery temper. He looked me over quickly.

"I hear you're a good tap dancer and want to work for me."

"I hope so, Mr. Prinz."

"Show me what you can do. Where's your music?"

I hadn't thought of that.

"I don't have any, Mr. Prinz—but I can dance to anything the pianist plays," I said with false courage.

"No music, no pianist," he said. "You'll have to dance without it."

So for my first audition I hummed my own music as I tapped around his studio . . . "Da-da-clickety-clack." . . . He tolerated this routine for about five steps before he said, "That's enough." It was enough for me too. I thought I was finished before I started. He walked up to me and looked straight into my eyes.

"How old are you?"

"Eighteen," I lied.

"You're sure?"

"Positive," I nodded, thinking he'd probably flogged people for less in the Foreign Legion.

"Well, you better keep saying that on the set," he warned, "or I could be in a lot of trouble."

Then he smiled for the first time. "You'll start working next week on *The Champagne Waltz.*"

I couldn't believe my ears. My first job. I had tap-danced my way into a Viennese Waltz.

The following day I received a call from Paramount to go to the Western Costume Company near the studio for a fitting. I was given several Johann Strauss period ball gowns to try on. They had all seen better days in previous films but still looked beautiful to me. The wardrobe mistress chose a lilac one nearest to my size, stuck a few pins in it and me, and I didn't see it again until the day of shooting. By then it had been completely renovated.

When I arrived for my first day's work I found there were hundreds of other male and female dancers. In fact, there were so many of us that we had to rehearse on the set, a large Viennese ballroom with crystal chandeliers. Mr. Prinz was on a rostrum shouting directions through a megaphone to his assistants who were on the dance floor with us. I was given a partner, Douglas, who was an old hand at dancing and extra work. I was lucky because he was able to lead me confidently into my first dance routine. The speakers blared out the "Blue Danube" and around and around we bobbed, for hours on end.

When the shooting of *Champagne Waltz* started I got my first glimpse of Leroy Prinz's reputed temper. Through his megaphone, for all to hear, he shouted at the girls who made mistakes.

"Left, Marianne, you silly bitch, I said turn left!" Or, "For Chrissakes, Joan, stop wiggling your ass, it's a goddam waltz!"

He sounded like Daddy. I was horrified, but glad he didn't shout at me. When he was moving among us on the floor all he ever said to me was in a whisper.

"How old are you?"

"Eighteen," I replied dutifully.

He would nod, pinch my cheek, and move off to shout at somebody else.

After we had danced and shot the opening waltz sequence, the film's director, Edward Sutherland, took over and the opera star, Gladys Swarthout, appeared on a balcony box to sing her number. We dancers were now asked to crowd around her to listen. It was the first time I had seen a star singing to her own playback, and I was curious to see how she did it. While the crew were setting up the shot my partner went off to powder his nose and I maneuvered myself into a front row position. When Douglas returned and spotted me he rushed over in a panic, grabbed my hand, and pulled me into the back of the crowd.

"For God's sake, Yolande, never stand near a star!"

"Why not?"

"You'll be seen in the camera."

"And that's bad?"

"Fatal. Once your face is established in a scene you won't get called back for the rest of the crowd work."

Douglas hid us both behind a pillar while they filmed Miss Swarthout's song. We stayed hidden for several shots when, during a break, a tall, good-looking man crept up beside us and leaned against our pillar to watch. Douglas took one look at him and clutched my hand.

"Hell," he whispered, "it's Fred MacMurray. He's playing her lover. We'll be surrounded by machinery any minute."

He raced me across the ballroom floor to the other side as the menacing camera trundled past us in the opposite direction. We found a lovely spot just behind the entrance doors. Douglas heaved a sigh of relief.

"One more minute over there and we'd be out of a job tomorrow."

Just as we'd settled, Jack Oakie bounced in beaming from ear to ear and stood bang in the middle of our entrance doors.

"Has the canary finished her warbling?" he asked.

"I think so," said Douglas as he whisked me back on to the dance floor.

"My God," he groaned, "that was the comic. They're coming at us from all directions."

I noticed that the crowd with whom I'd been standing earlier around the singer's box had all been dismissed from the picture once the camera had moved away. Douglas was right. The best way to stay in the movies was to stay out of them.

We took our last refuge in the empty balcony box, where we hid for three days. To while away the time Douglas gave me other tips for existing in the movie world. I couldn't depend on dancing jobs alone, he said, I would have to fill in as an extra between musicals. For extra work I must join Central Casting. This was the Hollywood agency for all people who appear in films without being seen: doubles, stand-ins, dancers, and the many hundreds of extras who were always in demand for background crowd scenes.

The trick of being a good extra, instructed Douglas, was to be a good liar. At the first interview the wise extra claimed to have an unbeatable wardrobe for all occasions, especially evening clothes because "dress" calls paid more. When a call demanding these clothes came through you made a last minute foray into your friends' wardrobes to borrow the necessary finery. Usually the only thing the excited friends asked in exchange was that you try to get them some autographs. But the master stroke of trickery was known as "telephone roulette."

To operate this plan you called Central Casting every fifteen minutes between 6 P.M. and 10 P.M. and said your name. Nothing else, just your name, every fifteen minutes. The lines were very busy at that time and it took about fifteen minutes to get through, but it was during the hours of six and ten that the film studios put in their orders for the people they required the following morning. And if they had just put in an order when you said your name you were almost certain to get the call, because it was easier for Central Casting to put you on it than to dial your number.

For the two weeks' work on *Champagne Waltz* I received two hundred dollars. It seemed a lot of money in those hard-up days. I was thrilled that at last I was able to pay Mother for my keep as well as contribute toward my back school fees. The rest went for dancing lessons. The sooner I joined Central Casting the better. I couldn't wait to start playing telephone roulette.

But before I could do any of this I had to finish school. My last term at Immaculate Heart felt like treading water. Most of the other girls were going on to college, while I was seeking a career of hiding in pictures. Nevertheless I managed to get the required credits and pass the university entrance exam. The family was pleased, but it didn't carry any weight with Central Casting.

Mother and Daddy showed up together for the graduation ceremony. Mother wore a hat and Daddy was sober. I was surprised he turned up at all considering how much money he owed them. Whenever our mother superior approached him he skirted deftly around her. He beamed all through our singing of "Ave Maria," pretending he liked it. We couldn't compete with Swarthout's rendering of "The Blue Danube," but we were better than Abigail's hillbilly group.

As I stepped up to receive my diploma, I glanced down at my white graduation dress. It could be useful for dress extra work, I thought, but I'll have to dye it yellow; cameramen hate white.

That evening Mary Inez's father took several of us girls and our boyfriends to celebrate at the Cocoanut Grove. Mother went home to cook for Grand'mère and Daddy got plastered and picked up a broad.

My schooldays were over.

The following week I was telephoning Central Casting every fifteen minutes chanting my name. If I heard there was a call for adagio dancers, figure skaters, acrobats, or jugglers I would get on the phone to my friends to find a professional for whatever was required so they could teach me how to do it before the audition. My mother thought I was mad saying "yes" to everything.

And perhaps I was, but we needed the dough. So, I spent a good deal of time in rehearsal halls, attempting to instantaneously master backbreaking feats. Then bruised, battered, and torn I would arrive at the audition. It only worked if the crowd needed was so large that I could get lost in the background.

My next dancing job was in one of the most extravagant musical numbers MGM had ever staged. It was the Cole Porter musical *Rosalie,* starring Eleanor Powell.

Every dancer in Hollywood was called to fill the enormous courtyard arena the studio had constructed on the back lot. Our dance director, the famed Albertina Rasch, wanted hundreds of whirling Gypsies for her opening shot. And she got them. Not only that, but all our Ruritanian costumes were custom-made in the studio wardrobe for each dancer.

Huge tents were erected on the lot to be used for dressing rooms, wardrobe, makeup, and hairdressing. They even had a canteen where all our meals were supplied. It felt like the Big Top had come to town.

Every morning we were picked up by the busload from MGM to be carted out for rehearsals in the *Rosalie* circus. Once deposited on that back lot there was no escape. It was too far to walk back.

One day, after a week of twirling and leaping around the courtyard like a Gypsy, I noticed another smaller group of girls had joined the circus. They were learning an entirely different routine, tap dancing down a wide, central staircase that led into the arena.

"What's all that about?" I asked our assistant.

"Oh, they come on just before Eleanor Powell's entrance, after we've finished shooting down here."

My cash register mind started ringing up the number of extra days they would be working after I'd finished being a revolving Ruritanian. And tap dancing, something I could really do, for a change. How was I going to maneuver myself into that routine once our Gypsy lark was over? I decided to try to learn the new girls' tap routine on my own. Whenever we had a break I went over to the bottom of the tall staircase, watched their steps, and practiced in a corner.

On the night we shot our opening number the lighting in the arena lit up the skies for miles around Culver City. There were cameras poised everywhere, shooting the scene from all directions. They said they were using more cameras than they'd used on the chariot race in *Ben Hur.* There was obviously going to be no hiding in *Rosalie.*

Dancing out of doors at night under the stars gave our work an added excitement. What with the music, the lights, and the hot meals served during the breaks, the atmosphere was more like a gigantic barbecue party. But because of those snooping cameras shooting everywhere at once, the party was over much too quickly.

On my last night as a whirling Gypsy I made a beeline for the tap-dancing director who was to start shooting his routine the following night. When I had him cornered I blurted it all out quickly in case I lost my nerve.

"Please, I would love to join your group tomorrow. I've learned the whole of your new tap number."

He was astonished. "How did you do that?"

"Between breaks, when you were too busy thinking it up to notice."

"I'll be damned," he muttered, and he paused while I held my breath. "I'm sorry, honey," he said at last, "but we have the exact number of girls we need already."

"Yeah, but what if one of them breaks a leg coming down those stairs?"

He smiled, then laughed.

"Okay, you win. You're hired."

I know he hired me more out of appreciation of my effort than out of fear that anything would happen to his dancers. I was thrilled, not only to get the extra three days' wages but because it gave me the opportunity to watch Eleanor Powell do her soon to be famous drum dance.

With lightning speed she beat out her sharp, staccato steps on a series of enormous drums that ran down the center of the arena. Of all the star tap dancers of that era—Ginger Rogers, Betty Grable, Ann Miller—to me it was Eleanor Powell who was the tops. No one else could match her technique, agility, and precision.

On the evening they were to shoot the tappers dancing down the stairs everything went smoothly during the rehearsals while they were lighting up. I sat on the sidelines like a reserve football player never expecting to get into the game.

During the very first take, one of the little tappers lost

her footing in the middle of the staircase and suddenly came tumbling down the rest of the stairs to the bottom. I couldn't believe it. Neither could the dance director. She wasn't hurt seriously, only a sprained ankle. As she was taken to first aid I heard director Woody Van Dyke's voice.

"Can we shoot without her?"

"Don't worry," said the dance director, "I've got a standby. . . . Yolande?" he called. "Where are you?"

I was standing right next to him, quaking. "You mean I'm on?"

"Right now. And I hope you weren't kidding."

I hoped so, too. The staircase now looked like Mount Everest. I was rushed into the dancer's costume. With my heart in my throat I raced to the top of the stairs and joined the other girls. The arcs spluttered on again, the cameras and playback rolled and then, like a starter's gun, I heard, "Action!"

We were off. As I clickety-clacked step by step down the staircase it seemed those stairs would never end. I reached the bottom huffing and puffing, and when the director shouted, "That's it. Print." I let out a sigh of relief. I was so pleased with myself you'd have thought I'd taken over for Eleanor Powell. I could almost see the headlines: "Chorus girl steps into star's shoes and becomes star overnight." Still in a trance as the camera trundled past me to pick up close shots of Miss Powell's number, I unpeeled the borrowed costume, collected my paycheck and climbed back onto the bus to oblivion. At least it was a new twist—chorus girl takes over for chorus girl and stays chorus girl.

Across the street from the side entrance of Metro there was a bar called Jim Stacy's. It was the meeting place for regular studio workers, from writers and directors to extras. It was also a handy drop-in for people who had just missed the bus and were waiting for the next one.

On this particular day I not only dropped in, I fell in, stumbling over somebody's foot and ending up flat on my eyelashes. The foot scrambled up, dusted me down, and full of apologies and felicitations sat me at the table he was sharing with another man who I remembered seeing around the

MGM writer's block. He introduced himself as Donald Ogden Stewart. The foot, who insisted on paying for my martini, had watery eyes like my old man and wore a shapeless pullover and a bow tie. He was drinking Coca Cola, which came as something of a surprise when he turned out to be F. Scott Fitzgerald. I can only recall him saying, "I suppose you came to Hollywood through a beauty contest." And me replying, "No, I just grew here, like Topsy."

"In that case," said Donald Ogden Stewart, "maybe you can tell me what the 'B' stands for in Louis B. Mayer."

Before I could even hazard a guess my bus arrived. I know now that what the B stood for depended on whether you were on your way into MGM or on your way out. But in the case of F. Scott Fitzgerald, for me F will always stand for "Foot."

At various other times in my Central Casting career I hid as a bobby-soxer in *Love Finds Andy Hardy*, a courtesan in *Sweethearts*, a normal person in *After the Thin Man*, and a something-or-other in *Pennies from Heaven*. Remembering my friend Douglas's tips I made sure I was never within shooting distance of Mickey Rooney, Jeanette MacDonald, William Powell, Myrna Loy, Bing Crosby, or any of the other stars in these films. As for Bing Crosby, he must have changed since my old man worked with him. He was so relaxed I wouldn't have known he was playing a scene if the director hadn't said, "Action."

Daddy had his own set ideas about the stars he worked with, and from these he wouldn't be dissuaded. For instance, back in 1934, when he was playing with Mae West in *Belle of the Nineties*, he insisted she was a man. He liked her, and referred to her as "a pocketful of fairies' delight," but nothing would shake his belief.

When Mae West first arrived in Hollywood her sizzling stage reputation had preceded her from New York. There she had written and staged many sexy sagas that had kept the box office busy and the police even busier. If the vice squad didn't attempt to close her down at least once a week she felt she was slipping. But Mae West a *man?*

"No woman," insisted Daddy, "would write a play called

Sex, star in it, bill it as 'The Greatest Sensation since the Armistice,' get thrown into the clink for it, and come out and do it all over again."

"Then why do they say she's the queen of sex if she's a man?"

"That's just it," he replied. "She *is* a queen—in drag. Always camping it up on the set with her hand on her hip, and wiggling her behind—you never saw a real dame act like that."

Out of sheer curiosity I visited him at the studio when he was working with her. She turned out to be a little lady of five-foot-two, although she gave the impression of being tall. Under her *Belle of the Nineties* costume she wore four-inch heels. She quietly dominated every scene, knew her lines, everyone else's, and how it should be played. Perhaps because she had written the screenplay, too. She saw to it that all the actors delivered their lines quickly so that she, by contrast, could take her time and give out that slow Mae West drawl.

I could see what my old man meant. All her feminine gestures were exaggerated in the same way a man overdoes it when he is dressed as a woman. Like Mother George, at Jimmie's Backyard, her eyelashes were a bit too long and her hair piled too high. We often wondered why she always wore floor-length dresses in the street regardless of the fashion. Daddy said it was probably because she had to hide her masculine thighs. I didn't agree. I think she wanted her fans to see her exactly as she was on the screen, and the Mae West screen image was always dressed in floor-length period costumes. However, Daddy was right about her being the fairies' delight. During her heyday there wasn't a female impersonator who didn't have Mae West in his act. Even today she has a legion of camp followers.

Strangely enough I never met the queen of sex during that picture. Maybe it was because Daddy couldn't bring himself to introduce Mr. West as Miss West. I finally met her in 1950 in London when I was starring in *To Dorothy a Son* with Richard Attenborough. Mae West and her manager, Jim Timminy, saw the show one night and came backstage. She was very shy and soft-spoken and asked if I would revive some of her former New York hits in London. Since she had written all her plays as starring vehicles for herself I felt there was only one Mae West who could play Mae West written by Mae West, and it wasn't me. So I didn't.

She still looked the same and dressed the same as she had in Hollywood all those years ago when she acted with my father. The long blonde hair, the highly madeup false eyelashes and the floor-length dress were rigidly in place. There in my dressing room it seemed that both the situation and she had emerged from another era. I felt I was standing in Tussaud's wax museum. She was a bit awesome. But definitely not a man.

At least my father didn't try to convince me that Spencer Tracy was a woman. When he first worked with Tracy, during the same year as *Belle of the Nineties,* on a picture called *Now I'll Tell,* he came home raving about him.

"You've got to come to the set and watch this Spencer Tracy," he enthused. "He just stands there looking at you and you can see what he's thinking!"

I wasn't keen on watching Mr. Tracy thinking on the set. Sitting on the sidelines while actors went over one scene all day from different angles wasn't my favorite occupation. Not until I started getting paid for it. As I had exams coming up at the time I used them as an excuse to avoid going to the studio. It wasn't until several years later, when I was working as a dress extra at MGM on *I Take This Woman,* that I first saw Spencer Tracy doing his secret emoting.

The set was a luxury nightclub and while we extras danced, Tracy played a love scene with Hedy Lamarr at a corner table. This Austrian beauty was MGM's newest love goddess. Under her real name of Hedwig Keisler she had already caused a nationwide furore by appearing in a Czech film called *Ecstasy* in which she not only swam in the nude, but indulged in simulated sex as well. Even Mae West had never gone that far.

After the first print had been privately viewed many times by the United States customs it was impounded on moral grounds; and after a few more screenings a United

States marshal said he had "inadvertently" burned it. A few people even believed him. Later a second print arrived from Prague, trimmed and censored sufficiently so that it could be shown without frightening the horses. Louis B. Mayer, who had seen the first fully frontal print, promptly signed up Fraulein Hedwig Keisler and renamed her Hedy Lamarr.

And now here she was, seated opposite craggy-faced Spencer Tracy at this nightclub table while he gazed into her deep, green-flecked, glacial eyes. With each hack-written word he caressed her, warming the scene with an inner glow which not only excluded the MGM sound stage but the whole world. For him there appeared to be no camera, no director, no crowd of dancing dress extras, only Miss Lamarr. All his tender attention was focused on this breathtakingly eye-boggling love goddess. From her rigid responses he might have been wooing a cadaver. She choked out her lines in a whisper like a frozen reindeer.

To the delight of us dress extras this two-minute scene was repeated for days on end. At eighteen dollars a day this job had turned into a bonanza. Occasionally Woody Van Dyke, the director, would send us away and join them at their table to rehearse the scene again quietly. But no matter how often that scene was played Tracy's performance was so fresh one would think he had never uttered the lines before. And Miss Lamarr remained a captivating stone.

I doubt if any of us would have changed places with Miss Lamarr. She was another highly paid casualty of a system that valued physical beauty above all else. The moguls demanded that their stars look like goddesses and act like humans.

One of the few female greats who achieved their impossible demands was Garbo, and even she had to pack it up at the peak of her career. I recently saw a Garbo revival and was astounded at her mastery of the most unspeakable dialogue. Most of the greats sank with their scenarios. But not Garbo. And not Spencer Tracy.

The only other great I was prodded into watching was Harold Lloyd. As it was the beginning of a lifetime friendship, I'm glad I was unable to wheedle my way out of it. He came into our lives shortly after the completion of *Belle of the Nineties* when Daddy landed a role in the new Lloyd picture, *The Cat's Paw*.

I was sitting on the set while my old man rehearsed a scene with a cellarful of Chinese, when a quiet man with a light makeup and an easy smile pulled up a canvas chair next to mine and asked me if I was interested in being a film star.

"Not today," I told him. "I'd rather be swimming."

"So would I," he laughed, "but I have to work for a living."

"Me, too, in a way—well, a future living. My father says I have to sit here and watch Harold Lloyd's timing. So I can learn to be a comic."

"No kidding," he said, and then suddenly, "Golly, you must be Jimmy's girl."

"That's right."

"Well, well," he smiled, offering me his hand, "welcome to the club."

"Thank you," I said as we shook hands. "Do you have a big part in this film?"

"Too big," he laughed, and at that point somebody called, "Ready, Harold," and my new friend got up, put on his horn-rimmed glasses, said, "See you later," and went on to the set to play a scene with Daddy and Alan Dinehart.

It was the first time I'd met Harold Lloyd and I hadn't known I'd met him. Without his trademark, the lensless spectacles, he looked like any normal human being.

The 1937 newspapers told us the Depression had gone forever. For the first time in years the film companies were showing a profit, and out of a record $108 million invested in new productions I collected a nonrecord $475. The studios turned out 588 pictures and Daddy Donlan only managed to get into three of them. When he wasn't chalking up performances, he was back chalking up tabs at his local bars, and as his debts got predictably higher his health got predictably lower.

It was the year we all danced the Big Apple while Roosevelt was inaugurated for a second term and I learned about unemployment insurance. (The first time I called at the bureau to collect my eighteen dollars Adolphe Menjou arrived in his chauffeur-driven limousine to pick up his.)

Daddy's carousing chum John Barrymore had been in and out of the hospital taking "the cure." He'd met a young student called Elaine Barrie and made her his fourth wife. Now, because of his failing memory, jobs were getting scarcer and he was nearly as broke as we were. His friend Ben Hecht made a rescue attempt by writing a special role for him in *Nothing Sacred*. Producer David Selznick had agreed to use the aging Profile provided he could learn and recite one twenty-line speech to him. Poor Mr. B. had even muffed that.

Craggy-faced Mr. Tracy won his first Academy Award for *Captains Courageous;* so did the world's first full-length cartoon, *Snow White and the Seven Dwarfs*. An unheralded program picture, *A Family Affair*, launched a new character and a way of life called Andy Hardy. The customers were flocking to see *The Good Earth, Lost Horizon, Topper, Dead End*, and *A Hundred Men and a Girl*. The girl was Deanna Durbin, and suddenly a star was born. Just as suddenly a star died—Jean Harlow, aged twenty-six, at the height of her career and in the middle of a picture which was finished by a double.

A graduate schoolgirl named Julie Turner, from Hollywood High, was renamed Lana for her debut, playing opposite Claude Raines in *They Won't Forget* at Warners. Another graduate called Yolande, from Immaculate Heart High, was still playing telephone roulette.

My first year out of school was one of utter confusion. It was time to start being an actress and I didn't know where to begin. There were no longer any permanent theater companies where I could start pushing a trunk onto the stage. On the other hand there were highly publicized stories of girls like Lana Turner being discovered on drugstore stools sipping a soda. (I tried sitting in Schwab's drugstore on Sunset Boulevard and drank dozens of ice-cream sodas to no avail.) Most of the studios signed up a few newcomer discoveries each year to be trained by the studio drama and singing coaches.

My father's agent, Sable Dunn, a plump, friendly, quietly go-getting lady, took me for interviews with every casting director in Hollywood, pushed me right in front of their noses. But even when I was all dressed up and wearing Mother's French hats they refused to discover me. Both Max Arnow at Warner Brothers and Bill Grady at Metro told me I should get experience and be seen in a play somewhere. I don't think the others even looked up from their desks.

Sable suggested the next step was to find a stage on which to be seen. Most of the stages belonged to what were called little theaters where students paid a monthly fee to rehearse and play roles in new plays. These were run by professional actors and directors who had come to Hollywood to work in pictures and found they needed another occupation to provide a regular income. One of these little theaters, which wasn't a fee-paying school, belonged to Mae West's manager, Jim Timminy. I saw him several times hoping to get into one of his plays and it was through him that I eventually met a playwright called L. I. Dunne who gave me my first speaking role. In an old, unused theater in Los Angeles he was trying out his new play *Oh, Mr. Randolph,* for which he was also the director. All the cast, except me, were professionals. I don't know whether or not they were paid; but I wasn't. Considering how green I was, he should have paid me to stay out of his play.

When I received the script I was both thrilled and apprehensive. I had never learned and spoken a speech out loud before and here was the ingenue role of Ann Gregory with three big scenes. I thought at last I had a problem I could share with my father. I hurried excitedly to the La Paula apartment to ask his advice.

He wasn't where he usually was, in the kitchen huddled over his pie tin, but sitting in an armchair in his living room with his feet up on another chair.

"What are you doing in an armchair like normal people?" I asked.

"The old ticker is acting up. Doctor says I have to take it easy—and not worry."

"Maybe you can stop worrying soon," I said as I handed him the play. "Look, my first stage role—Ann Gregory—and you can show me how to play it."

He flicked through the play, scanned Ann Gregory's three main scenes and threw the script aside on the couch.

"It's not worth playing," he shrugged. "You should go up for Scarlett O'Hara in *Gone With the Wind.*"

At that time Hollywood was in the throes of the search for Scarlett. Practically every female star in the business considered herself the only possible choice and producer David O. Selznick was testing everybody who was somebody and a lot who were nobody. It was the lead story in all the film papers. Would it be Bette Davis? Paulette Goddard? Tallulah Bankhead? One thing was certain, it wouldn't be me. The only thing I had in common with Scarlett was that we were both female. I couldn't even read Ann Gregory in *Oh, Mr. Randolph*, let alone attempt the most sought after role in filmland. As usual Daddy Donlan was asking for the impossible. He had no memory of what it was like to be an inexperienced beginner.

I picked up my first play, kissed him good-bye and left him with his dreams of his daughter playing Scarlett O'Hara while I got on with learning Ann Gregory's lines. Mother helped me with the memorizing and the leading man taught me how to say them. I fell in love with him for the duration of the play—one week. In the beginning I was always falling in love with whoever was playing the leading man. It wasn't until I became a leading lady that I went off them. Curious.

On the opening night of *Oh, Mr. Randolph* there were only about fifty people in the audience, in a theater which held a thousand. Most of them were relatives of the actors. I said my lines as quickly as I could to get them over with, before I forgot them. I was glad my old man wasn't there, it would have shattered his illusions. Mother, Aunty, and Jack and a few friends came to my dressing room afterward. They said I looked all right but they couldn't understand a word I said.

After my debut debacle, I decided to enroll in one of the fee-paying little theaters. I chose the Edward Clark school. Mr. Clark had been a director in New York before coming to Hollywood. He put on a new play every four weeks, rehearsing his students as they would work in a professional company, except that we had to learn all the roles and exchange parts every week so that everyone would get a chance to play the leads. When I'd been there six months Daddy Donlan came to see the third generation of Donlans doing her turn at the leading role. This time the rest of the family didn't come.

They'd seen me act once and didn't wish to repeat the experience.

That night I gave my all and could almost be heard past the third row where my old man was sitting. After the show he came backstage.

"Well, you've got the spark all right," he said, "but for God's sake make your entrance onto the stage with authority—as if you knew what you were doing, even if you don't."

With him out front he was lucky I hadn't sneaked onto the stage on my hands and knees.

At the end of that week he sent Sable Dunn to see the show. My entrance had improved but what I did afterward hadn't. We both agreed over an aftershow hamburger that I wasn't fit to be seen yet. She said my father had been on to her about sending me up for Scarlett. They were now testing anybody. I told her to forget it, he was having illusions of my grandeur. It was then Sable broke it to me how ill he really was now. What's more she was having difficulty getting him even a few days' work because news of his heart trouble had spread through the studio casting departments. What he had feared most had happened; he was no longer insurable. But now Harold Lloyd had asked for him specially to appear in his next film, and she didn't know whether to tell Lloyd about my father's illness and chance his losing the job, or risk having Lloyd find out later. We decided it was only fair Harold should know before the picture started and I offered to go and see him personally with the hope of persuading him to take a chance. I knew how much it would mean to my old man's morale.

Fortunately, when I saw Harold at Paramount the following week I didn't have to persuade him.

"Yolande," he said reassuringly, "if Jimmy can walk and talk he's the man I want." And as he led me to the door he clasped my hand, "Don't worry, I'll have my friend Doctor Toma look after him."

And that is how James Donlan made *Professor Beware.* Every day he was called, Harold called Dr. Toma as well. My

121
☆

old man perked up during the film and was his old laughing and joking self, giving his usual lift to the scenes he was in. Harold had taken a chance, it worked and I was grateful. After the film was over Harold arranged for me to meet Dr. Toma privately to find out the true facts of Daddy's illness.

It was raining that January 1938 day when I took the bus to Dr. Toma's office on Sunset Boulevard. He was a robust young surgeon, only recently in practice but with all the warmth and understanding of a dedicated doctor. I'm sure that's why Harold was so fond of him. He broke the bad news gently but firmly. James Donlan could die within six months if he worried unduly or went back on the bottle.

I rode back on the bus with my mind in a turmoil. He owed weeks in rent, income tax men were after him; how could he *not* worry himself to death? How, in that situation, could he keep off his last friend, the bottle? It was a destructive circle I couldn't break. I fretted. I must work quickly, I thought, anywhere, anything to save him, pay the rent, pay the doctor, the drink bills, the tax—anything to keep him alive. I called up Central Casting every night for extra work, went on every dancing interview, but the jobs I did were not frequent enough to support us all.

Every day as I came back from auditions or the odd day's work I stopped by to see him. Usually, he would be sitting in his armchair, his feet up on a stool, alone, down. I was so worried for him. No one to share his loneliness. I had left him; I'd broken my promise and now there was no one.

Often if I came early I would see him in the distance crossing the street, walking slowly as he had been told to do because of his heart. As he looked healthy on the outside angry drivers would toot and yell at him for not moving across it quickly. If he'd had a white stick, a limp, or a crutch they wouldn't have done it. How could they know he was dying? It broke my heart and I wanted to scream, "Stop yelling at my Daddy, you mean bastards! You're in a hurry to get from nowhere to nowhere in the rush of life, and you're killing the pride and soul of a lonely, dying man! Goddam you all!"

Sometimes if I arrived late I saw him staggering drunkenly out of Ace Cain's, the nearest bar where he had an account and could charge his booze . . . oh, no, he's killing himself. But how could I stop him, poor, sad clown.

That spring, thanks to George Cunningham, who had directed the dances in Daddy's show *Oh Kay!*, I landed a dancing job in Edwin Lester's operetta season at the Philharmonic Auditorium in Los Angeles. It was an annual event that provided dancers and singers with at least six weeks' steady work. This year they were doing *New Moon* and *Roberta*, and George had been signed as choreographer for both. He knew the financial mess we Donlans were in and I was lucky he remembered to call me for these shows.

I was now able to pay off some of the food and medicine bills. Also to contribute toward Dr. Toma's fees, although he insisted he would look after my old man regardless. At last our future seemed brighter.

On the opening night of *New Moon* Sigmund Romberg himself conducted the orchestra. The excitement in the star-studded audience was electric. I have never since heard his music played with such great feeling and zest. Our dance numbers were mainly with the comedian, Sterling Holloway. We tossed him around like a rag doll and sang lyrics at him. Sterling was lean, lanky, and with a mop of almost white hair which always hung down over one eye. He specialized in playing likable goofnuts, a trademark he had already established in several films, including *Professor Beware* with Lloyd and Daddy Donlan.

Every night during the run of *New Moon* I stood in the wings and swooned when the romantic leading man sang "Wanting You." As usual I fell out of love with him as soon as that show was over. By comparison the leading man in *Roberta* was a romantic letdown. His name was Bob Hope and none of us had ever heard of him. He was friendly and funny with his slick delivery, but not swoon material.

At the end of one of our numbers a chorus boy and I were left alone onstage, sitting on a lovers' lane bench, smooching. It was the cue for Bob Hope's entrance, which he

123
☆

made from the curtains directly behind us. Many nights he would delay his entrance and we could hear him back there whispering nonsense at us, trying to give us the giggles.

"Go on, you can do better than that," he'd hiss, secretly nudging the boy through the curtains. Or, "Close your eyes when you kiss—now open them and tell me what the house is like."

When he eventually came on we were able to run off. While the chorus boy pattered away to report Mr. Hope's latest devilments to his fairy-footed colleagues I would stand in the wings watching this new comedian, hoping to pick up some of the ease and subtlety with which he delivered a gag.

The telephone call came at 4 A.M.

I was in a deep, exhausted sleep when I heard the phone ringing. I had been out late that night. After the show George Cunningham had taken some of us girls to one of the Mexican clubs on Alvera Street. Half awake I reached out for the alarm clock to check the time. The telephone continued to ring. Mother was either asleep or refusing to answer it so I pulled myself out of bed. In a sleepy daze I wandered into the hall and picked up the shrilling receiver. It was the night porter of the La Paula apartments.

"Your father's died—alone—in the bathroom on the floor. He's in the morgue."

He explained how my father had called a nurse who lived in the same apartment block to get him a shot, a pill. She was out. He had to wait for her to get back. When she did it was too late.

I replaced the receiver, my mind a jumble of despairing thoughts. . . . If only I'd been there I could have saved him. . . . "What have I done?" I ruminated guiltily, "I've killed my father. . . ."

The autopsy said cirrhosis of the liver, hardening of the arteries, coronary thrombosis—God knows what. I telephoned Sable Dunn.

"How do I bury him with no money?"

"The Screen Actors Benevolent Fund," she consoled. "I'll make the arrangements for you."

Aunty showed up for the funeral to say good-bye to her brother before they shut the coffin lid. Having remarked how well Jimmy looked considering he was dead, she added she was sure he would be delighted to see her at the service as they wouldn't allow grudges in Heaven.

After the funeral Uncle Jack drove me in his Yellow Cab to the La Paula apartments to collect my father's trunk and my own small desk, which I had left there. I was shocked when the receptionist told me they had been sold in lieu of rent. Daddy Donlan had owed seven months. He had nothing of value; his possessions couldn't have fetched more than a couple of dollars from a junk dealer, but it was the law. I felt so empty leaving without a memento, not a photograph, a press cutting, or even a pie tin.

I was doing a show that night. He was dead. I didn't dare tell anyone in the chorus or cast in case they sympathized. I couldn't have stood it. The curtain had come down for James Donlan, but it was going up for *Roberta,* so I went on and smiled and danced.

Left with the responsibility of carrying on the family profession, I obviously needed the best advice I could get. The first person I sought out was Harold Lloyd. Of all the super stars of the era, to me he was the most super of them all. At the time of Daddy Donlan's death Harold was installed as a producer at RKO studios and was preparing a film for Lucille Ball, *A Girl, A Guy and A Gob.* Busy as he was he always found time to see me.

Harold was a joyful optimist who had fulfilled all our American dreams by rising from an unemployed extra, like myself, to becoming the wealthiest and best loved star in Hollywood. He had outearned every other star of the Golden Era, including such Hollywood moneybags as Mary Pickford, Douglas Fairbanks, Gloria Swanson, and even Charlie Chaplin.

Around his thirty-two-room Italian Renaissance home in the Green Acre section of Beverly Hills, twenty acres of almost unpriceable land sprouted with fountains, forests, swimming pools, tennis and handball courts, a golf course, and all other kinds of buildings for staff and guests. He even had a chemistry lab where he could play medicine with Dr. Toma. And unlike so many of the stars he hadn't built this showpiece for show. He did it, as he did most things in his life, because he liked it.

What's more he believed if he could do it anybody could do it, including me. All it required was a bit of luck and a great deal of determination.

"I started as an extra disguised as a Red Indian," he told me and his warm, kindly eyes twinkled at the memory. "Not that I particularly wanted to be an Indian, but I was determined to get into the movie business."

A film company which had been shooting in his home town, San Diego, had announced that they needed a group of Indians as extras. So Harold got out his war paint and feathers, joined the real Indians, was selected, and earned himself three dollars for the day's work. But it wasn't always that easy. After that he spent weeks without work, standing outside the studio gates with no hope of getting inside.

In those days, before the Actors Union and Central Casting were functioning, the assistant directors often chose their extras from the crowds who hung around all day outside the various studio gates. But you could stand there for six months without results. As Harold discovered.

"I got so fed up," he told me, "that one day when I was waiting outside Universal and a group of extras came out of the studio to have lunch in the restaurant opposite, I followed them. I slipped into the men's room, put on some makeup and then rejoined them, mingling with their painted faces on their trek back to the studio. I managed to slip past the gateman and get my name on the extra list for the following day's work."

I had to admit this was determination. It was also Harold's lucky day in more senses than one. He made friends with one of the other extras who had landed himself a job as a stock cowboy at $25 a week. His name was Hal Roach and he was later to father hundreds of successful comedies including the *Our Gang* series and the Laurel and Hardy pictures. He also launched such historical comic personalities as Charlie Chase, Snub Pollard, Bebe Daniels, Jackie Cooper, Patsy Kelly, Will Rogers and, of course, Harold Lloyd.

But when Harold and Hal first met they were both milling around in the crowds looking for work. It was only through an unexpected small inheritance that Roach was suddenly able to pull out of the crowd and set himself up as a producer. At that time being a producer bore no resemblance to the image we have today. The money they spent on the whole picture then wouldn't even pay for a film trailer now. So when Hal offered Harold five dollars a day and a percentage of any profits to try his hand at a comedy short, it was an offer he couldn't refuse.

In those days, according to Harold, film making was much more fun and spontaneous. As he recounted it, it sounded like Home Movies to me.

"There was no such thing as a script. We just set off down the road with a camera and a couple of actors and tossed around ideas. Something outside might spark us off, a junk heap, an old car, a monument—anything we could climb over, fall off, or throw."

Roach was always inventive and quick to grasp a comic situation. Then he would let the camera roll and the actors improvise. But out of the chaos of pratfalls, climbs, and chases came those early comic gems.

"We sold that first picture for eight hundred and fifty dollars," he laughed. "As that was about five hundred percent profit we thought we'd struck El Dorado!"

In later years Harold was to turn up at many unexpected times in my life and listen to my confusions with understanding and humor. By then he had spectacles with lenses.

It was no surprise to me when in 1952 they decided to give Harold a special Oscar. On the base of the gold statuette they had inscribed the words: *Master Comedian and Good Citizen.*

When *Roberta* had finished its run Aunty and Uncle Jack moved into Mother's apartment with Grand'mère and myself to help share expenses. Uncle drove his cab on the night shift as the fares were higher and Aunty and I took it in turn to dial Central Casting every night while Mother did the cooking.

Under the influence of the French Mollots, Aunty and Jack had quieted down considerably and no longer indulged in nocturnal duels. Unlike the Irish Donlans, the French Mollots were early risers. Mother joined a hiking club and first thing every morning, after she'd done her exercises, she climbed up the Hollywood hills while Grand'mère beetled off to Mass.

In the afternoon Mother attended healthy cookery classes where she learned about black strap molasses and wheat germ. To Grand'mère's horror Mother began to sneak these elixirs of youth and longevity into her classic French cooking.

"*C'est affreux, Thérèse!*" Grand'mère croaked, stomping her feet. While Mother cooked, the old lady followed her around the kitchen spying on her, complaining she had lived quite long enough already without the help of California health freaks.

On one of Mother's hiking jaunts she found a new boyfriend, Jerry Sands, who was a car salesman and had a dimpled smile like Gable's. We all liked him in spite of the fact that he was a health fanatic, too. He and Mother often joined my boyfriend, Wesley, and me when we went dancing or to the movies. When the four of us double-dated, everyone remarked how young Mother looked. "Just like your sister," they would say to me and Mother would preen with pride and flash her flirtatious eyes at Jerry. He melted under her glance and obviously adored her. We all expected nuptial bells for Mother again and were ready to welcome him into our family.

Her feet hardly touched the ground as she planned her stone ground wholemeal wedding cake. Everything smelled of roses; until the fatal weekend when Wesley invited us to his bungalow at Hermosa beach to celebrate passing his calculus exam.

On our first evening he mixed up a harmless wine punch and had some of his student and tennis chums in to drink it.

Mother and Jerry, the two health fanatics who normally didn't touch alcohol, were in a frivolous mood and joined the rest of us in a couple of rounds. We all laughed, talked, danced, and Mother sang "Chiri-biri-bin," and apart from that the party was a festive success.

In our twin-bedded room Mother and I giggled and whispered like schoolgirls in the dorm. Then came the dawn. Bright and early Mother and I crept down to the kitchen to brew her dandelion coffee for her yoghourt, prunes and bran breakfast; and who should we find slouched across the kitchen table? Jerry. And on the table, an almost empty bottle of wine, and in the health-crazed lover's hand a glass of the demon contents. Jerry didn't appear at all healthy anymore. He looked up at us with his Gable grin.

"A hair of the doggie," he slubbered, and I noticed his dimples were sagging. Shakily he poured two glasses of wine for us. "Come along, kiddies," he chortled, "a little drinkie for the doggie."

Mother was stunned. "Drink?" she quailed. "At eight in the morning? Oh, heavens, you're not another one?"

" 'Nother what?"

"Drunk, like her father!"

"That's not nicey, Terry, honey," he protested, slid off the stool onto the floor and passed out.

We spent the remainder of that weekend fighting a losing battle trying to keep Mother's lover sober, to no avail. Every time he awakened he sneaked out to buy another bottle and he stopped eating anything, not even black strap molasses or wheat germ. It became his lost weekend in every way as Mother refused to see him ever again.

"Once was enough," she told me later. "I've certainly been unlucky with my men."

I had to agree she was a bad picker but I didn't realize she was going to shut men out of her life completely, forever after, which she did. It seemed a sad waste of an attractive woman. I can remember her saying, "Yolande, you must work to be independent, you can never rely on any man."

With renewed effort I badgered Central Casting. It took weeks of dialing before I landed my next job, as stand-in for the Hungarian actress Steffi Duna. It was a Western movie at Republic studios. The only requirements of a stand-in are to be the same coloring and size as the actress playing the scene, and to stand in the same places while the cameraman does his lighting. I was such a newcomer that I learned Steffi's lines and played her scenes as well, not realizing that the prime reason for my standing there was so that the lamps would melt *my* make-up and not hers.

Nineteen thirty-eight looked like it was going to be my Western year because I was shuttled right off this one onto *The Oklahoma Kid* at Warners, in which I played one of my hiding-as-an-extra parts trying to keep out of the way of James Cagney and Humphrey Bogart. Just which of the many Warner brothers decided to make their two favorite gangsters into cowboys nobody seemed to know. Least of all Cagney and Bogart.

The scene was at night at an outdoor barn dance where we extras hopped about yipping festively while the two stars stalked each other. Bogart must have been the villain because he was dressed in cowboy black. Both of them were like a couple of kids playing cowboys. They kept breaking into guffaws at each other's handling of their unaccustomed spurs, chaps, and six shooters, as well as their gangsterese accents. I wondered whether these two gangster stars had collapsed with glee or kept straight faces the first time either of them had to go bang-bang-you're-dead in a cops-and-robbers movie. I remember wondering the same thing about Edward G. Robinson when my old man worked with him in *The Whole Town's Talking*. He was the most sinister gangster actor of that period but in real life he was the least likely candidate for such villainy. It was always a shock to meet this mild-mannered, soft-spoken art connoisseur. As the Hollywood star system was mainly based on typecasting, it wasn't often one found this striking contrast between the screen image and the real person.

As for me, I would have settled for any casting. I wasn't even a type yet. One of the recent discoveries was Veronica Lake who had become a type by wearing long blonde hair hanging over one eye. I heard she had been found acting under her real name, Connie something, at the Bliss-Hayden Little Theater School. So after the operetta season I signed up with them. It was a snobbier version of the Edward Clark school and "them" were Lela Bliss, a tall, blonde actress with a lah-de-dah accent, and her husband Harry Hayden, a short, plump, jolly actor. Harry directed the plays and they both appeared in all of them in the plum parts. It was good experience for us, acting with these two excellent professionals; and even better for them because by comparison to us they looked so good they were always getting discovered and acting in films.

In my first Bliss-Hayden role I had a scene in which I sat in a railroad station waiting room and said, "I think seeing people off is awful." Lela Bliss, who was out front teaching, said, "Stop acting!" This confused me as I thought that was what I was there to do.

"Stop acting and be yourself," she explained.

I tried, but I didn't know what myself was. She gave up on that one and concentrated on teaching me how to say "orange." Apparently in one of the lines I had said "arnge" and Lela insisted it should be "ahr-rahnge." I learned that. In fact, I became the best "orange" sayer in the class. It's a shame I've never been in a play about oranges where I could say it. In one of the productions I had to play the role of a temperamental actress. I found that a great problem, too. It's difficult to play a temperamental actress if you're not an actress.

But not as difficult as the antics I was asked to perform for a few lessons under the teaching of the distinguished Russian actress Maria Ouspenskaya. Her method of teaching was called Stanislavsky. This was the name of the distinguished Russian gentleman whose ideas started all the latter-day Method-acting shenanigans. Stanislavsky insisted it wasn't enough just to walk on a stage and say, "Dinner is served"; one had to be aware of *why* it was served and what the cook's grandmother had said in 1894 when grandfather had come home roaring drunk on vodka.

As Madame Ouspenskaya couldn't afford a theater to put plays on and try this out on a stage, she kept us busy offstage

131
☆

doing Stanislavsky exercises. We sat around the room trying to pretend to be seashells. I tried and tried but never became one. We also had to hop about like a frog and croak. It was said to be good for breaking down our inhibitions, and there is nothing more inhibiting for an actor than to be not-acting.

The main problem most actors have to face is that unlike an artist who can paint at home, and a writer who can write at home, when an actor pretends to be a seashell or a croaking frog at home he is likely to be carted away. So the frustrated actors formed little groups to act at each other. They adopted this Stanislavsky offstage system to keep themselves busy when they weren't. But as Americans were keen on nicknames and not so keen on Russians they called it The Method.

Since those days I have been wined, dined, hired, fired, romanced in the dressing room, directed, misdirected and chased around the casting couch by exponents of *all* methods. Sometimes I chased the methods around. Between being a frustrated seashell and a croaking frog I ran across the most exciting method of all. It was called the Group Theater. This group thing was a gathering of actors that sprang up during the Depression and presented plays about sexy labor problems. But as soon as America was prosperous again most of the Group, including playwright Clifford Odets and actor John Garfield, were lured to Hollywood and took to swimming pools or drink: and so the outfit disintegrated.

I had a thrilling interlude with an ex-director of this Group Theater. Undaunted by the breakup of the Group he had become a drama coach at Columbia studios. Here he carried on in his office with his old Group methods—sexy labor problems. To evaluate my talents he asked me to play a love scene from the Odets play *Golden Boy*. He read the role of the boy and I, the girl. I must have been real convincing because when he came to the kissing bit he lost his head and kissed me bang on my gaping mouth. I don't know whether it was the Method or not, but I made a film at his studio.

Today, anytime I get really bewildered by acting methods my mind goes back to a story Garson Kanin told me about a luncheon party at Claridge's in London. Around the table were Spencer Tracy, Gar, Katharine Hepburn, and director George Cukor. They were discussing the important facets of acting and everyone was flinging around fancy phrases like "unconscious motivation," "rhythm of speech," and "character delineation." Everyone except Spencer Tracy, who sat listening silently. When the coffee came around Kanin turned to him and said, "What about you, Spence? You've earned your living at it long enough. What do you think is most important?"

"Learn the fucking words," said Spencer Tracy, and poured some more coffee.

Although I hadn't had the benefit of Mr. Tracy's pithy advice when it was my turn to play the lead at Bliss-Hayden's Little Theater I had a survival instinct that warned me to learn the lines first before I could play them. So on the days I did extra work I took the play with me to study in hidden corners between takes. I was nearly put off learning any of them on a film called *The Great Man Votes*. We crowd were seated on bleachers in an outdoor arena. As usual I sat as far away from the star as possible. Only in this case it was our old friend John Barrymore, who had fallen apart considerably. I didn't bother to say hello as he was having enough problems already. He was no longer even attempting to learn his speeches.

"I've learned enough words in my life," he told the director, who happened to be Garson Kanin. So he had all his lines written on blackboards which were held next to the camera or wherever his eyeline happened to be. They used three boards, in assorted sizes, according to the length of his speeches. I heard later from Gar Kanin that during the film Barrymore had a short scene in which a character came on and said to him, "Are you Gregory Vance?" All Barrymore had to answer was, "Yes." When Kanin saw them writing a huge *Yes* on the blackboard he thought things were going too far.

"You don't need just 'Yes' on the board, Jack."

"Why not?" demanded Barrymore.

"What else could you possibly say?"

Barrymore reflected for a moment and answered, "Well, I could say No."

I noticed from my bleacher seat that Mr. B. often couldn't see the blackboard, let alone the lines. It was a harrowing experience for a budding thespian and I buried my nose in my play. There were no blackboards at Bliss-Hayden.

I was slightly disconcerted when Central Casting sent me for crowd work at MGM on *Idiot's Delight* because when I arrived on the set I found I was the one and only crowd and couldn't hide. It was a backstage set with a dressing room door and a circular iron staircase. I was hustled into a showgirl's spangled leotard with feathers and told to walk up the staircase during the scene. The only other person in the scene was a good-looking guy who had to hurry through the dressing room door. He was the big-eared cowboy villain from *The Painted Desert* and now the king, Clark Gable.

I was thrilled. Just the two of us, me the crowd, and Gable the star, playing our scene. My heart thumped beneath the spangles and my feathers stood on end as I climbed the stairs and Gable walked through the door. It was only a one-minute take but for that minute we costarred, Gable and me. After our scene we sat on a couple of old stage trunks and had a do-you-remember-when chat.

"My God, I would never have recognized you," grinned my costar. "Just caught a glimpse at your old man's funeral but, hell, you've filled out!"

"Well, I've grown up a couple of feet and two bumps. You look gorgeous. Not so thin."

He smiled. "Yeah, I've filled out, too. Been able to eat regular meals since I had this regular work."

His next regular work was to be *Gone With the Wind* as soon as he'd finished *Idiot's Delight*. He told me he was looking forward to it.

"Great subject, great part. But at the moment we're having a kind of a hassle." His eyes crinkled and his dimples puckered. "They're insisting I play Rhett Butler with a Southern accent and I'm insisting I don't. Crissakes, can you imagine me attempting a Southern accent?"

I could imagine him attempting anything. I told him so and he gave me that don't-give-me-that smile. The property men arrived to shift our two stage trunks to get some lamps around to the dressing room.

"On a backstage set like this, does it make you nostalgic to be back in the theater?" I asked.

"Hell, no," said Gable, "I never liked acting in the theater."

"My father always missed it."

"Your father was a good stage actor. I could never have made it like this without MGM and Hollywood."

"You didn't just 'make it'—you're the king here."

"All that king stuff is publicity crap," he laughed. "I was just lucky to be in the right place at the right time."

Director Clarence Brown called him back on the set to do a scene in the dressing room with Marjorie Rambeau. He squeezed my hand and wished me luck as he left to do his king thing. My stint was over but I stayed and watched and pondered. Hollywood was the right place, now was the right time. But how many more Donlans would become paupers here for the few Gables who became kings? Maybe for me the theater was a better bet.

I went back to Bliss-Hayden's to learn how to act being myself on the stage.

To this day I don't know exactly how it happened. Maybe Sable Dunn spoke to somebody who talked to somebody else who had seen me saying "ahr-rahnge" at Bliss-Hayden's. Anyway, we were in the last week of rehearsing when a call came through that I had actually been booked for a *Gone With the Wind* test. I was to be at Selznick studios the day after our play opened and might even be directed by George Cukor.

Panic.

I telephoned Will Price, a Southern friend, to come to our apartment that night and teach me an instant Southern accent. Will later became the dialogue director on the actual film. When I broke the news at home pandemonium set in. Mother kept dashing from the kitchen to the living room saying, "For Dear's sake, I can't believe it," and burned the dinner while Grand'mère followed me around excitedly cackling, "Clock Gobble?" By the time Will Price left us that evening the whole family was talking with a Southern accent. Except Grand'mère who just went Gobbling on.

I rehearsed the play all day and read *Gone With the Wind* all night. On opening night I kept slipping into the Scarlett O'Hara accent and every time I did Lela Bliss gave me a sharp dig in the ribs. I felt a bit stomachachey after the show and attributed it to Lela's boney elbow. I raced home, gulped down Mother's dinner, which promptly came up again, washed and pinned up my hair, leaped into bed and stayed awake all night saying, "Ah do declare, Ashley Wilkes, ah don't for the life of me understand what yo see in that skinny little Melanie."

After a while I imagined Clark Gable carrying me through the fire on his horse. I looked up into his sexy brown eyes and he looked down at me in horror and said, "Yo not Scarlett, yo is Yolande," and dropped me into the burning cinders. I broke into a hot sweat. I could see Gable riding on Poncho into Selznick's office and tearing up his Rhett Butler contract. I felt a pain in my stomach which made me dizzy; and then another, and before long I had forgotten all about Clark Gable and was longing for Dr. Toma.

We called him that morning and I spent the day of my *Gone With the Wind* test on an operating table with Dr. Toma removing my appendix.

Among the many celebrities who planed, trained, and trekked West to pick up the gold during the Hollywood boomtime was a tall, slim, middle-aged man with a balding, skeletal head and sunken cheeks who was destined to set the night life of our little hick town on its celluloid ear.

His name was Earl Carroll and he had already become something of a legend in his own lifetime. For years he had dazzled New York with the most extravagant girlie shows since the great Ziegfeld. To be a "Carroll Girl" was said to be the accolade bestowed only on those who could look the best, dance the best, and protrude in the best places.

Over all his stage doors was a sign that proudly stated: THROUGH THESE PORTALS PASS THE MOST BEAUTIFUL GIRLS IN THE WORLD. And surrounded by such goodies it seemed Mr. Carroll just couldn't stop nibbling at them. His conquests of beautiful women both on- and offstage invariably made headline news. Particularly the time he was sent to jail for allowing one of his beauties to take a nude dip in a tubful of champagne at one of his equally notorious parties. As it had occurred during Prohibition I'm not sure whether he had been sentenced because the girl was nude, underage, or because champagne was illegal even for washing.

So naturally the Hollywood papers were full of his arrival. They were also full of his new plan. Casanova Carroll was going to build a theater restaurant that would out-Hollywood Hollywood. It was to be the largest and most glamorous of its kind, with the best food, the finest talent, and, of course, the most beautiful girls in the world. Since there was practically no night life in Hollywood, and as most of its inhabitants, contrary to their image, were usually in bed by ten o'clock, everyone thought Mr. Carroll was out of his skeletal head.

However, they conceded, if he was looking for the most beautiful girls in the world what better spot to find them? Every beauty queen from the forty-eight States had migrated to Hollywood to seek her fortune in the movies. These beautiful girls were everywhere; working as waitresses, usherettes, salesladies; and all hoping to be discovered. There wasn't a crooked nose or a set of uneven teeth in sight. So when Carroll announced in the papers that he was holding open auditions to find forty girls for his new show they turned up in the thousands.

I joined them and no one was more surprised than I when after two weeks' weeding out I was among the chosen forty. I was also surprised to find that the wicked Mr. Carroll with the naughty reputation looked and acted very much like the mother superior of my convent. He wafted around us during rehearsals wearing an artist's smock. His voice was soft and gentle. And so were his effeminate hands. His attitude was that of a coddling custodian and we were later to find out that stage-door callers, notes from customers, and sometimes even our incoming telephone calls were discreetly scrutinized.

Carroll's relationship with his girls was unlike that of any other producer. Immediately we were hired he told us we were the most important attraction in his shows. His audience would come primarily to see us, not the stars.

"You must treat your positions with responsibility," he told us gently but firmly.

The first of these responsibilities, we found, was that we

were not allowed to expose our beautiful bodies to the sun. Mr. Carroll didn't want his lovelies to appear with red, brown, and white strap marks. In California this was a great hardship as recreation centered around swimming and sun. There were little yelps of disapproval. We were also to be weighed every week like jockeys to keep our figures under his control. The stage manager was in charge of this ritual. He stood by the scales with his notebook of weights and checked us off on his weekly tally. It wasn't long before the girls who had put on weight found that a bottle of whisky was the acceptable bribe to stop him marking it down. The only Carroll girl I recall being fired for putting on weight was Yvonne de Carlo. Maybe she was lucky because she didn't do too badly after that.

Mr. Carroll arranged for our hair to be individually styled at one of the top hairdressing salons and once he had selected our hairstyle we were not allowed to change one wisp of it. He then had portrait photos taken of each girl and covered the walls of the entrance bar with them. Using heads, he said, instead of the usual pinup pictures gave his girls class and an elusive glamour.

Although his nightclub was constructed like a normal theater it had tiers of tables instead of seats descending toward the enormous stage. And unlike most theaters the girls' dressing room was on stage level. Carroll said it was to save his lovelies from climbing stairs after a strenuous dance number. Perhaps it was to save himself since he was our most regular visitor. Whenever he appeared we were usually in various stages of nudity and in the early days the very sight of him started pandemonium. Shrieking and giggling, the girls toppled over each other to grab their dressing gowns or hide behind their costumes. Mr. Carroll couldn't understand what they were all fussing about.

"You little angels have the most beautiful bodies in the world," he said gently. "You shouldn't be ashamed of them."

It was his way of skinning an angel.

The opening of the new show, called *The World's Fairest,* was certainly a gala occasion. Every available searchlight flashed across the sky from Hollywood to Beverly Hills beckoning the stars out of each other's beds and into the limelight. The milling crowd of borrowed diamonds and rented furs weaved happily through the radio interviewers and photographers' flashbulbs. As far as the eye could see there were stars, droves of producers, directors, and moguls' mistresses.

Backstage, as we powdered our makeup and preened our feathers, odd bits of news kept filtering through. "Marlene's at a front table!" "Guess who Errol Flynn's brought!" "It can't be Garbo but it looks like her!" Most of us had friends or relatives somewhere out there at the cheaper tables. The principal male singer had invited his new agent who had actually brought a movie talent scout to hear him sing. Poor guy—he was to be the first of the casualties.

Mr. Carroll popped in to cheer us up before the last call. As usual he was suave, serene, and self-possessed, he had discarded his smock for an impeccable tuxedo.

"Just remember this," he purred. "They're all here just to see one thing—my beautiful angels."

Then the orchestra struck up and we angels took flight. The show was on. The man waving the baton was Ray Noble, that clever Englishman who was already famous for writing such smoochy ballads as "Love Is the Sweetest Thing," "The Very Thought of You," and "Love in Bloom," so at least we knew the music was in capable hands.

For the opening number Carroll had had individual costumes designed for each of the forty girls according to her coloring, personality, and individual hairstyle. And every girl in turn was given her own entrance down the central staircase while the principal singer sang Carroll's own special number, "The Most Beautiful Girls." The singing stars popped up and down on elevators that came up through two sections of stage jutting out on either side of a smaller staircase leading to the audience.

Everything was going smoothly until one of these elevators refused to come up, the one on which the principal singer was supposed to sing his solo number while the girls did a quick change onstage behind the curtain. The poor man was left to sing the whole of his number unseen in the basement.

And worse was to come. In the backstage chaos of attempting to get the elevator working somebody pressed the wrong button and opened the curtains instead. There we were, all forty of us, with our backs to the audience and our bottoms bare.

It is quite a shock to glance over your shoulder and find a gala-dressed audience gazing with astonishment as you struggle to get your bare bottom into the next costume. I wondered if anything else could go wrong. It did. We had a gay little Tyrolean number in which we revolved onto stage center backed by a cutout set of Austrian Alps, trees, and chalets. The revolve wouldn't seem to stay center. It kept switching from right to left. Every time it moved it jerked and down would come an Alp, a tree, or a chalet on top of Carroll's Tyrolean angels.

In turn we picked up ourselves, our various pieces of set and carried on singing and dancing and doing our Tyrolean "Yoodle-eee-ooo-hoo-hoo." By the end of the number the whole set had come down, the revolve had packed up altogether and we Tyrolean angels just had to scamper off clutching our various pieces of Alps while we sang our last "Yoodle-eee-ooo-hoo-hoo."

The girls who shared that vast, mirror-lined dressing room were a strangely mixed group. Surprisingly only three of us had ambitions to achieve success in show business. Most of them wanted to make a successful marriage and had varying fantasies about the way it would happen.

Perhaps the most memorable character was Lili, one of the few girls Carroll had brought from New York. Lili was a past master, or mistress, at wheedling expensive gifts out of her escorts. It was usually jewelry which she promptly sold back to the shops as soon as the romance was over. The money went straight into the bank for her dowry. She used to say she put up with her rich, elderly men while she was young and beautiful so that she could afford a young, dreamy-eyed man when she was rich and elderly. Fortunately she invested her money in California property and was able to buy herself a young man long before she was elderly. In fact when she finally handed in her feathers she retired with her dreamy pauper to a Beverly Hills mansion almost as big as carnal Carroll's.

There was Mary, blonde, blue-eyed, and beautiful, who eventually married screen actor Robert Cummings; and her friend Patsy, who married National Yeast millionaire Frank Hale; Lois, who walked up the aisle with comedian George Jessel and later walked down it again to divorce him; and Patti Sachs, a tall, willowy blonde with finely chiseled features. Patti was the surprise of them all. She is now a top-ranking California lawyer.

Vicky was the only girl who gave Mr. Carroll any trouble. She was forever cutting her wrists over this or that romance and arriving at the theater with bandaged arms. The third time she cut her wrists Mr. Carroll dashed into our dressing room in a highly emotional state.

"Vicky," he said tremulously, "the next time you do that you'll have to leave my show. And that goes for the rest of you girls. I will not allow my angels to damage their beautiful arms."

Lili gave a snort as he flounced out. "Oh, she only does it to get his attention!"

At the beginning there was always talk and speculation about the famous Carroll parties. It was Lili who gave us our first unexpurgated eyewitness account. "He doesn't just have daisy chains," she concluded with a sigh, "he has dahlia chains."

Little Jasmine, who sat next to me in the dressing room, was always horrified at Lili's sex chatter. Jasmine was a tiny, delicate redhead with green eyes permanently wide open with shock. Her soft-spoken drawl and ladylike manner gave her the airs of a Southern belle. One night Lili slipped in carrying a large photograph of Carroll. She was a little high and singing, "He kissed me here, he kissed me there, he kissed me everywhere. . . ." She used his photograph to indicate the various portions of her anatomy which had been blessed by his patronage.

In the mirror I saw Jasmine's face smoldering. She leaned over and whispered, "She's a liar! Mr. Carroll is too fine a gentleman to consort with such a vulgar girl."

From where I sat Lili seemed the ideal playmate for him. Nevertheless, whenever Carroll opened our door all I could see of him were two horns and a tail, although Jasmine, who had known him for some time, insisted it was all false gossip. To her he was the fatherly Messiah spreading beauty and love throughout his kingdom. I soon realized that she was secretly in love with him.

It was Jasmine who persuaded me to risk my virtue on his Christmas Eve party. And it turned out to be quite a production. Early Christmas Eve morning Carroll bundled himself and us into an enormous sleigh. An actor rigged out as Santa Claus drove us up and down Hollywood Boulevard while we waved and squealed at the shoppers. Later in the evening, when we'd finished prancing around the stage and wiggling our feathers, Mr. Carroll appeared at our dressing room door laden with magnums of champagne.

"I want my little angels to be in the right spirits for the Christmas party," he purred.

As soon as we had unplucked our feathers and slithered into our party gowns, sleek limousines whisked us up to his extravaganza home above Sunset Boulevard and straight out of a movie magazine.

One Christmas tree wasn't enough for Carroll's little angels so he had every tree in his estate lit up and twinkling like a Palladium pantomime. And all the barbecue grills surrounding his waterfalled swimming pool were spinning with Hollywood-sized turkeys. By the time the party was rolling and our fiancés or boyfriends had arrived, Carroll had draped himself in his favorite Chinese robe, led us down to his Chinese throne and played Father Christmas with an enormous lucky-dip-grab-bag.

One by one we dipped our little manicured mitts into Santa Teachum-Yung's satchel and out came boxes of French perfume, Paris hats, or diamanté-studded evening bags. And somewhere among the presents were two extra-special gift baubles of rubies and emeralds donated by one of Carroll's male angels who backed his shows. Somehow Lili walked off with both these Number One dips. She was obviously well organized in these matters. True to form, as soon as Christmas was over, she was back in the shops with her gift baubles tucked under her arm and before you could say Happy New Year she had cashed her gifts into cash and the cash was in her bank.

Our first Carroll party was frivolously gay, but not at all wicked. We were almost disappointed. The only shock I had that evening was when one of the backers offered me a cigarette. I enquired what brand it was.

"Marijuana," he said nonchalantly.

I was frightened of any form of dope, but in order to appear sophisticated I answered, just as nonchalantly, "No, thank you, I just put one out."

The only taste we acquired from his Christmas Eve party was for lucky-dip-grab-bags. What's more the news of our addiction was spread swiftly around the wealthy playboy circuit, mainly by Lili. Soon it became impossible to lure the girls to a party without one.

A few days later Father O'Sullivan suddenly appeared at my home. He was a little high and took me out for a wino's lunch. He was still deliciously attractive, but now that I had grown up I realized the schoolgirl crush had faded. He was in a jolly mood and delighted I was in a show with so many beautiful girls. He told me he had a fellow priest who was leading a dull life and needed an outing and asked if I could fix him up with a double date. Although I was deeply sympathetic I said I didn't think he had a hope as the girls were mainly interested in grab-bags, and priests who were likely to be defrocked were not grab-bag potentials. He took it in good spirit. .

I never did mix-match the chorus girls and the padres. The last I heard of Horatio Macgillicuddy he had moved to his new parish in San Francisco on his way to the Holy See.

Frugal Lili also taught us another habit—clearing the

remains of the lavish buffets into our makeup kits to take home to mother. I remember doing this at one of the Marx Brothers' parties and suddenly finding Chico, or was it Harpo, helping me. That night I arrived home clutching a whole Virginia baked ham to my bosom!

In between lucky-dip hijinks most of us dated normal fellows nearer our own age and income. A few girls had millionaire appeal, but obviously I wasn't one of them. If there was a man around with an empty pocket I found him. And because of our late hours the selection of boyfriends was limited to night people. One of my first dates at Carroll's was a trombone player in Ray Noble's orchestra. The flirtation started when he began pointing his trombone at me whenever I danced on. Soon he had introduced me to his fellow blowers in the wind section and we all went out together to black nightclubs to listen to black hornblowers. The white blowers all felt they had a lot to learn about jazz from the black blowers.

While all of them made lovely noises when they were blowing, as soon as they took their horns out of their mouths it seemed that all they could talk about was their mouthpieces. My trombone player must have had a major mouthpiece problem because he always had sore lips. Somehow the romance didn't survive.

My other suitor was a screenwriter named Wally Sullivan. He had recently written a successful film called *Libeled Lady* for Jean Harlow, Spencer Tracy, and William Powell, and was therefore able to wine and dine me in the kind of places to which I would later become accustomed—I hoped. His friend, Howard Snyder, wrote funnies for Bob Hope and often joined us with sweet little Southern belle Jasmine.

We usually had a late night snack around the corner from the theater at the Brown Derby restaurant on Vine Street. The Derby was famous as a lunchtime rendezvous for all the Hollywood names and gossip journalists. It provided individual telephones that could be plugged into any one of the tables and if you received a call your name was paged until they found your table. So of course all the no-names and

145
☆

agents had their friends and relatives telephone them during lunch as a sort of status symbol.

By the time we arrived at the Brown Derby after the show it was almost empty except for us night people and a gaggle of gangsters huddled around their tables. For ogle appeal the gangsters had now replaced the stars. Wally and Howard pointed out which one was Bugsey-the-Boob or Maxie-the-Mint and warned us to nod a smile if they looked our way. So Jasmine and I gawked and smiled dutifully as we munched our Monte Cristo sandwiches, which were a mixture of cheese, chicken, and ham on layers of bread dipped in egg yolk, fried and served with jam. Only in Hollywood could you find a Monte Cristo sandwich.

But not even in Hollywood would the Brown Derby serve you with drinks after 2 A.M., so we night people had to move on to the illegal, gangster-owned clubs, which was why it was necessary to have a nodding acquaintance with Bugsey and Maxie. I always enjoyed the rituals getting into those clubs. The darkened secret doors, the man who looked you over through the secret grills, and the private key handed over to open your own booze locker. If they hadn't been illegal we would never have stayed up in them, jabbering and drinking until five in the morning.

As sweet little Jasmine never touched a drop of booze Howard thought it was an awful lot of fuss to go through for a lady who didn't drink. But his main complaint was that she would only let him kiss her hand. It was making him neurotic. I could tell because he started wearing dark glasses and only taking us to dark places. Wally, on the other hand, began appearing in daylight. He brought his typewriter to my place each day to work on his scenarios and he bought me an Easter bonnet. Things were beginning to look serious. However, we didn't dash impetuously to the altar because Wally was an old man of thirty-seven, which was almost twenty years older than I. The relationship needed a pause for reflection.

It was just as well. On Easter Sunday I put on my new Easter bonnet and Wallace took me to Easter Sunday Mass. It was good and beautiful. After which he took me to see the fatal film. It was Shaw's *Pygmalion* in which Leslie Howard as Professor Higgins taught Wendy Hiller as Eliza Doolittle how to speak English.

Wally went into the movie house as Wallace Sullivan, scriptwriter, and came out as Professor Higgins, elocution teacher. And I was his Eliza Doolittle. He decided that my western Californian accent was an impediment to my dramatic career. With such a drawl, he said, the most I could hope for was a horse between my legs at Republic studios with the rest of the cowboys. Therefore Wallace, with his Irish-English accent, would teach me to broaden my A's and soften the R's so I could play Queen Victoria. During the days we did the rains-in-Spain scene from the film and at night, when I tried out my new accent in the dressing room, I caught absolute hell from the girls.

"Oh, the queen's arrived," said Lili whenever I came in, "with legs all the way up to her ass and a plum in her mouth."

The rest of the girls would chorus, "Hya, Highness, when's Prince Wallace taking us to Ascot?" or some such endearments.

But the crunch came when Wallace began inviting newly arrived starlets from England to dine with us so I could listen to their accents. Every time I opened my mouth he put his big Irish foot in it. Somehow that romance didn't survive either.

Years later on a return trip to Hollywood I ran into Howard Snyder, who by then had become a top TV writer. He took me to the Cocoanut Grove to see the opening night of Frank Sinatra's first comeback. Howard, who had written the dialog for Sinatra's act, told me that Frankie was feeling nervous and insecure, so he wanted friendly faces at the ringside tables.

While I was being a "friendly face," I asked Howard, "Whatever happened to Wally Sullivan?"

"Oh, he's now running a school for speech and elocution," said Howard. He couldn't understand why it made me laugh.

After the rains had stopped falling in the plains with

Wallace, I spent most of my days studying drama and singing and often taking on an extra-curricular assignment at the film studios. My new drama teacher was Dr. Fleishman, who was the most popular film dramatic coach in Hollywood. He rehearsed us in duologues from recent films and we acted the scenes *sotto voce* as they did in the movies. Once a week he recorded the scenes on discs. I played Bette Davis in *Dark Victory* and *Petrified Forest*, Katharine Hepburn in *Bill of Divorcement*, and Amanda in Noël Coward's *Private Lives*. It was an exciting change playing these starring roles instead of hiding behind pillars as an extra.

With the combined income derived from lucky-dip-grab-bags, scavenging buffets, and Carroll's wages my first purchase was a secondhand Ford. Most of the other girls bought themselves new noses. You would imagine that lovely looking girls, who had already been selected from the best that Hollywood could provide, would leave their appearance alone. But one of the girl's boyfriend was a cosmetic surgeon and had offered them a 50 per cent discount by the dozen. As the ideal Hollywood nose of the moment was short and turned up, they arrived back in the dressing room one by one with identical noses. The Donlan nose had already been born short and turned up so this bargain bobbing didn't affect me. But eventually I succumbed to the Hollywood even-teeth propaganda and had four perfectly healthy teeth filed down and capped because two of them protruded slightly. I'm sure if the Hollywood standards had demanded it we would have joyfully cut off our ears.

So, with my new teeth and my old car I would drive to the studios at 5 A.M. for daylight work and back home at 2 A.M. from the moonlight work. I needed that car because Hollywood's public transportation couldn't keep up with my hours. Apart from camel caravans in the Sahara Desert, it was and still is the worst in the world.

One of those early daylight stints was in Paramount's *Man About Town* starring Dorothy Lamour, Jack Benny, and the friendly blonde from Ernest Belcher's dance school, Betty Grable. Originally Betty had been going to star in the film, then suddenly, like me, her appendix popped. So they gave the role to Lamour and Betty had to take the lesser part. I had to dance around Dorothy Lamour who was always a dusky lady singing in a sarong. In those days if you found yourself in a musical sequence with Dorothy Lamour you became a dusky lady, too. Which meant standing naked at six o'clock in the morning in a large, drafty dressing room getting sponged all over with dusky maiden paint. Then on went your black wig and your sarong. For the rest of the day you hula-hulaed your hips and mouthed umpa-woola-moola sounds to Miss Lamour's playback.

At lunch break we nibbled our tuna sandwiches and chef's salad in the hubble-bubble of the studio commissary. The tables were always alive with the munching of Paramount's golden names. Bing Crosby, Bob Hope, Ray Milland, Claudette Colbert, Fred MacMurray, W. C. Fields—and always Cecil B. de Mille. But did the great de Mille pluck any of us dusky maidens out of our Hawaiian chorus into Cleopatra's solo barge? Not a hope, we told ourselves, those things only happen in movies. As soon as the day's hulas were over I had to scurry across the road to the Turkish baths and steam off the dusky maiden paint, rattle across Hollywood to the theater, slap on the white body makeup and become one of Carroll's little angels again for the twice nightly shows.

And practically every night was another uncharted adventure. If it wasn't Vicky building up to another slashed wrist it was Jasmine working up to a Southern swoon from the shock of Lili's blow-by-blow account of her latest bed ball. There were also the birthdays. For each of the girls' birthdays Carroll appeared with a specially designed cake and bottles of champagne.

It was Lili who made the rule that only virgins were allowed to cut the cake, although I suspect it was Carroll who suggested it. It was one way of checking up on his angels' sex lives. He was totally immersed in the girls' activities both on- and offstage. The six girls he had brought from New York were from his regular harem and they were sprinkled among the new girls to collect dressing room gossip and bring it back to Caliph Carroll. As it was mostly about husbands and lovers he could time his approach to suit their moods.

His number one girl was Beryl Wallace and she was the only one who had a private dressing room. She also had a solo spot in the show and was looked on as the wife figure. But unlike most wives she too would collect beautiful girls for Carroll to sample.

Earl Carroll really loved all forty of his girls and he would have had all forty at once if they had let him. As it was, the frustrated impresario had to settle for groups of two or six at a time. I was surprised there was so little rivalry among his concubines. Perhaps his secret was in letting his girls choose the next particular partner for him.

Between my own romances I often went out after the show with Jasmine, a couple of the other Carroll girls and Mr. Carroll. Jasmine was proving to me what a kind, celibate gentleman he was and how lucky she was because he really loved only her. Nevertheless when Mr. Carroll kissed me "hello" I spent the rest of the week washing my mouth with Listerine because the nuns or someone had told me all promiscuous men had V.D. With his history he seemed a likely candidate.

One of the evenings he took us to a club run by beautiful young ladies for other beautiful young ladies. They were all extremely fond of Mr. Carroll's girls, for as soon as they joined our table they began kissing and fondling them affectionately. Mr. Carroll sat in the middle like a happy Maharishi blessing them all with double Scotches all around.

Nothing made Carroll happier than seeing his angels spreading his message of love to each other and anyone else who came along. But Jasmine only had eyes for Mr. Carroll, which left me to concentrate on my Scotch.

Then came Jasmine's birthday party. It was to be a weekend do with a large supper party at Carroll's house on Saturday night. The guests were to spend the night in the various colored bedrooms and bring their swimming and tennis gear for the following day. The way Jasmine explained it to me it sounded very much like the Christmas party. But still, all the week before I pestered her for details of the sleeping accommodations.

"Where do I sleep?" I asked.

"In the blue room," she answered.

"Where does your celibate Messiah sleep?"

"In the gold room."

"How far is the gold room from the blue room?"

"At the opposite end of the house." Jasmine sighed with exasperation. She felt I'd been out with Mr. Carroll often enough now to know my virtue was safe.

With trepidation I packed my overnight case and under my party dress I wore two pairs of panties and a panty girdle. During the show the birthday cake and the champagne were brought around as usual. Lili decided I was the one to cut the cake.

When I arrived at the house the butler took me upstairs to the blue room where I left my case and coat. When I started down the stairs to the party room the butler said, "No, miss, the guests are in the gold room."

The gold room, I thought; what's this? That's Mr. Carroll's room. To *end* a party, maybe. But to start a party?

When the butler opened the door I saw the gold room was as large as the party room—only it had a six-foot bed in the center and at the foot of the bed was the buffet table laden with caviar, champagne, and more cakes and goodies. The only guests present were Jasmine and the two shapely secretaries.

Mr. Carroll greeted me with open arms.

"Ah, my little angel," he said, "kiss your host hello."

Which I did, reluctantly. I was dying to rush down the hall to the blue room and wash out my mouth with Listerine. Instead I gargled with the champagne he handed me. We toasted Jasmine's birthday a couple of dozen times, gnawed on the caviar, and the two secretaries started getting giggly. Jasmine's eyes were sparkling, in fact too sparkling. Miss Southern Lemonade was sloshed.

"Where is everybody?" I asked stupidly.

"Honey child," Jasmine slurred happily, "my divine Earl has asked them all to come tomorrow. So I could have him all to myself on my birthday. It's a surprise."

It certainly was. And I was glad it wasn't my birthday. Mr. Carroll then decided we should all save our party dresses for tomorrow and wear his pajama tops instead.

"We'll make tonight's party a pajama party," he said gleefully.

He handed each of us a silk top and we all went to our respective blue, pink, and yellow rooms to get undressed. I put my pajama top over my dress and tucked the skirt into my panty girdle. I was now more dressed than ever.

When we returned to the gold room the celibate Messiah was in his pajama top stalking about the room on his long white legs and burning incense. And the delicate, wide-eyed birthday girl was dancing bare-assed on the foot of the bed. Mr. Carroll thought it highly amusing that I had returned looking like Humpty Dumpty with all my clothes on under my top. I became his little Eskimo angel.

Two bottles of champagne later Mr. Carroll decided it was time for the two secretaries to go to bed—their beds—as they had to be up early in the morning. As they started for the door I scurried after them calling, "Me too, me too. . . ." Mr. Carroll caught my hand as I reached the door.

"Not yet, my little Eskimo angel. You haven't kissed the birthday girl goodnight."

I trekked back to kiss the birthday girl goodnight. She had stopped dancing on the bed and had collapsed happily into it. As I reached the side of the bed the lights went out and I heard the latch on the door lock.

I leaned over and whispered, "Your celibate Messiah has just locked the door and I'm not in the blue room."

To which Jasmine sang happily, "Happy Birthday."

Daddy-Long-Legs put the key in his pajama pocket, handed me a piece of cake and told me how much I loved Jasmine and he loved Jasmine and Jasmine loved me. I was sleepy and hated everybody. I reached over for the brandy bottle, poured myself a brandy, which always keeps me awake, and sat on the edge of the bed. Before I got the glass

to my lips old Daddy-Long-Legs and Miss Southern Lemonade were entangled in a lover's knot and the bed was bouncing up and down spilling my nightcap all over my issue of
Mr. Carroll's pajama tops.

Mid the tumult I crawled across the bed to get a napkin
from the buffet and Carroll's great long arm reached out and
pulled me back by my brandy-soaked tail. It seemed to me
he had enough to keep him occupied without interfering
with my ablutions.

When the storm subsided I whispered to Jasmine that
she should get me out of there and she whispered back that
the divine Mr. Carroll loved me, she loved me, and that I
should go to sleep.

"Nobody sleeps in the gold room," I mumbled into my
half-empty brandy glass.

I figured that my only chance now was to snatch the key
from Daddy-Long-Legs's pajama top pocket. I crawled into
my cocoon on the left side of the bed and played 'possum.
Jasmine was in the middle and Carroll was on her right murmuring into her ear what a heavenly little cherub I was and
how she should kiss me for him. Instead, Miss Southern
Lemonade rose from the waves of the golden bed like Lore-
lei out of the sea and finished bang on top of the celibate
Messiah chanting, "Hallelujah."

The Messiah, who was now in the center court next to
me, began whispering celestial eulogies in my ethereal ears
as I groped for the key in his pocket.

At last I snaffled the key of his earldom, capered across
the bed and over the buffet, bringing most of our Last Supper
tumbling down behind me. I was in such a hurry I didn't
even have time to scavenge the jar of caviar.

I raced to the blue room, grabbed my weekend case, shot
down the stairs three at a time, out of the door, into my car
and drove home still in Daddy-Long-Legs's pajama top.

The following day I received two dozen chrysan-
themums from Mr. Carroll with apologies for disrupting my
sleep. That evening in the dressing room Jasmine was as
wide-eyed and shockable as ever, and Mr. Carroll, immaculate again in his tuxedo, appeared to tell us he was taking our

153
☆

present show to New York and all his angels were free either to go with it or appear in the new show in Hollywood. I decided it was high time to leave Earl Carroll's, hand in my dancing shoes, and try my luck as a film actress.

The last I heard of the Carroll girls they had followed their fortunes down varied and sometimes surprising paths. Wide-eyed and shockable Jasmine Shelton married a Mormon deacon, moved to Utah and raised seven children. I never made it there for tea and temple.

Little Lois Andrews, who had married George Jessel when she was sixteen, achieved an uneventful contract with 20th-Century Fox and three more husbands before she died of lung cancer in 1968. Evelyn Moriarty was also signed for a build-up by Fox and finally became Marilyn Monroe's stand-in in her last three pictures.

Then there was Jean Wallace, the platinum blonde with the sexy figure, who during my day was dating movie star Franchot Tone. She later married him, produced two sons and continued her film career which included starring opposite her husband in *The Man on the Eiffel Tower*. She must have been keen on actors as no sooner had she divorced Franchot Tone than she was married to Cornel Wilde and began appearing in his films.

Sandra Jolly, another collector of actors, married Forrest Tucker and later Jack Carson. Marilyn Buford became the 1946 Miss America; Peggy Satterlee made more headlines than any of the girls when she sued Errol Flynn for rape; and Beverly Carroll, the celibate Messiah's niece, wedded Academy Award-winning composer Lionel Newman.

Beryl Wallace, Earl Carroll's number one girl friend and constant companion, had a steady if unspectacular film career and died with him in a plane crash in 1948. They lie side by side in the Garden of Memory at Forest Lawn Cemetery. A nude statue of Beryl, which Carroll commissioned before his untimely death, stands watchfully over his grave.

During my period at Carroll's we were able to buy my most longed-for possession—a home. We had it built in Studio City in the San Fernando Valley, which was just becoming a residential area. The Valley was a hive of bulldozers, vacant lots, and freshly painted pink, blue, and white bungalows, all with "For Sale" or "Just Sold" signs on them.

Our little white house had five rooms, two bathrooms, garage, patio and a front and back garden. All that for only five thousand dollars. And for the first time I had my own bedroom and bathroom. On the day we moved in I ran into the house and skipped around the packing cases shouting, "Our own roof over our heads forever, FOREVER!" To me, after living in all those hotel rooms and apartments, owning a house meant security and foreverness. Never dying owing seven months' rent.

In the move to the valley we lost Aunty and Jack as lodgers and collected a new one, a handsome British wrestler and drama school chum named Bob Gregory. He was jolly company and we females felt safe with a wrestler in residence. He could also speak French, which was a great asset with Grand'mère and, fortunately for him, he loved opera because he had to listen to it loud and clear every Saturday. That was my rest day and the day Mother always tuned in to the matinee broadcasts from the Metropolitan Opera House in New York. Since New York was so far away she felt she had to turn the sound up to its full volume. After which she went outside to do her gardening and was joined by Grand'mère who sat in the patio crocheting doilies. The noise was deafening and I can still recall the screeching of Valkyries racing through my rattled brain as I lay tossing in my new blue bedroom. It was enough to make Daddy Donlan curse in his grave, and it put me off opera for twenty years.

Early in my trying-to-be-an-actress period I did my first screen test. Well, almost did it. While I was in my last week at Carroll's I had an interview with the casting director at Republic studios for the lead in a Western. He told me I would be screen-tested for it the following day and he would have the test scene script delivered at my house that evening. All during my dance routines at Carroll's my mind was on the test, wondering how long the scene would be and would I have time to learn it before the 6 A.M. call for makeup at Republic.

After our second show I raced home at about two in the morning, and alas no script. Mother gave me a bite to eat and we waited. Grand'mère, who was a night prowler, crept into the kitchen in her purple silk negligée to munch a crab's claw. Three o'clock, still no scene. There was no one I could telephone at that hour to find out what had happened. Mother suggested I try to get some sleep so that at least I would look good. Grand'mère offered me her wine as a sedative and we all had a couple of swigs. It sent them both straight off to sleep, but not me. I went to bed and tossed all night listening for the bell to ring.

By five thirty I was up and dressed to go to the studio regardless. Just as I was about to leave, a third assistant casting director arrived at the door, blind drunk and full of apologies. He'd been to a party and forgotten to deliver the scene until now. He handed me some torn bits of script covered with ashes and alcohol and buzzed off. I could hardly read the scene let alone learn it.

When I arrived in the makeup room, there were five other girls there all testing for the same role. Every one of them looked beautiful, healthy, and happy and had had their scenes for a week. I wanted to crawl under the makeup chair and cut my throat, but I studied the booze-soaked scene instead.

We were all put into long cotton covered-wagon-type dresses. One by one the others were led to the set to play their scene and all came back smiling. I felt as if I was waiting my turn to go to the gallows, and the more I studied the scene the less I could learn it.

I was the last one to be led to the slaughter. The set was a ranch house porch. The leading cowboy, who I think was Roy Rogers, was now fed up doing this all day. He had a Coca Cola in one hand and was munching a hamburger from the other. The director was tired of the scene too, so he didn't want to rehearse. He just said, "Shoot," and I gabbled my lines at the cowboy who munched his answers back at me through the hamburger. All my lines came out fine except one. No matter how many times we shot that scene I couldn't remember it. Roy Rogers got through three hamburgers before we all packed it up.

I never did say that damn line then, but I've remembered it ever since—"I'm the scrawny little girl who tagged at your heels when I was in pigtails." Along with "ahr-rahnge" it has haunted my brain all my life with other forgettable sayings I can't forget. That day was the beginning and end of my career in Westerns.

By comparison my first test at MGM was a snap. It was for one of the Andy Hardy pictures. There was no scene to study. All I had to do was to try to look beautiful so I could be one of his girl friends. I was put in the hands of the studio makeup and hairdressing experts, Jack Dawn and Sydney Guilaroff. Between them I was given Joan Crawford's mouth, Hedy Lamarr's eyebrows, and Garbo's hairstyle. With all that

157
☆

help I finished up looking like Boris Karloff. The director spun this new monster around on a chair three times in front of the camera and gave the role to Ann Rutherford.

When I tested at Paramount for the leading role in Cecil B. de Mille's *Northwest Mounted Police* they didn't waste their dough on cameras and sound. I was given the part of the native half-caste to learn three days before the test. For a change I had time to work on the scene. On the day of the test I was put on the stage of a small theater in the studio and braced myself for the great de Mille's arrival. Instead, the casting director wandered in and sat out in front.

"Okay, kid," he said. "Action."

I actioned. I gave my all and remembered every line and when I'd finished he congratulated my performance profusely and gave the part to Paulette Goddard.

In the meantime, my next-door neighbor in Studio City, who was an insurance broker and had never considered an acting career, was persuaded to take a test at Fox and was signed up immediately with a seven-year contract.

You see in Hollywood it could happen to anybody, as long as anybody didn't want it to happen. And it didn't happen to me until February in 1940 when Hal Roach, now a legendary Hollywood tycoon with his own Hal Roach Studios, was preparing to direct a Thorn Smith comedy called *Turnabout* with Carol Landis, Mary Astor, and Adolphe Menjou. An agent, for whom I'd danced when he was directing the stage musical *Roberta*, telephoned me to say that Hal Roach was looking for an authentic French girl for the film and did I know of anyone?

"Yes, me!" I squealed.

"But Roach doesn't want an American girl speaking with a French accent," the agent explained patiently, "he wants a French girl speaking American with a French accent."

Eventually I persuaded him that with three years of school French and a French grandmother who lived with us who couldn't speak English, I was almost type casting.

But we both agreed that in order to get away with fooling Mr. Roach I would have to do all the interviews and small talk with a French accent, as well as the dialogue in the film test. Also I was to take on my grandmother's name, Mollot. I worked on my accent by forcing poor old grandmother to try to speak English so that I could copy her inflections. Soon I became quite proficient at speaking English with a French accent. But I knew if I should meet anyone who spoke fluent French the game would be over. In a last-minute flurry of doubts I confided the plot and my fears to Harold Lloyd.

"Hell," he said cheerfully, "if I could be an Indian, you can be French."

On my first interview with Mr. Roach I was so frightened I became deaf and dumb as well as French. All I could whisper was, *"oui, oui,"* or *"non, non."* Whenever Roach spoke to me, which fortunately was in English, I turned to my agent with a puzzled look as though I couldn't understand. Then the agent would repeat very slowly what Roach had said. So I would say *"Oui, oui,"* again. Mr. Roach wasn't ready to put up with this for long so he cut the interview short by giving me the test scene to take home and learn.

It was the role of a French maid called Marie and the scene was set in Carol Landis's bathroom. By the day of the test my Grand'mère was word perfect as the maid and I still couldn't speak French.

When I arrived in the make-up room I was horrified to find six other girls hanging about in maid's uniforms just like mine and all of them chatting in perfect French. I not only had six competitors but six authentic competitors. To avoid getting caught in a conversation and giving myself away I pointed to my throat and emitted a series of guttural French hisses indicating a touch of laryngitis.

As soon as I was made up I hid in my dressing room until I was called on the set. My turn came at the end of the day when the only ones left to test were myself and a Great Dane dog called Dopey. To save time they tested the dog during my scene with Miss Landis. In careful pidgin English Mr. Roach explained that I was to carry on talking and dressing Miss Landis after her bath, as per script, and ignore the dog. Which I did. But it wasn't easy because all through the scene the huge Great Dane kept jumping in and out of the

159
☆

bath water, standing on my mark and shaking himself all over me. By the end of the scene my hair and false eyelashes were dripping and the uniform soaked. I could have been speaking Chinese.

To my great surprise the agent telephoned me the following day to say I'd won the role. I leaped about the house with glee and bought Grand'mère a bottle of California wine made with authentic French grapes. We celebrated by singing the "Marseillaise" and drinking toasts to Dopey the Great Dane dog. I'm sure it was his performance that did the trick. In any case Dopey and I were put under contract for the film.

But now I would have to keep up the hoax both on and off the set for the next four weeks. My only chance was to speak as little as possible except for the lines in the script. For the first weeks I kept to myself, ate lunch alone and stayed off the set except when I was needed to rehearse a scene. I made communication so impossible that the other actors soon ignored the foreigner.

One day while I was getting my film face done in the make-up room Mary Astor plunked herself next to me to ferret among the makeup man's tubes and do her own face. She explained to me that as she had been in films for so long she knew every hazard on her face far better than any make-up man who was seeing it for the first time, and didn't I agree? Panic. And then I gave her my no-comprend stare and said, *"Non, non, madame,* ze dog he eez not *dangereuse!"* It was a line from the script and proved to be an invaluable conversation stopper. But later when I tried it on Adolphe Menjou he just slipped into fluent French, cornering me into speaking my "native tongue." At first I thought I was getting away with it until he asked me what part of France I came from. I answered in French that I came from Lyon.

Menjou said: "With that accent you mean Lyon, New Jersey."

The game was over. Fortunately by that time most of my scenes were already shot and everyone enjoyed the hoax, including Hal Roach. But the one who enjoyed it most was Harold Lloyd.

Miss Nothing was delighted to see her name on the screen cast list for the first time, even though half of it belonged to Grand'mère. On the Hollywood ladder to success a Miss Nothing with a speaking role was a good step up from a dancing Miss Nothing in the chorus. I thought each new role would lead to a larger one and eventually to a hacienda with swimming pool compris.

But the French accent that had opened the first door now managed to close the rest of the doors. The casting directors of the other studios were convinced I was really French and wouldn't let me play Americans. As I couldn't very well ask Adolphe Menjou to call around dispelling their belief I was only summoned if there was a small French role going. For cornering this unique market my agent soon succeeded in raising my wages from $50 per day to $100 per day. But there was an acute shortage of French Fifi roles being written and earning $100 a day for three days out of three months wasn't enough to keep us in California wine and bouillabaisse.

I spent more time signing unemployment insurance forms than Hollywood contracts. It wasn't long before I was back off the ladder and into the chorus again. This time for a six-week stint for $50 a week at the Cocoanut Grove nightclub. Now, while the Cocoanut Grove was a fine setting for the stars to receive their Oscars at the Academy Awards dinners then held there, it was no place for an aspiring award winner to be found kicking her heels in the line. To avoid recognition by my agent or any film moguls I changed my name again. This time I was Joycelyn Day and borrowed a blonde wig for the job.

And no sooner had Joycelyn Day opened at the Grove than Yolande Mollot was cast in another French role at Universal Studios. It was a second lead in a film titled *Dark Streets of Cairo*. And the role was bigger and better than any before. After six months of no work at all I was suddenly doing two jobs as two different people at the same time.

From six in the morning I was Yolande Mollot, emoting at Universal with all the side benefits that go with a featured role—private dressing room, hairdresser, makeup man, lunch interviews with the press, chair with Grand'mère's name on it, and a stand-in. At night I was Joycelyn Day, back in the chorus girls' dressing room, slapping on my own makeup, dance costumes and borrowed hair, trying to hide during the routines.

It wasn't easy to hide when I was one of only twelve girls in the middle of a dance floor with all the spotlights on us. I was forever getting ticked off for wearing my feathers down the front of my face instead of the back of my head. And most of all for cringing under my cloak during the "Three Musketeers" number.

After six weeks of hiding my face by night at the Grove and showing it by day in *The Dark Streets of Cairo* I might as well have saved myself the effort because the film was such a dud that my appearance in it was as secret as the dancing.

So back I went to the French maid market, of which there wasn't much. I French-maided for RKO in a Binnie Barnes picture for two days. For a week I parlez-voused with Bela Lugosi in a horror film called *Devil Bat*. In it he played a mad doctor instead of Dracula. But he looked the same and every morning he kissed my hand, lingering over it a little longer than was necessary for a platonic friendship. One more second and I felt I might turn into a bat. When he wasn't in a scene his penetrating eyes followed me around the set. It was only a mild flirtation. But I found it ironic that of all the handsome stars, the one I appealed to most was Dracula.

The end of the *Devil Bat* led me straight back to the unemployment bureau to collect my weekly checks until I was rescued by Hal Roach again to play John Hubbard's nurse in *Roadshow*. The role had only a few lines, but at last they were without a French accent. I hoped that after *Roadshow* the news would spread through the industry that here was a genuine American girl who could speak genuine American English. Now anything could happen. But all that happened was I didn't get any roles at all, either French or American.

Except for a brief interval in a Roach comedy short in which I had to run around the set in a temper and long underwear, I didn't work for four months. But fortunately I acquired some fun playmates during my Roach stints. For, unlike the other studios, the Hal Roach studio was more intimate and had a family atmosphere. Most of us who worked there became friends.

Hal Roach, Jr. had us over to his father's house for swimming parties. Their home was in the luxury Hollywood tradition with acres of gardens and a heated outdoor swimming pool where we dunked at the end of the evening. Victor Mature was a newcomer star and shared a small rented bungalow with the publicity man, Homer McCoy, who later became a top film and TV writer. The two of them used to organize impromptu supper parties at which I remember Victor putting mayonnaise on all his food, even liver and bacon. Having just finished *One Million Years B.C.* he was being publicized as the "Beautiful Hunk of Man" and had a complicated love life with most of the young glamour stars. There was usually one at the party, another pestering him on the telephone, and a third driving around the block outside his house spying on him.

They certainly weren't after his money because he was known as the first of the big no-spenders. Even at the peak of his career he lived for a while in a chauffeur's room above the garage of one of his pals.

"Gotta watch it," he told me. "This star shit can't last."

It didn't matter to us whether you were a star, a hairdresser, a small part player, publicity man, assistant director, or one of the famous juniors, we all played together. At most of the other Hollywood studios the employees only associated according to income and status. So our gang at Roach was unique.

When we moved to the valley Aunty and Jack found themselves a furnished bungalow in Los Angeles and acquired a wire-haired terrier called Popeye. Uncle Jack said the dog was my replacement. But Aunty insisted that Popeye had taken the place of all the other women in Jack's affections. Everywhere that Jack went Popeye went, and Jack bought him only the finest fillet steaks for his dinner. Jack taught

163
☆

him to sit up and laugh at his jokes and his raspberry noises. At least, Jack *said* Popeye was laughing, but to an outsider like me the noises emanating from the terrier sounded like good old-fashioned barking.

On Sundays they came to our valley home for dinner and we all played cards afterward—all except Popeye who ran through the house laughing at all the cars that passed. So it was a sad day when Uncle Jack telephoned to say that his Popeye had died suddenly. It was an even sadder day when Aunty telephoned a week later to say that Uncle Jack had died, too.

"Would you believe it," she sobbed, "he died of a broken heart mourning that damned Popeye. That dog was the only thing he really loved."

She organized a slap-up Requiem Mass for Jack and a Catholic burial, even though I had never seen him in a church before. I asked her how she had managed to get the church service as I hadn't been able to swing it for Daddy.

"Oh, I've never bothered with nonsensical church laws," she said. "I just told the priest he'd been a devout Catholic."

On the three evenings before the funeral Mother and I sat with her in the funeral parlor where Uncle Jack was laid out in his coffin. Aunty felt he needed company. When the parlor was empty Aunty left her pew to go over to the corpse and shake her fist at him.

"That sonofabitch ruined my life!" she exploded. "Always chasing other women, gambling with the money I got from my first husband . . . !"

Whenever outside mourners reappeared she quickly knelt down, crossed herself, and shed a few tears. But the minute they left she was back on her feet cursing and shaking her fist again at the stony-faced Useless.

"What a bastard he was! I'll never forget the day he sniveled around in the sand looking for his whore's ring. And I was in the goddam tent cooking his Italian shit stuffing!"

Mother was shocked. "Imagine," she whispered to me, "shouting and cursing like that in front of the dead."

Three weeks after the funeral Aunty picked up her third husband in a bar in Las Vegas. Later she confided to me that he was a drunk just like she had been and that God had found him for her as a punishment.

In 1941, life in sunny Studio City was quietly suburban. Our neighbors were doctors, dentists, accountants, policemen, and salesmen with wives, children, dogs, chickens, and rabbits. There were no swimming pools yet. And aside from the Fox-contract player-insurance-broker next door, no one else in our small community was in the film business—including me.

Mother bought herself a bicycle to get to the shopping center which was half a mile away and had a sprinkling of shops, one movie house, a couple of small banks, and a drive-in restaurant. Grand'mère, who by then was eighty-nine, walked the same distance most days to catch the bus to Los Angeles to hear a concert or see a show. As the bus stop on Ventura Boulevard had no bench and the service was so erratic that she often had to wait there for an hour, Grand'mère, dressed up in all her Parisian finery, hat, gloves, and umbrella, took to sitting on the curb in defiance.

This infuriated Mother whenever she caught her at it, and the two of them had fiery French quarrels about it during the evening meals. It had no effect on Grand'mère but it gave me indigestion. Mother would tell her sitting on the curb was uncivilized, to which Grand'mère would tell Mother that living in Hollywood was uncivilized. What kind of a place, she demanded, had no orchestra, no opera company, no ballet company, no theater, and when a visiting company came to Los Angeles, no decent transportation to get you there? Paris, proclaimed Grand'mère, was never like this.

My impression was that Mother and the old lady didn't get along together as they were always screaming at each other in French and Grand'mère always stamped both feet to punctuate her points. But maybe they were just having an ordinary Continental conversation.

Grand'mère made no concessions to living in California. She never attempted to learn English, read only French books and newspapers, ate only French food, and always drank wine with her meals. In spite of the sunny climate she

165
☆

always carried an umbrella as she had done in Paris. Mother could never persuade her that it didn't rain in California. She paid her share of the housekeeping expenses and lived a life entirely independent from us. Even though she couldn't speak the language she bought all her own tickets for her shows and negotiated her transportation all over the southern coast.

Every night she pinned up her iron gray poodle-cut hair and creamed her face. In the morning she was up at dawn taking a perfumed oil bath before putting on a full makeup. When she had finished her toilette she always looked immaculately fashionable. If she had a flaw in her aristocratic face it was her sunken cheeks. These were caused by a complete lack of teeth and her refusal to wear false ones.

Dentures, she insisted, were for people who couldn't eat without them and her gums were tough enough to eat anything. And she was so right. I often sat and watched with hypnotic fascination as she cracked Pacific prawn shells with them. And having cracked them she would munch firmly and swallow the lot, shells and all. Years later when I was bored with peeling dozens of prawns in a Barcelona fish restaurant I recalled her success and finished the rest of my prawns with their shells on. Unlike Grand'mère I was sick for three days and held up shooting on an expensive film, while she lived on in perfect health until she was ninety-six.

Aside from being physically healthy she was mentally alert, too. She kept up with the news through her French papers and was interested in all the new fashions. Maybe her faith in the Holy Boss gave her this astounding strength. Although she never tried to be a God salesman she was the only Catholic in the family who beetled off to mass regularly every Sunday, even if she had to hitchhike, which she often did, shaking her umbrella at the passing cars.

I was beginning to think it might help if I took Grand'mère's magic umbrella and shook it at the studio casting directors. Just as I was becoming the star performer at the unemployment bureau, Max Arnow of Columbia suffered a moment of aberration and offered me a job in their picture *Under Age*. Surprisingly the thing that landed me the role was the *Golden Boy* love scene I had read for the kissing Columbia drama coach. However, there was no love scene for me in *Under Age*. I played a wisecracking, heart-of-gold leader of a group of teen-age girls that included Nan Grey and Mary Anderson.

I can't remember where I was leading them, but according to the few stills I have left it must have been something sinful because we were in a motel; as well as illegal because we were also in a courtroom. The only other thing I recall about this movie is that Columbia had decided to give it to a promising newcomer for his first directorial break. His name was Edward Dmytryk, and judging from Eddie's later films *Under Age* must have had a message, too. But the best message I got from it was a weekly contract for the run of the film—my longest work stint to date.

My agent and I were excited about this movie because my scenes in it were long enough to be shown as test scenes for the other studios. Unfortunately we couldn't get any of the other studios to look at them. Not even Lew Shreiber at Fox who had signed up my next door neighbor.

After *Under Age* I landed a couple of days' work at Universal playing a manicurist in a scene with Irene Dunne and Walter Catlett in *Unfinished Business*. The director was Gregory La Cava, who years back had failed to discover Aunty as the new Marie Dressler; he also failed to discover me. But I was fascinated to find that Mr. La Cava never worked from the script. He had the actors improvise the scene with their own words. And it worked. The effect was natural and spontaneous.

It was also a little shattering for me because for my first scene no one troubled to let me into the secret and I couldn't understand why Walter Catlett kept giving me cues that weren't in my script. Somehow I struggled through the rehearsals, but in the actual take he gave me different lines again. I looked at him blankly.

"Did you hear what I said?" he ad libbed.

"I did," I cried in desperation, "but I don't know what you're talking about!"

"Great," said Gregory La Cava. "We'll print that one."

When *Unfinished Business* was finished there was no business in show business for me again. But having begun playing speaking roles, I tried not to go back to chorus and extra work. Instead I took odd jobs outside the film world. For several weeks I modeled dresses in a wholesale house for five dollars a day. We worked from eight in the morning until six in the evening with a half-hour break for lunch. Every second of that time was used putting on one dress after another as quickly as possible, walking into the buyers' room, saying the number and price of the dress before hurrying back into the dressing room and into another outfit. It was much more exhausting than dancing. I began to feel and look like a coat hanger because the buyers never looked at the person wearing the clothes. They were there to buy the dress not the girl.

The only exception was when one girl slipped hurriedly into a backless evening gown and was already in the buyers' room saying the number and price before she realized her gown was on back to front. They sold a lot of that model.

During a Los Angeles motor show I got a job on one of the stands advertising oil. On the customers' side of the stand were large signs with questions about the oil written on them. There was a button to press on each sign for the answer. I stood just beneath the sign and out of sight. As soon as the button lit up on my side, I crawled on to an elevator which brought me up through the center of the platform—shades of Earl Carroll!—to answer the question. It wasn't too difficult as the answers were printed in front of me on the opposite side of the question. The customers were not so much interested in the answers as they were in seeing a nincompoop in an evening gown appear through the floor and talk a lot of guff about oil that she didn't understand.

On the days when there were no odd jobs I continued with my tap and ballet classes. I even had instruction from ballet heartthrob David Lichine, who had followed in the leaps of Massine and Nijinsky and was the lover-boy-Nureyev of the forties. His *pièce-de-résistance* was his dancing of Nijinsky's famous *L'Après-Midi d'un Faune*.

I had enrolled as a pupil at Nico Charise's dance school

when Lichine was the visiting celebrity who gave us ballet lessons. In return I tried to teach him how to tap. And again in return he brought me a solitary rose and took me out on a picnic up in the hills behind the umpteen-feet-high "Hollywood" sign. I remember sitting on the grass among the ants, clutching my single rose while Lichine tried to clutch me. After a burst of pas-de-no-deuxing in and out of the sign I found that although Lichine was a great dancer I was the better runner.

What an *Après-midi* it was with that *Faune* chasing me around. I'm here to tell you that all male dancers are *not* gay.

The various ballet masters under whom I had studied had all agreed I was the right height and weight for the male dancers to lug about. That was before my bra changed to a size thirty-eight. It was then I got the message that as an aspiring ballerina I might as well stop aspiring because my boobs kept bumping into my partner in the *pas-de-deux*. (The *pas-de-deux* is the ballet term for the girl and boy running toward each other and the girl finishing up ass-over-appetite in the air. She then uses her partner as a sort of exercise bar and his job is to keep her from falling on her face.)

An additional hazard, of course, was that when these great boobs bobbed up and down they were not always in time to the music. On top of this my bloody toes bled and I had trouble with my *fouettés,* those one-legged toplike spins ballerinas always do when they're showing off. The trick here is to look at one object, point your foot at it, spin and snap your foot and your head around to find the same object. They call this "spotting." But I was never able to spot it before throwing up. Today I can't think why I never see the Royal Ballet Company throwing up—at least not on the stage.

In between my visions of Dame Donlan in her tutu gliding through *Giselle* I did more modeling and more demonstrating. At least it kept a few nickels coming in during 1941 so we wouldn't have to spend a Charlie Chaplin Christmas eating our shoelaces. Instead we spent a Japanese one. On December 7 they blew up the United States navy in Pearl Harbor and we spent that night huddled around our radios listening to President Roosevelt telling us we were at war.

169
☆

We were supposed to instantly start disliking the Japanese. This was damned inconvenient for many Californians who lost their Japanese gardeners when they were immediately locked up, and equally inconvenient for thousands of Americans who had the misfortune to be of Japanese origin.

There were growing rumors that California would be the next target. So we had a few air raid practice alerts and learned how to black out our homes. The inhabitants of our quiet Studio City were in varying states of flusteration. Except Grand'mère. She had already lived through a war or two, or even three because I can't believe she wasn't around when Napoleon was playing soldiers. In any case, she was sure no one would attack California as it was too far from civilization.

Pretty soon gasoline was rationed and so were our boyfriends. One by one they were drafted or joined the services. Even the Hollywood studios began losing their male stars. James Stewart, William Holden, Burgess Meredith, and Ronald Reagan were some of the first to join the army. The navy collected Robert Montgomery, Doug Fairbanks, Jr., Gene Raymond, Wayne Morris, and Tony Martin. Everyone started making war pictures to stir up our patriotism but I couldn't get a role as a WAC, a WAVE, or even a French Resistance heroine. Then one day MGM decided America's best secret weapon for morale should be bigger, better, and starrier musicals. It was a decision that was destined to change not only my life but what was loosely called my career.

Metro-Goldwyn-Mayer was a walled-in, impregnable empire of treeless streets lined with office buildings for executives, senior writers, junior writers, rehearsal studios, wardrobe factories, and hangarlike sound stages. A network of studio trolleybuses operated day and night and carried you from point A to point Z with the minimum wear and tear on the legs.

And like all other cities the kids played in the streets. Only many of the "kids" in this case had world famous names and would spend their lunch break playing ball games or sitting on benches munching their hamburgers and sandwiches watching the trolleys and the costumes go by.

One of the sitters was Buster Keaton. This great come-dian, whom the studio now considered "old-fashioned," had fallen on hard times and somebody in the MGM empire had shown a surprising streak of compassion by putting him under contract as a writer. But here the compassion ended. They gave him a small room in the junior writers' block. I never heard whether or not he had any writing accepted, but he turned up every day like the pro that he was and ate his little picnic lunch on the concrete streets of the studio he had helped to make famous.

The senior writers' block lured a stream of gold-seeking literary giants into its tempting but fickle corridors. Daily it emitted the cream of best-selling authors and playwrights such as Ben Hecht, Charles McArthur, Anita Loos, Frances Marion, Dorothy Parker, Dashiell Hammett, and Robert Benchley. Every now and then they would emerge in vary-ing stages of shock, frustration, or elation depending on the acceptance or rejection of their latest inspirations.

The offices of the junior writers' block resembled small prison cells. There was room in them for only a desk and a chair. After six months' working in them the occupants came out either as monks or alcoholics—sometimes both. Only the strong survivors became senior screenwriters.

Most of the junior writers were young trainees who came from a variety of professions. One of my boyfriends was in the junior block. His name was Jim Hill and before coming to Hollywood he had been a guide at Radio City. Apparently in-experienced contract writers were chosen with the same abandon as the inexperienced contract-players. Anyway, Jim was happy to be paid for learning the film business from the inside. It came in handy later when he became a producer with Burt Lancaster, married and divorced Rita Hayworth, and bought a block of apartments in Santa Monica.

According to Jim his job at Metro was to rewrite small emergency scenes after the senior writers had delivered their scripts and were busy on other projects. For instance, if a film was in production and the director came to a problem scene on the floor, a copy of it was immediately sent to each of the junior writers, who were told to have a go at their own rewrite version while the director shot around the trouble-some scene. The best one was then selected and shot—the scene, that is, not the junior writer.

Beyond the hub of this celluloid metropolis were miles and miles of studio suburbia known as "the lot," where clusters of backless foreign cities and Western ghost towns sprouted in plaster and wooden confusion. Beyond these were acres of countryside, all part of the empire, where grown-up cowboys and Indians could play cowboys and Indians.

The president and lord-king-almighty of this walled kingdom was a plump little family tyrant named Louis B. Mayer. Mr. Mayer believed in God, Mickey Rooney, and the immortality of MGM, although not always in the same order. Within the closely guarded walls of Mr. Mayer's empire, he manufactured the hallucinatory drug of the thirties and forties—the American dream films. All the lovers were beautiful and had even teeth. They were good men who married gorgeous girls, became billionaires, and went to heaven. Bad men lost their penthouses, were shot, and went to hell. Black was black, white was white, and everything else was either funny or you could hum it. And to keep the balance Louis B. Mayer peopled his domain with ugly executives and pretty girls and thousands of drones who assembled his dream capsules.

When Hitler started rolling across Europe as though he owned Metro, Mr. Mayer retaliated by rolling out the famous MGM musicals. *Babes on Broadway, DuBarry Was a Lady, Ziegfeld Follies,* and *Meet Me in St. Louis* were a few of the tranquilizers he pushed into film history. And that's where I came in.

The summons had come through the MGM musical department, which had sent out a call to all dancers registered with them. By then I had decided that even dancing was better than modeling on the run or trying to sell oil on an elevator. So there we were, hundreds of us, being checked in by name through a side gate at MGM. Dancers I'd never seen before had come in from the sands of Santa Monica beach, from under the rocks of Laurel Canyon, and the cacti of the

San Fernando Valley. Most of the girls, including myself, wore the interview costume of the day, a fox jacket over a pair of shorts and high-heel shoes. The fox fur was to show you had a fox fur and the shorts and high heels were to show you had legs to go with it.

This particular call, it transpired, wasn't for just a day's work or even a few weeks' dancing in one musical sequence. It was a call to be seen and tested for a yearly MGM dancing contract with options for up to seven years. For the chosen twenty it would mean at least a year's steady paychecks.

We all hopped on the studio trolleybus which dropped us off at the dancers' rehearsal room, an enormous sound stage with one wall completely mirrored and practice bars attached to the other three. At one end sat Arthur Freed, Metro's top musical producer who was also justly famous as the writer of such international song hits as "You Were Meant for Me," "The Doll Dance," "Singing in the Rain," and a whole slew of standard golden disc world hits. Flanking him was the dance director Chuck Walters, and Freed's right-hand man, composer-arranger and lyricist Roger Edens.

We were paraded in front of these merrymakers and weeded out according to the beauty standards of the era which were big boobs, big grins, and long legs. Those who passed the beauty contest then had to pass the dancing test. Each one in turn had to do several steps including the standard time-step. The lucky survivors were given a seventy-five-dollar-a-week contract and a clocking-in card to get us in and out of the factory. I was one of the lucky survivors.

Mother had become a survivor, too, at another factory called Lockheed. Because of the war effort she had learned to make airplanes; not the whole plane, mind you, just a piece of it. So while Mother was working for Lockheed, I was working for Metro, and you could hardly tell the difference between our two factories.

With high hopes of becoming one of MGM's future musical stars we clocked in every morning, hopped the trolley to our rehearsal stage and were given practice classes by the studio dancing teacher. Often we were joined by Gene Kelly, MGM's newest dancing discovery. He was an all-American,

173
☆

good-guy type whom we all liked. He usually worked out his routines in the smaller stage next to ours. Sometimes I joined him, using another corner to rehearse my own. It was interesting to notice that his dancing style was heavier than Fred Astaire's, and I remember wondering how he was ever going to make it. In view of what he eventually achieved I should have got on with my own terpsichoring. I remember Bob Hope saying, "Every time Kelly starts to dance Astaire starts counting his money."

Whenever a musical number was about to go into production Arthur Freed, Roger Edens, and Co. would wander in and discuss the stars and the style of dance sequence planned with our choreographer. For the first few musicals it was Chuck Walters. He was another new boy who had just arrived from his triumph as Betty Grable's dance partner in the New York stage success *DuBarry Was a Lady*, and his first assignment was to direct the dances for the film version.

Serious rehearsals began about four to six weeks before shooting was due to commence. And while Chuck created his routines he used one of the girls to work out the role to be danced by the female star. This was in order to save the expensive lady from learning a whole lot of steps that might later be thrown out. But this had its other side. By the time the star arrived on the scene the dance numbers were already well rehearsed and it could be rather inhibiting for her to watch a Miss Nobody executing her dancing role to perfection.

Even Judy Garland, who was always serious, tense, quiet, and hardworking when she rehearsed with us, said she invariably felt like the new girl at school when she first tried to pick up the routines. And she'd been virtually brought up by MGM through the *Andy Hardy* series to *The Wizard of Oz*.

Once when Lucille Ball was rehearsing her numbers with us for *DuBarry Was a Lady* she stopped in the middle of a routine and said, "I bet you girls wonder how the hell I happen to be the star of this thing. So do I!"

Lucille was another new star at Metro and *DuBarry* was her first big musical film, so she was quite nervous. But she covered it up with her sense of humor. It was for this movie that they dyed her brown-bleached-blonde hair the wild strawberry pink she's been sporting ever since. Then, having dyed it, they kept it hidden under a white wig for most of the film.

By the time the stars joined the rehearsals we were usually dancing to the playback recording of the numbers with full orchestra and their prerecorded songs. This is what they'd been up to while we'd been working out the dance section. And this is why in the final picture you never see the stars huffing and puffing through their lyrics after leaping about in some strenuous dance routine.

In spite of the cast of Ball, Red Skelton, Tommy Dorsey, and the two talented newcomers, Gene Kelly and Virginia O'Brien, *DuBarry* turned into one of Metro's less than greatest musicals. The best thing that happened to Lucy Ball on that film was the rollicking friendship she struck up with the work-starved Buster Keaton. He was the one person at MGM who recognized her comedy potential. And, since he was so bored doing nothing, whenever she wasn't shooting he spent hours teaching her how to get visual comedy out of handling props. Lucy is the first to acknowledge that his coaching had a lot to do with her eventually becoming America's top female clown.

Of the twenty contract dancers my closest chum was a tall, slim, Finnish blonde, Pat Patelson. She had been a Rockette at the Radio City Music Hall and as the Rockettes had a worldwide reputation for expert precision dancing, the MGM choreographers were delighted to get her. However, Pat was a newcomer to Hollywood and the movie world and somehow I took over the role of guide and taught her some of the tricks of our trade, which had peculiar results. I was still convinced that if a dancer aspired to become an actress she shouldn't be seen on the screen as a chorus girl. I must have convinced Pat, too, because she followed me into my hiding-from-the-camera positions in our dance routines. So although we danced in numerous musicals we could not be seen dancing in them.

Today Pat has two grown daughters, one of them a ballerina, who would both love to see their mother dancing on the screen. Pat tells me they search frantically for her whenever those old musical numbers we were in are revived on TV or in the movie houses, but thanks to me they cannot find her anywhere!

While we were working on *DuBarry*, the director, Roy del Ruth, stopped by our rehearsal one morning.

"I need the best dancer you have," he told Chuck Walters, "and I need her urgently."

As he hurried off there was a muffled huddle between Chuck and a couple of other musical bigwigs and we all held our breath. When Chuck came out of his huddle, he chose Pat. She was quaking with excitement as he escorted her outside to a chauffeur-driven limousine. We all followed to wish her good luck. We thought for sure she was on her way to becoming the future Eleanor Powell.

When Pat arrived at the sound stage an assistant director led her to a dance mat in the center of the floor. There were no lights, no cameras, only a sound boom over the mat and a beam of light projecting a screenful of Red Skelton at the other end of the stage. He was doing a knockabout comedy routine in which he kept skidding. Mr. del Ruth asked Pat to watch the screen carefully and told her that every time Skelton skidded on the screen she should skid on the mat so they could record the sound. The disillusioned "best dancer" had to skid around for hours before she hopped the trolleybus back to our rehearsal room to spread her sad tale.

But Pat has now come to terms with her skids and is rather pleased about them. Because whenever *DuBarry Was a Lady* is revived and her daughters cannot see her in the dance routines, at least they can hear her in Red Skelton's routine.

Another of the dancing girls who had dramatic aspirations was Mary Jo, a short angel-faced ladylike blonde. Unlike me, she believed in being seen on the screen with the hope that Louis B. Mayer would discover her emoting through the song and dance numbers, tear up her dancer contract, and give her the dramatic star buildup. So wherever the stars moved during a number, there was Mary Jo right beside them, sparkling away with all her eyelashes standing to attention.

After nine months of knocking herself out, and some of the stars, with her exuberant dancing, and getting no reaction from Louis B. Mayer, she eventually persuaded Arthur Freed to give her a line to say. The picture chosen for Mary Jo's line was the now historic Judy Garland musical *Meet Me in St. Louis*. On the day of The Line the girls were all atwitter as they maneuvered themselves into their period costumes. It took some maneuvering, too, as the designer insisted they wear period underwear for authenticity. Under each dress went a bodice, bloomers, petticoats, and a laced-up corset. Since Mary Jo was speaking, her corset was laced up tighter than anyone else's as her authenticity would be showing directly in front of the camera.

During the rehearsals of the scene, in which a few of the girls clustered around while Mary Jo said her line to Judy Garland, all went well and director Vincent Minelli was so pleased, he said, "Let's shoot it." So the cameras rolled for the first take. When Mr. Minelli said, "Action," Mary Jo passed right out in a dead faint. There was a rush of antifaint remedies from all directions and within a few minutes she was up again. She said it was a combination of the excitement, the extra hot lights for the color film, and most of all the tightly laced corset that had knocked her out. The wardrobe lady removed the corset and for the next take, although Mary Jo didn't look so authentic, she stayed on her feet and spoke her line like a veteran.

After all that effort, and her stellar performance in the face of extreme difficulties, Mr. Mayer still didn't see her. But *you* can see her the next time they screen the "Trolley Song." She is the effervescent blonde bubbling, "Clang, clang, clang," on Judy Garland's right and on your left.

We didn't have as many rules to break at Metro as we had at Carroll's, but just enough to keep it interesting. For instance, on shooting days we were sent to the makeup and hairdressing departments to get prettied up for the color cameras. In those days colors showed up much stronger on film than they actually were, so screen makeup was muted down and the offscreen result was drearily drab. Then one by one our makeups were carefully inspected by one of the assistants. As soon as we'd been passed we rushed away, wiped it all off and put on our own red lips, eyeshadow, and color on our cheeks. We knew we weren't going to be seen on the screen so we felt we might as well look good off it.

In any case it was difficult to identify ourselves with the final MGM product to be shown on the screens of the world. We seldom knew whether we were in a comedy or a drama; we just had our numbers to learn and that was the end of it.

Between musicals the contract girls were often sent to the various stages for extra work. And those were the days Pat and I played hooky. We would get to the studio, clock in with our cards and then sneak out, spend the day at Malibu beach, and race back just in time to clock out again.

All work and no play makes a girl monotonous, so I was ecstatic when a handsome young sergeant showed up at my door in the valley. His name was Philip Truex and we had met a few years before at the house of his father, actor Ernest Truex. Philip had given me a brief whirl around Hollywood and then disappeared to New York to act with Maurice Evans's Shakespeare Company.

Now he was back defending our country in Irving Berlin's all-soldier musical hit *This Is the Army*. This smash success, in which Irving Berlin himself appeared, had been touring the country raising millions of dollars for the war charities. They were now playing in Los Angeles and were about to make the film version in Hollywood.

Philip was gentle, well educated—he'd been to school in England—and well mannered. He was everything that most men were not in Hollywood. So it was instant-in-love.

I was also fond of his father, who had starred in dozens of stage comedy hits both in New York and London, including *Whistling in the Dark* and *George Washington Slept Here*. Ernie was a cuddly family man and never brought his actor side into his home. Now he was dividing his time between the theater in New York and playing comedy roles in films. Most people remember him as Gary Cooper's very

funny sidekick in the movie *The Adventures of Marco Polo*.
His wife, Sylvia Fields, was a much admired stage
actress and she was just as cozy as Ernie. Sylvia was one of
the few actresses who could forget her career when she
wasn't working and get on with her dusting happily. She was
always cooking, sewing, darning, knitting, and homemaking.
Everybody loved everybody and I loved the Truex family.

Philip organized seats for Mother and me to see him in
This Is the Army. In one of the sketches he had to dress up as
a girl so the tenor could sing to him/her the famous Berlin
song "I left my heart at the Stage Door Canteen—I left my
heart with a girl called Eileen." During the number Philip,
as Eileen, sat on a bench wearing a long blonde wig and a
pinafore dress. He looked like Alice in Wonderland. I remember nudging Mother during the song and saying, "I'm
going to marry that girl."

Philip took me out dining and dancing whenever he
could get leave from his camp. On Sundays we had family
dinners with Ernie and Sylvia; otherwise we raced around
the Sunset Strip in my car, taking in the Player's Club, Dave
Chasen's, Ciro's, or the Mocambo. When Philip ran out of his
soldier's pay we used my MGM wages. Nothing mattered except doing everything *now*. In wartime there are no tomor-
rows.

Meanwhile, back at the fable factory, we had just started
rehearsals for Arthur Freed's production of Gershwin's *Girl
Crazy*. Norman Taurog was the director and Busby Berkeley,
Chuck Walters, and Jack Donahue shared us dancers between them—technically speaking, of course. The only thing
I recall about this picture was jitterbugging in some spectacular Western number. Dozens of outside dancers had in-
truded on us, as well as Judy Garland, Mickey Rooney, and
Tommy Dorsey's orchestra. We were all wearing cowboy costumes and doing peculiar things with whips—Buzz Berkeley
liked using props to make his patterns.

I don't know what kind of patterns we made with our
whips as I never saw the movie. In fact, I never saw any of
these musicals I hid in—any more than I saw the directors
who made them. Like Busby Berkeley they always seemed to

be up in the air somewhere on a crane or a rostrum and had an earthbound person to execute the actual steps for them. In this case it was Jack Donahue who, every time he passed me, said, "Yo, your dancing is getting awful close to the ground."

It was, too. I could barely lift my feet up with the ennui of being the other end of a prop.

Then suddenly out of nowhere, during the last week of production, came an offer which was to change everything. On the way back from the studio I dropped one of the dancers off at her boyfriend's house in Beverly Hills. He was a Hollywood agent named Howard Lang, and he asked us both in for a drink. He was brimming over with excitement and celebrating the success of a show he had coproduced with Al Rosen in Chicago. It was a farce called *Goodnight Ladies* starring Skeets Gallagher and Buddy Ebsen and for a year it had been breaking box-office records at the Blackstone Theater.

We all drank to its continued success. During the course of our celebrating I told him how I had longed to get into a New York show and how frustrating it had been going back to dancing at MGM after beginning to play speaking roles.

"Okay," said Howard suddenly, "why not join my play in Chicago?" I looked at him in stunned amazement. "At least it's on the way to New York," he added with a smile.

"You can't be serious."

"Never more so," he laughed. "The ingenue, Gloria Grahame, is leaving. So's the girl playing the French maid. If you can clear your Metro contract you can pick which you want to play."

He sent me home with the play under my arm and bubbling over with anticipation.

I shook the play at Mother's surprised face. "Look," I gurgled, "a real live professional play with words to say!" I couldn't eat I was so anxious to read this farce which was rocking the whole of Chicago with sidesplitting laughter. Excitedly, I devoured all three acts and didn't laugh once. I was so puzzled—but I put it down to lack of experience. Who was I to question such a success? The following day when I spoke to Howard Lang I made a really stupid mistake. I chose to play the French maid instead of the ingenue. It was mostly lack of confidence and at least I knew I was safe as a French maid. Nevertheless, it would be my first step into the theater. I'd now done over a year of terpsichoring in Arthur Freed's musicals. I'd tapped, waltzed, Tico-Ticoed, and pirouetted, all to no avail. Enough, I decided, was enough and caught the next trolley to Mr. Freed's office.

Arthur Freed couldn't believe his ears when I told him I wished to leave MGM. Firstly, he didn't know I was there to leave, and, secondly, no one, not even invisible chorus girls, left the mostest, giganticest film studio in Hollywood unless by request—the studio's request.

"Leave?" he repeated faintly.

"I want to go on the stage," I said meekly.

Mr. Freed poured us a drink in case one of us was suffering from shock.

"Do you realize, Miss . . . er . . . er . . ." I filled in the "er" for him. ". . . that people all over the world are clamoring for your opportunity of being here in Hollywood under contract to MGM?"

The mere idea of someone asking permission to leave his Shangri-La seemed to numb him for a moment and he took a deep gulp from his glass.

"I've been offered a role in a play in Chicago and I really ought to do it," I said. Mr. Freed said people in plays in Chicago all wanted to come to Hollywood and MGM. I said, "Yes, but not with a dancer's contract and no prospects. I want to become an actress."

He smiled reassuringly as he took stock of me for the first time. "Perhaps we at Metro have plans for you."

I tried a smile back and explained that aside from dancing behind the stars and often behind the scenery, I'd only had three hopeful opportunities so far. These had occurred during the intervals between musicals when we clocked in, had our dancing lesson, and sat on our benches all afternoon crocheting and watching the stars go by. The first time I was picked off my bench I was told to hurry over to another stage for a close-up. I dropped six stitches, moistened my lips, and ran. I couldn't wait for the trolley.

I arrived breathless to find the set lit and the camera ready. It was a Regency drawing room and the lights were focused on a lady's Sheraton escritoire. I was laced into an Edwardian costume, had my nail varnish removed, and was placed at the desk. I was then given a quill pen, some delicate stationery and told to write a letter. It didn't matter what I wrote, the director said, because the contents wouldn't be read as the camera was facing me. But the camera wasn't facing my face. It was focused on the bottom half of my right arm. It was an "insert" shot. Probably of Greer Garson's hand writing to Walter Pidgeon, or perhaps Jeanette MacDonald writing to Nelson Eddy. Those were the two MGM ladies who usually wore the period clothes. I didn't ask. I didn't care.

The next time I was hauled off my bench I was in no hurry. I waited for the trolley. When I arrived on the set I found it was a modern luxury bathroom. Both my legs were hurriedly painted Max Factor's Tan No. 2 and I was wrapped in a huge bathtowel. As none of the rest of me had been painted it didn't take Sherlock Holmes to deduce which section of my anatomy was required. I was asked to step out of the bath, which I did. In fact I did it three times. The director said I had stepped out very well and should go far and sent me back to my bench. The wardrobe lady who wrapped the towel said the legs were supposed to be Lana Turner's. Not that Miss Turner didn't have lovely legs, she said, but she'd taken them on vacation to Palm Springs. Lucky stars, I thought, they can go away between pictures, not like us dancers who waited around to replace the missing parts of their anatomies.

So the third time I was sent to another set I crawled off my bench and dragged my disillusioned feet onto the trolley. But this time when I arrived I was grabbed by the makeup man and hairdresser and painted and coiffed from the neck up. The makeup man even cut me a special pair of eyelashes which I kept blinking in amazement. Then I was put into a sweater and skirt and led on to the set. As usual it was lit and ready. This time it was a park bench in a clearing of plastic grass and rubber trees. In the middle of it all was a young man in an officer's uniform. I'd never seen him before but I knew he was an actor because his face was painted Max Factor's No. 3. The director called me into the scene.

"Hey you, honey," he said, "I want you to meet Peter Lawford." Then he explained to Hey-you-honey and Peter what was required. Peter was supposed to cuddle and kiss this young high school girl on the park bench. At first she enjoys it. Then she gets angry, shouts at him, and walks out of the scene.

"You mean I have lines to say?" I asked excitedly.

"No, honey," he answered patiently, "it's a silent shot. No sound. We just want the action. So just say whatever comes into your head."

We ran the scene a couple of times and then tried the first take. After the kiss I must have become overexcited in the angry shouting bit because instead of saying something simple like, "How dare you kiss me when we've only just met—I'll go home and tell my mother," I said, "Hey, you creepy damn wolf, I'm getting the hell out of here!"

The director said, "Cut." He then made it quite clear that although there was no sound many people could lip read. Not even MGM gangsters were allowed to say "damn" or "hell" on the screen let alone young high-school girls. The Hollywood censor and that family man, Mr. Mayer, wouldn't like it. I stopped swearing and completed the scene as requested. Although my right arm, two legs, and eventually my face had been seen in three different projection rooms by a pride of Metro lions, not once did Mr. Louis B. Mayer have me swept off my bench into the arms of King Gable with equal billing.

No, somehow I didn't think anyone at MGM had plans for me.

Arthur Freed waited until I'd finished my story and drink before rising and extending a hand. "Okay," he sighed, like a man who had finally accepted the fact that one of his contract dancers was feeble-minded, "and good luck."

He even helped me to the door in case I wasn't capable of finding it for myself. "And if you ever want to come back, the job's still there," he added gallantly.

183
☆

Many years later, when I was appearing in a play in London, Arthur Freed and Gene Kelly came back to see me in my dressing room at the Vaudeville Theater. "This is the only girl I ever made a star by firing her," he laughed to my other visitors. Even all those years later he still couldn't believe anyone could really have left MGM at her own request.

Yolande (circled) in *Rosalie*. "Stay away from the camera!" (MGM)

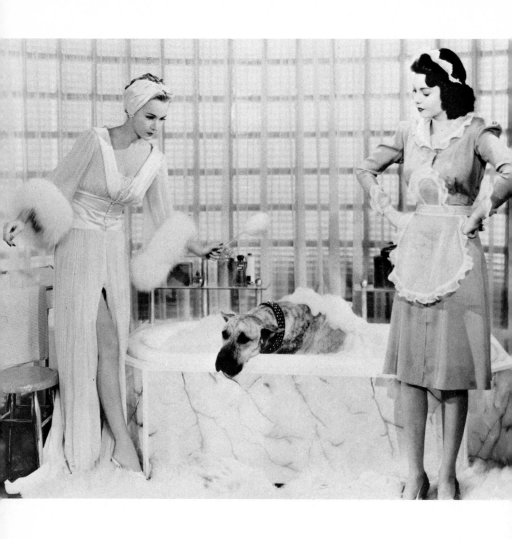

Carole Landis, "Dopey" the Great Dane and Yolande "Mollot"
in *Turnabout*, 1940 (HAL ROACH STUDIOS INC.)

DuBarry Was a Lady, 1942 (Yolande is seated at Red Skelton's feet. The girl lying above is Mary Jo, who fainted in *Meet Me in St. Louis!*) (MGM)

Yolande and friends in *Good Night Ladies* in its second year at the Blackstone Theatre, Chicago (BLOOM, CHICAGO)

(*Opposite, above*) Miss "Mollot" again, with Mary Anderson and Alan Baxter in *Under Age*, 1941 (COPYRIGHT 1974 COLUMBIA PICTURES INDUSTRIES, INC.)

(*Opposite, below*) Dizzy days in Earl Carroll's "Vanities" with the author at back right enmeshed in the collapsing scenery revolve! (NEW YORK PUBLIC LIBRARY)

Olivier and his new star. "But not, Madame, at the Connaught!"
(RADIO TIMES HULTON PICTURE LIBRARY)

Born Yesterday and its female lead whooping it up on tour in England

Yolande with Bill Kemp in *Born Yesterday*, Yo wearing the Buchanan tartan (JOHN VICKERS)

The day of my departure on the *Super Chief* for Chicago Philip took me to lunch at the Brown Derby and afterward bought me a gold, ruby, and diamond cocktail ring to celebrate our engagement. Life was a joy. We were in love, I was an actress again, and Philip promised to spend all his future leaves in Chicago.

On the train I met the film star comedian Stuart Erwin who was going to replace Buddy Ebsen opposite Skeets Gallagher. Even he was elated with the prospect of joining a hit show. As he was the star he and his wife, June Collyer, were given a private compartment where he spent most of the three-day journey studying his part. The ingenue, Peggy Drake, and I shared first-class pullman seats which turned into upper and lower berths at night. Peggy had done a few roles in movies, but not much more than I had. She was just braver. We were both leaving our homes for the first time to live on our own in the big city. As neither of us had any money, and both of us would have to send some of our wages back to our mothers, we decided to room together and share expenses.

Our first night on the train we met a marvelous army major. He was middle-aged but attractive in a sort of Spencer Tracy way and turned out to be a doctor. He took us to a bang-up dinner in the dining car and when he found we were young hicks on our first big adventure, with no money to spend, he took us under his wing and gave us a three-day train spree. That evening when we went to our berths we were greeted by the porter who escorted us to a private compartment, like Stu Erwin's, where our things had already been moved. He said it was ours for the trip with the compliments of the major. I was surprised to find that one of the things he had not moved in was the major.

"We better watch it," frowned Peggy when the porter had gone.

"Sure, nothing is for nothing," I agreed with foreboding.

But no; although he plied us with drinks through all the dry states, treated us to every meal, and fed us benzedrine for our hangovers, our major made nary a pass.

At the Chicago station we were met by the stage manager, a wrinkled, meticulous, but kindly little man called Myles Putnam. He hustled us into a taxi, dropped our luggage at the Blackstone Hotel lobby and whisked us off to the costumiers for fittings. During the drive we kept our greenhorn noses pressed to the taxi windows gaping at the skyscrapers, the huge neon signs, and the busy streets bustling with Chicagoans wearing hats, coats, and gloves. We couldn't tell which ones were the gangsters, but they were a change from the Hollywoodians in their playclothes.

When we finally arrived back in our hotel room we found a huge bouquet of flowers waiting for us on the dressing room table. There were also a couple of bottles of whisky and two envelopes. They were all from the major. In each envelope was a hundred-dollar bill and a note from him wishing us luck in the play. It was the last we heard from our jolly benefactor.

For a week we rehearsed every day with the understudies and watched the play at night. And it was all true—the theater was packed and the audience rolled about laughing. One by one we took over our roles from the departing cast, but I cannot recall one happening of my opening night, so it must have breezed along all right. If it hadn't I would have recalled every disastrous detail.

But I do recall what happened after the show. Peggy and I were slipping out of our stage clothes and planning how we would celebrate by treating ourselves to a couple of T-bone steaks at Tommy's bar-restaurant when a message came down from the stage door.

"There's a gentleman for Miss Donlan. Name of Lloyd."

I shrugged my shoulders at Peggy. Neither of us knew anyone in Chicago yet—maybe it was a friend of the major's. I asked one of the departing girls if she'd mind sending the gentleman up while Peggy and I slipped into our dressing gowns.

When I answered the tap on our door I stood for a moment open mouthed. It was Harold. He smiled and shook both my hands warmly.

"Well, you're on your way now."

"Harold! What are you doing in Chicago?"

"I'm here for a Shriners' convention. So naturally I had to see the show." He was so pleased I had a stage role. "And you're working with Skeets Gallagher, the finest farceur in the business. He can teach you everything," he added.

Coming from Harold this was high praise for another comedian and Skeets deserved it. He had the lightest, freshest, most unforced touch in his playing of any actor I have ever seen. He was also a sweet guy whom we all loved.

That evening Harold took Peggy and me to dinner at the Blackstone, where he was also staying, and I decided to order oysters for the first time. They seemed the right type of sophisticated dish that a sophisticated actress should eat. When those gray slurpy blobs arrived in their shells in front of me I thought I was never going to make it. I tried to swallow each one without biting into it, as that would have been disaster. Harold noticed the difficulty I was having.

"No good?"

"They're excellent."

"Why are you making such a face then?"

"I can't stand them."

"Well, order something else," laughed Harold.

"No," I insisted, "everybody loves oysters, why shouldn't I?"

"It's an acquired taste," said Peggy.

"Then I'm going to acquire it," I said defiantly, and glurped down the rest.

Eventually I learned to like these awful blobs; which shows if you take an adult with the mental age of under seven you can teach it to like anything. I was also told never to mix oysters with whisky. One evening, against everybody's advice, I ordered oysters while drinking whisky. Everybody was right. They didn't mix. Since then I have given up oysters—but not whisky.

Once Peggy and I had settled down in the show we found ourselves a two-roomed furnished apartment at the Canterbury Court on the north side of the city and felt we were now really in residence.

Life in Chicago was so completely different from Hollywood. Instead of everything folding up at 10 P.M. the whole town was lit up from midnight onward and the streets were packed with people going to the all-night restaurants, bars, supper clubs, and movie houses. The hotels were always packed with conventions of some kind or other and men poured out of them wearing their funny hats and blowing paper whistles. Mingling with them were the soldiers and sailors who came to this lively city for their leave. Chicago seemed to be in a constant state of celebration. Everybody was crowding to see the new smash films, *For Whom the Bell Tolls* and *Casablanca*. Dance orchestras never stopped playing its theme song, "As Time Goes By." Hit shows from New York, such as Rodgers and Hammerstein's *Oklahoma* and George Abbott's *Kiss and Tell* came there for runs of at least six months. An unknown playwright named Tennessee Williams was also there, trying out his first play, *The Glass Menagerie* with Laurette Taylor. Most of our cast who saw it thought it was a great play, but would never make it in New York.

We often joined the casts of these other shows for impromptu supper parties in each other's apartments; or for nights on the prowl. It was fun going to our theater without having to lug a trunk onto the stage. I was learning the trade in the way Daddy Donlan had said I should—with a live, pulsating audience, and actually being paid for it. To gain more experience I understudied Peggy's ingenue role as well.

Almost every evening after the show we were taken out to supper. Most of Hollywood stopped by in Chicago on their way to New York, and most of them looked us up—including my friends from the MGM junior writers' block, Jim Hill and Co. Wealthy Chicagoans took us boating on Lake Michigan on Sundays. We were constantly celebrating weddings, as the girls in the cast married boys in the services who kissed them good-bye and returned to their camps or went off to war. When they returned on leave they were usually accompanied by their buddies and we celebrated all over again.

Peggy and I enjoyed our newfound freedom away from our home nests. We played all night and slept all morning. Neither of us could cook anything except French toast, so whoever was up first made French toast for breakfast. And if we ever had guests for breakfast, lunch, or supper they got French toast, too.

When Philip arrived on a two-week furlough we leaped into each other's arms and never stopped hugging, kissing, and loving, and eating French toast. Our young love was so potent that Peggy obligingly moved in with one of the other actresses so we could have the apartment to ourselves. Every night after the show Philip and I joined the rest of the cast for spareribs at Tommy's bar, waltzed around the beer gardens by the lake, or held hands at the Balinese supper club while the orchestra played "People Will Say We're in Love" from *Oklahoma*.

Yes, we were in love and we didn't care what tomorrow brought until tomorrow brought a letter from Mother. She was coming to Chicago in four weeks' time to look after me. Chaos erupted. Mother would never approve of our "living in sin" on Philip's visits just as Grand'mère wouldn't have approved of Mother living with Jim Ferrier—so, just like Mother did, we decided to get married right away.

It was a quick justice-of-the-peace marriage, and to a Catholic it wasn't valid. I would worry about that later. In the meantime, it was enough to ease Mother's conscience and permit me to be permissive in our unpermissive society. After the wedding Philip left for his army air base in Sacramento and I was another lovelorn war bride.

No sooner had my mother announced her arrival than Peggy's mother announced hers. Now two mother storks were coming to hover over us. It was obvious we could no longer share the two-room apartment, so we ordered two singles in the same block. As mine was vacant first, Peggy moved in with me to await the invasion of mothers. The day after we moved was a day of panic. Peggy came down with a cold which made her deaf as well as dumb. Laryngitis set in and she couldn't speak a word. I left her in the big Murphy bed and rushed to the theater to take over her role. I knew it as I had been well rehearsed by Myles, the stage manager, so it would make a fun change, although Daddy Donlan would have said it wasn't worth playing.

Just before the curtain went up Harold Lloyd telephoned. He was in Chicago consorting with those Shriners again, or counting his bowling alleys, or had some millionaire's business up his loaded sleeve, and he invited Peggy and me out to supper afterward. I told him about our calamity and how I couldn't go out after the show and leave Peggy alone, especially as she was unspeakable.

"Don't worry," said Harold cheerfully, "I'll pick up some food at the coffee bar and we can all eat at your place."

Before I could explain that my "place" was a small cupboard filled with a large bed I was called onstage to play Peggy's ingenue.

After the show, flushed with the success of having remembered the words and not knocked over the furniture or the actors, I taxied home to the apartment. Peggy was lying prone, alive but silent in the all-encompassing bed. Once it was down out of the wall one side of it blocked the passage to the tiny kitchenette and the other side blocked the door to the bathroom. Any space that was left seemed to be filled with Peggy's baggage, most of which she hadn't been able to unpack.

When $75 million worth of Harold Lloyd arrived he was laden with paper bags of fried chicken, cole slaw, French fries, and cartons of coffee. I maneuvered him around the wardrobe trunk, suitcases, and makeup boxes to the only available chair, on which were two more suitcases. I relieved him of his bags of food and left him perched on the cases on the chair talking in sign language to Peggy. At this he was an expert, after all those silent films.

To get to the plates and cutlery and things in the kitchenette I had to clamber back and forth across the bed and Peggy before I could serve our esteemed guest with his buffet supper. And whenever I forgot the pepper or salt or something Harold climbed down, joined in and helped to get it. Before we'd even started the meal we had crawled over the bed, over Peggy, around the fridge, around each other, and over the bed again.

We all laughed so much we had to go to the bathroom— which meant trekking over that damned bed again. By the time we'd finished we were all slightly hysterical.

"My God," gasped Harold weakly, "what the Marx Brothers could do with this setup!"

I played the ingenue for a week before returning to the French maid and was furious with myself for not having accepted it when it was originally offered. It made me restless to get to New York where all the best theater roles were cast and where Philip and I planned to live happily ever after and replace the Lunts.

To collect extra money for my dowry I signed with a modeling agency and spent my free days as a photographic model. At the same time, because of the upsurge of American musicals, I decided to take singing lessons as an investment in the future. Some of the *Oklahoma* cast told me about a Signora Chiarni who was reputed to be one of the best singing teachers in Chicago. So I searched her out and enrolled for some lessons. Mother was terribly pleased about this, but Signora Chiarni wasn't.

She was rather a formidable Italian lady with more bosom than height, and the walls of her *conservatorio* were covered with signed photos of famous voices, ranging from Lily Pons, Lawrence Tibbett, and Grace Moore to Dinah Shore, Tony Martin, and the Andrews Sisters. Whether she had taught them all or not it had me standing somewhat apprehensively in front of her grand piano for my first lesson.

I had brought along a piano copy of "I'm Just a Girl Who Can't Say No" and had emitted no more than eight bars of it before she rapped the piano with her fan. For some reason she always carried this closed fan, even though we were well into a shivery December. Maybe she kept it to strike really bad pupils.

"When you sing," she exhaled, "why do you open your mouth so wide?"

"To let my voice out, I guess."

"Every time you open your mouth you close your throat!"

"I do?"

The signora took a deep breath and clicked her tongue.

"What do you do when you eat?" she asked as though dealing with some particularly backward child. "You open your mouth and close your throat. You do not open your throat until you close your mouth. It is the same with singing."

I closed my throat and opened my mouth and told her I'd go home and do her breathing exercises and try to coordinate opening my mouth and throat in the right order. By the time I went for lesson number two I was feeling slightly more confident for having done my breathing homework. But the signora didn't want to hear any more *Oklahoma*. Instead she sat at the piano and banged out a C.

"Sing that." I did. "You feel it coming nicely out of your throat?"

"Yes, I do."

"That is just where it should not come from!" she thun-

dered, her fan slapping the piano top. "From your diaphragm, girl. You have a diaphragm, have you not?"

"Uh huh."

"Every note should start from the diaphragm. You push
it up and up until you can almost feel it coming out between
your eyebrows. . . . There you feel it growing, growing, like
a bubble. Then—suddenly—strong, crystal clear, you let it
go!"

I think it was during my fourth or fifth lesson that I did
let it go. I was screeching Betty Hutton's "Murder He Says"
when Signora Chiarni suddenly stopped playing, threw her
music in the air, and collapsed on the floor. She was taken to
the Menninger Clinic where they said she was suffering from
a nervous complaint. Her sister, with whom she lived, assured me the signora had had this complaint for several years
and that it wasn't my fault.

After a year's run in Chicago the show moved off on the road
and Mother moved back to California leaving unchaperoned
me to play Milwaukee, St. Louis, Cincinnati, Pittsburgh,
Cleveland and Detroit. I loved the train journeys and seeing
all these new cities.

I can still recall the heightened sense of expectation as I
walked through the rat-infested alleys to the stage doors of
each new theater. The musty smell of size and stale makeup
that permeates every backstage; the feel of the stage boards
when the theater is empty and the curtain up. I often stood
alone on these stages trying to drink in a sip of the magic the
greats might have left there for us beginners to taste. Every
eminent star had played these theaters, maybe even Daddy
Donlan when he and Mother were battling across America.

The show had reached St. Louis when I received the sad
letter from Mother saying Grand'mère had died. It seemed
that on one of her night prowls to the refrigerator she had
caught a chill while chumping a pig's trotter vinaigrette. The
chill had led to a cold which led to her snuffling out in her
sleep. I felt that Grand'mère's journey to harpsville at ninety-

six was as happily inspiring as her lively adjustment to old age had been.

The highlights of the *Goodnight Ladies* tour were Philip's furlough visits. On these weekends I always booked a double room and bath for a single person and then sneaked him into the hotel. The possibility of a house detective banging on our door added zest to our intermittent honeymoons. And the saving added extra money to our New York dowry. It was a terrible wrench whenever he left for camp, but I was lucky to be traveling with such a jolly cast. We were never bored. Although none of the other cities were as lively as Chicago, there were always plenty of new sights to see.

When we reached Detroit, where Sally Rand was doing her fan dance, it was time to renegotiate all our contracts for another possible nine months. Decisions, decisions. Should I go to New York and chance getting a better role there, or play this French maid on the road for the rest of my life? I decided to ask for a fifty-dollar raise and see what happened. What happened was Al Rosen, the other partner, gave me the sack and brought back the girl I had replaced.

I was out of work, just like that. It was a frightening shock and I couldn't sleep for my last week's run. Now I was going to have to go to New York alone, and the rest of the cast had warned me it was the city where everybody pushed you off the sidewalks, swore at you on buses; where waiters snatched away your food if you didn't gobble it quickly, and salesladies chased you out of their shops screaming if you didn't purchase their goods. I was already a nervous wreck.

On the way to New York I stopped in Dayton, Ohio, where Philip was stationed, to spend two weeks with him recovering from my unemployment. It was June and we drank May wine, picnicked in the park, paddled a canoe around the lake, and pondered how long it would be before the war was over and we both had jobs.

The morning I was packing to leave for the battle of New York a happy surprise telegram arrived. It was from Howard Lang, the producer who had hired me for *Goodnight Ladies*. He had just opened a new farce in Chicago, *School for Brides*, starring Roscoe Karns. It was due to open in New

York in six weeks' time and Howard wanted me to hurry back to Chicago to replace one of the girls. I couldn't believe my good luck. I was sure the Holy Boss had organized the whole deal, so I promised that in return I would get my non-Catholic husband to marry me in a church.

Philip changed the train tickets, which were pointing in the wrong direction. We kissed good-bye again and that night I was back in Chicago. And that week Chicago was being conventional again and there wasn't a hotel room to be had anywhere.

One of the actresses in the new show, Jenny, had been in the original *Goodnight Ladies* before it took to the road. She was an easygoing chum and offered to share her room with me. I was grateful, even though it was a single and we had to take turns sleeping on the floor. But I hadn't counted on Jenny's new boyfriend. He was an actor in the current Mae West play *Catherine Was Great,* which was running at the same time as ours. In it he played one of Mae West's lovers, and after it he continued as Jenny's lover. Which was lovely—but not in a single room when I had to be up early for rehearsals and learn new lines.

The two of them would arrive all tipsy and giggly around 3 A.M. and they could never remember whether it was Jenny's turn on the floor or in the bed. By the time they had either sat on me in the bed or walked over me on the floor and found their proper niche, I was wide awake.

Although this held none of the problems of my *soirée* with Earl Carroll, I wondered how many more times I was going to end up as the unnecessary, wide-awake *trois* of somebody else's *ménage.*

By the following week the funny convention hats had departed and left me a hotel room, and I had opened in another role my old man would have said wasn't worth playing. Obviously the director didn't think it was worth directing either because he used an assumed name on the program.

To me, *School for Brides* was just like the last play, *Goodnight Ladies*—a mixture of pretty girls and comics getting tangled up with indiscretions and untangling into goody-goodies. Nevertheless my role as the prospective bride of a

195
☆

millionaire was much better than the French maid. Howard had given me the extra fifty dollars a week and we were definitely going to open in New York. I was so grateful I went banging on the door of the local parish priest to organize our Catholic marriage.

When Philip arrived on his next leave I dragged him to the priest for instructions on the rules for non-Catholics to follow when they marry Catholics. According to the Church the prospective spouses have to know what they're getting into before they get into it. Most of the dos and don'ts have to do with sex, birth control and the raising of offspring in the faith. For instance, they wouldn't want Philip to encourage Earl Carroll and his mob to join us. And I don't think they would approve of him procreating Catholics while dressed as Eileen from the Stage Door Canteen.

Under my persuasion Philip, who listened to all of it and believed none of it, passed his exams and before he returned to his camp we were married by the priest. Now I was square with the Holy Boss and ready to tackle New York.

New York, New York, was a wonderful town.

It was also hot and dirty when the train arrived at Pennsylvania Station. I straightened my shoulders, flexed my muscles, clenched my fist, made ready for battle, and climbed into a taxi.

"Don't argue with me," I said to the driver, "just drive me to the Algonquin Hotel."

"Who argues in this heat?" he shrugged. "You must be a tourist."

"No, I'm working here," I said proudly.

"That's your tough luck, kid," he said, and drove me through the streets of the giant Meccano set.

The skyscrapers on either side rose defiantly from the steaming sidewalks, daring you to conquer them. I had chosen the Algonquin Hotel because I had read it was New York's most famous rendezvous for the dazzling theater stars and literary nobs. When my taxi pulled up at the Algonquin, Mother was there to meet me. I hadn't seen her since she'd left Chicago when I went on the road with *Goodnight La-*

dies. After Grand'mère's death she had sold our forever house, which now gave me pangs of insecurity.

While the porter was fussing around the luggage Mother whispered, "Are you sure this is the right hotel? It's quite expensive."

"Yes, I know," I told her, "but I couldn't come to New York for the first time and not stay here."

"I'd better start looking for an apartment right away," she said.

"Fine," I agreed. "And we'll leave here as soon as I've heard a spectacular personality say something witty."

Our room was pretty old and scruffy. But I was told by a genuine New Yorker that was the charm of the Algonquin. It was so homey it reminded the literary intellectuals of their scruffy old rooms at home.

The greatest thrill for us young actresses was laying out our makeup in the dressing rooms of our first New York theater—the Royale, in the heart of theaterland on West Forty-fifth Street. Until then I had always thought theaterland was on Broadway. All those old backstage movies were centered around it, they had written songs about it, and my California friends had wished me luck on it.

I took a hurried walk up Broadway to see if it was still there. And there wasn't a live theater in sight. It had nothing but second-rate movie houses, cheap snack joints, and tatty shops selling unmentionables. It looked even shabbier than Hollywood Boulevard. We were glad our Royale Theater was on West Forty-fifth. And no matter what happened afterward we could all say we had played New York.

At a couple of preview performances we gave before opening I was surprised to hear the audience laughing and clapping, just as they had in Chicago. Perhaps, we told ourselves, New Yorkers weren't so sophisticated after all.

On the opening night we all received greeting telegrams from our families and a few flowers. But no one planned a champagne supper party for us afterward. Even our opening was nothing like those we had seen in the movies. The play was greeted with polite chuckles and muffled applause. I had still to find out there was quite a difference between Ameri-

can and European audiences. In Europe, if they are not enjoying a play, people whistle, stamp, boo, and shout, "It's a
disgrace!" or, "Rubbish!" In America—at least, in those
days—they sat and suffered in deafening silence—until they
decided they'd suffered enough, at which point they would
quietly and decorously walk out.

When the curtain rose on our second act I noticed quite a
few seats were already empty. When it fell at the end of the
last act I noticed almost one third of the seats were empty.
Later on I was to go to opening nights in New York where, at
the end of the play, only one third of the seats were *occupied.* So we were lucky.

We newcomers, undeterred by the cool reception, gathered at Sardi's restaurant around the corner to dine and wait
for the early newspaper reviews. When the first paper arrived
we pounced on it and laid it spread-eagled across the table. It
was Burton Rascoe's review and it said: "Unfunny. Not so
much corny as mildewed." We all ordered another drink. In
paper number two, critic John Chapman's considered opinion was that *School for Brides* was "an ill-conceived hunk of
cheese." It hardly seemed worthwhile opening the third
paper. But we did. "One of those things," wrote Robert Cole-
man, "that's likely to pester Broadway in summer along with
horseflies, and gnats and heatwaves." At least George Jean
Nathan was kind enough to say I was "a piquant little package with numerous points to recommend her."

By the time we'd gone through the rest of the reviews
and our table was littered with such unusable quotes as
"Amateurish," "Puerile," and "For backward audiences,"
this "piquant little package" had a feeling she'd have to get
up early and trudge her "numerous points" around the
agents' offices looking for another piquant job.

But what happened to *School for Brides* after its critical
clobbering? It ran for one year, to solid sellout houses. *Goodnight Ladies* came into town and opened shortly after us. But
New York couldn't take two loads of crap in one season, so it
flopped.

When it became obvious, even to me, that we were in for
a run, Mother and I spent our days scurrying around looking

for somewhere to live. And I was as thrilled to find an apartment in Greenwich Village as I had been to stay at the Algonquin. All my life I had dreamed of living in this reputed Bohemian quarter where painters, poets, and actors frolicked together, communicating with their muses and casting aside conventions.

The apartment in which I was hoping to frolic was on the fourth floor of a nineteenth-century converted terrace house on Washington Square. All it had was one large studio room and a single bedroom with a kitchenette and bath. Its greatest asset was a good-sized roof terrace overlooking the back courtyard gardens.

My first purchases were a garden swing seat for the terrace and flower-filled window boxes. By the time Philip arrived for his first visit, the apartment had been freshly painted and all the new furnishings from Macy's were in their places awaiting him. Our first love nest looked warm, inviting, and romantic. We loved *it*, New York, and each other. Now all we needed was an heir to share it. While we were busy making an heir Mother moved in with her friend, Rella, who lived in the adjacent building.

However, we couldn't carry on creating all the time, I still had a show to do, and after it we frolicked in the Village clubs with the Bohemians. Ernie and Sylvia, who were now living in New York, took us to the Stork Club or the 21. These were places where Ernie was well known and which we couldn't afford. Life was merry and Philip's visits were always honeymoons. After he had returned to his camp this time I was surprised to find I hadn't become pregnant. "How come?" I asked Mother and Rella. "Everyone always warned me if I carried on the way we've been carrying on I would get pregnant. The first time I've thrown precaution to the wind—nothing!"

I figured I'd been conned. Had I not been creating correctly? Mother assured me that was the way I had arrived and Rella suggested I should stop worrying and buy a mink coat instead. Rella was a typical New Yorker who had just returned from a two-year trip around the world. She had a theory that whether it was New York, London, or Paris, having a mink was the American equivalent to having a title. Doors opened quicker, tables appeared faster, full hotels expanded at the sight of it, and young fortune hunters paid for your drinks.

Furthermore, no matter how much you couldn't afford it, it was a good investment because it covered a multitude of old worn clothes and everyone assumed your fake jewelry came from Cartier's.

"So draw out your savings, come along to Maxie's and invest," said Rella.

Trembling, I drew out the notes one by one from my savings bank and Rella marched me up New York's Mink Alley. We weaved our way around hundreds of trundling fur carts hung with skins, coats, and stoles of every description, up three flights of stairs and into Maxie's mink joint.

"Never in a lifetime a bargain like this," said Maxie, when he heard what I was afraid I wanted.

He flung the mink coat on the floor and walked over it to show how healthy it was.

"Because you're a friend of Rella's who buys dresses from Abie whom I love like a brother, this you can have brand new for half the price," he continued, rolling it into a ball to show me how light it was.

Before he had a chance to kick the ball across the room I bought it. This never-in-a-lifetime bargain was possible because it was a small-size model specially made up for a stockbroker's girl friend.

"Crazy woman," shrugged Maxie. "Not after the coat is finished does she walk out on him, but before yet!"

So out I went with my savings on my back, thanks to Rella who bought her dresses from Abie, and Maxie who loved him like a brother, and the crazy woman who walked out on a stockbroker yet.

Before the year was over I had an heir brewing under the mink. Happily I carried the new Truex through the last three months of *School for Brides*, and just as the heir was becoming apparent, Philip was discharged from the army. It was a day of joyful celebration, the end of our honeymoon, and the

201
☆

beginning of married bliss. There were only two complications; we were both out of work, and I had never played the role of a housewife.

While Philip did the rounds of the theatrical agents, job hunting, I put on my new apron-and-oven mitts set and dusted. When I went to the butcher's I couldn't tell a pork chop from a lamb chop from a sirloin of beef. They all looked the same without their furs on. Having selected one of these beasts I usually brought home enough for eight. When Philip refused to eat the same meal twice running I accused him of being uneconomical. It was a miracle he ate it once. The meat was often so underdone it was ready to crawl back into its fur and go back to pasture again. And my cocked-up *au vin* was usually swimming in oil.

By the end of that year Philip had a stomach ulcer, a role in a play about Oliver Wendell Holmes with Louis Calhern, and our heir was kicking up a fuss in my stomach. My first thought was that this poor little citizen-to-be didn't know what it was in for. It was about to have a mother who not only couldn't cook, but hardly knew which end to pin the nappy on. I boned up with the usual books on *Baby and What To Do With It When You've Had It* and Philip soothed my worried brow with the usual, "Don't panic, darling. You'll know what to do. You're a woman. It's intuition."

Why men's intuition was that women's intuition would tell them how to handle a baby was something my intuition wasn't able to understand. So, as I didn't want to be as unprepared for the mother role as I had been for that of the housewife, I soon found myself a how-to-be-a-mother school. It was organized by the Red Cross. Every Tuesday at 2 P.M. all us prospective mothers waddled down Fifth Avenue to our classroom, and when we'd maneuvered ourselves into our straight-backed chairs, a trim little nurse skipped onto the dais carrying a toy baby doll in her arms. With the greatest of ease she showed us how simple it was to strip it, dunk it, oil it, dust it, diaper it, milk it, burp it, and eventually crib it.

Then came the hygiene course. We were all warned that at the whiff of a germ baby might easily disintegrate in our arms; that kissing relatives should be banished; that if mother even *thought* she was catching a cold she should cover her motherly mug with a mask, and at all times everything should be boiled—except the baby.

After six weeks of this we were given inscribed diplomas certifying that we were mothers and we all shuffled home and waited to be one. When I was finally presented with my cuddly, wrinkled, pink bundle known as Christopher, he looked nothing like the doll on the dais. However, the doctors assured me that within three months Christopher would look just like a baby.

That January afternoon Philip breezed into the hospital room. His overcoat was speckled with snow and his deep blue eyes, fringed with mile-long black eyelashes, were alive with exaltation.

"You've done it," he smiled. "It's a miracle. Just born and you can see he's a Truex. The image of Ernie."

"Yeah," I grinned, "wrinkles and everything, all he needs is a moustache. I only hope he turns out to be as handsome and well-mannered as you are."

Philip kissed me gently and stroked my now flattened stomach which he had massaged with oil all through the pregnancy.

"Was it awful?" he asked.

"Unbelievable," I groaned. "Hurt like hell. Whatever we did that caused it, remind me we shouldn't do it again."

"I'll try," he grinned, and he opened a bottle of May wine as the nurse brought in our progeny.

Elated, we counted Christopher's fingers and toes to see if they were all there and they were. Joyfulness reigned at Manhattan's French Hospital on January 14, 1946.

Because of my rigid hygiene instructions, I spent the next three months rushing around in a mask, boiling my fingers, washing down all our visiting relatives, and practically picking Christopher up with tweezers. The result was that Christopher grew, gurgled, and guzzled himself into a beaming, healthy baby while I shriveled into a wrinkled pink bundle, catching every germ in New York.

On one of Mother's baby-sitting nights Philip took me to see the new hit comedy *Born Yesterday* by Garson Kanin. It had only just opened and its smash success was the talk of New York. Its two unknown leads, Judy Holliday and Paul Douglas, had become stars overnight. I remember Philip and I holding hands and laughing until we cried at Kanin's crackling, hilarious dialogue. Set in Washington it was the tale of Harry Brock, a rich, crooked junk dealer who gets his dumb, not-couth broad, Billie Dawn, educated to the point where she is smart enough to walk out on him.

The Billie Dawn role was the finest comedienne's part in the best comedy I'd ever seen. I couldn't get it out of my mind. It was the only role I had ever seen that I really wanted to play. But how? Where? I couldn't stop talking about it on the subway going home. I even told Christopher about it when I was nursing him, but he just burped and fell asleep.

Philip's play had finished its run, so now we both had to go out job hunting, and we took turns looking after Christopher. Our savings were dwindling and I began to feel guilty about the mink. Although it was the beginning of summer I wore it to all the agents' offices to prove to myself what a good investment it was. Naturally the first agent I took it to was the William Morris office which had handled the casting for *Born Yesterday*.

The waiting room was full of girls just as eager and broke as I was, but none of them were wearing mink coats. Maybe they didn't have any—or it could be because the temperature was in the seventies. However, I'm sure I'd never have got in for the interview at all wearing my California trench coat. Agents and producers, being notoriously naïve, believe that no brunette can be a blonde, no blonde can be a brunette, and no mink-coated broad can be played by a girl who only has a trench coat. As it was, the secretary whisked the one with the mink out of the corner and deposited me in front of the Big Man's desk.

"What can we do for you, Miss Donlan?" he asked with the mirthless charm-smile of a busy agent.

"When Mr. Kanin casts the *Born Yesterday* road company I'd like to audition for it."

The smile sagged a little as though I'd already taken up too much of its time.

"You make the twentieth this week," it flashed, "but leave your number with Miss Goodyear and we'll call you when the time comes."

I thanked him and hurried out so he could stop smiling. Miss Goodyear promised she wouldn't forget to call me, but somehow I knew she would. I'd have to think up some other means of entry.

It was late June when Myles Putnam, our stage manager from *Goodnight Ladies,* telephoned to say he had work for me. It was for producer Jules Leventhal, a Broadway showman known as Papa Jules, who had theaters in places like Brooklyn and the Bronx, which were always referred to as the "subway circuit"—probably because they could be reached from Manhattan by subway. Papa Jules, said Myles, was sending *Goodnight Ladies* out on a six weeks' tour on his circuit with comedian Kenny Baker, and I was offered the ingenue lead.

Although it seemed I might spend the rest of my professional life hopping from *Ladies* to *Brides* and back again, it was a lifesaver and I took it. But as I had to do ten shows a week it didn't allow much time for domestic bliss. After three weeks of subways and shows and trying to be a wife and mother, I was dusting Christopher, nursing Philip, and feeding the mice that had suddenly joined us in our apartment. To add to the turmoil I read in *Cue* magazine that Garson Kanin had been holding auditions at the Lyceum Theater for the second company of *Born Yesterday.* So much for Miss Goodyear's promise! I threw on the mink and rushed to the theater hoping to find Garson Kanin, or producer Max Gordon, or anyone who could get me on the audition list. Their offices were empty. The only one around was Kanin's assistant, Hal Gerson.

"Sorry, show's already been cast," he told me and my heart sank. "Everything except understudies."

"When are they being picked?"

"Tomorrow morning."

205
☆

"Please," I begged, "put me in the understudy audition."

"You want to understudy?"

"Anything to get near that marvelous role."

I'm sure it was my overwhelming enthusiasm that not only persuaded him to put me on the list, but to let me have the script and show me the key scenes used in the audition. Normally, unknown actresses are not given a script to study until five minutes before they are due to read it. There are just not enough scripts to go around to the hundreds of girls who apply for these readings. I was lucky.

After the two shows in Brooklyn I stayed up most of the night memorizing the scenes so I could play them freely without burying my nose in the book. I also bleached my hair for the part. It came out a fiery red blonde. Philip was horrified when he woke up to find his brunette wife had turned into a wild, red blonde trollop.

"All that crazy hair," he cried in disbelief, "just for a reading? You must be mad!"

I was mad. Possessed. I put on my tartiest dress under the mink and flew off on a cloud of hope to the Lyceum Theater.

The darkened orchestra seats were spotted with groups of tarted-up blondes like me. There were about fifty of them, all with their agents. I saw the Big Man from the Morris office sitting there with his protegées. The charm-smile was in temporary storage. The curtain was up, disclosing the set of the luxury Washington hotel suite with the elegant staircase used in the play. It looked so empty and drab now with only the rehearsal lights on it. A tarty blonde was sitting on the stage sofa reading one of the scenes with the stage manager, who walked around her in his shirt sleeves reading the other roles from his prompt book. I saw Garson Kanin's fair head bobbing about in the second row. I had last seen it bobbing around Barrymore and all those blackboards on the set of *The Great Man Votes*. Gar, who looked like a kindly New York leprechaun, had been the youngest top-ranking comedy film director before he joined the armed forces, and had guided stars like Carole Lombard and Ginger Rogers through some of their best comedies. And his reputation for being gentle and patient with his fellow workers had preceded him to New York.

One by one I watched the girls read their scenes under the dismal rehearsal light, stop for a word with Kanin and then exit. When the tension became too much I went out to the foyer for a cigarette. At last I heard the stage manager call out, "Yvonne Dolan, please." Over the years I had learned to answer to anything so I took a deep breath, raced up to the stage and bellowed out the scene loud enough to shake Times Square. It didn't come out as I had planned. Much too noisy. The tension of waiting had built up the explosion. Garson Kanin called me to the footlights. I thought it was to say good-bye.

"Now do it again, honey," he said, with an understanding smile, "and this time just relax."

I was so grateful to this kind man for giving me a second chance that I forgot all about me and my silly nerves and played the role I loved with the ease and fun with which it had been written. This time when he called me to the footlights he said, "The job's yours if you want it." Want it? What kind of talk was that! "You'll have to start right away," Kanin was saying, and I faltered suddenly.

"Right away like when?"

"Tomorrow morning."

"You see, I'm on a subway circuit contract. I have to try to get out of it."

He nodded understandingly. "I'm afraid I have to know, honey," he said gently. "We open in New Haven in three weeks."

"Give me a day," I begged him.

"You can have to the end of the week," he smiled, "and good luck."

I raced over to Papa Jules's office on Broadway. He and a group of Damon Runyon characters were huddled around his desk drinking beer and playing cards.

"Papa Jules," I panted, "please, I have a chance of a lifetime to play in *Born Yesterday*. Can you replace me?"

Reluctantly he put down his cards and escorted me into the hall. "What's this in *Born Yesterday?*" he asked.

"Understudy Billie Dawn," I burbled. "Isn't it wonderful?"

"Why so wonderful?" he shrugged. "You give up the lead in my show for an understudy? You're crazy."

"I might get the chance to play it in one of the companies. Judy Holliday got the part when Jean Arthur walked out on it. You never know."

"Thirty years I'm in the business, I know once an understudy always an understudy." He started to go back to his cards and then, as an afterthought, turned and said, "I'm too busy for auditions. Find me a girl today to take over your role this week and you're free."

"Oh, thank you, Papa Jules," I said shaking both his hands. I ran out into the streets of Manhattan on another impossible quest. But as I hadn't time to think how impossible it was, it became possible.

I covered all the actors' haunts; Ralph's Bar, Sardi's, and finally Walgreen's drugstore, searching for the ideal actress who could take over my role quickly. And who should be sitting on a stool at Walgreen's soda fountain but Mary Ellen, the girl who had replaced me when I was fired in Detroit. I knew she could play the part in *Goodnight Ladies* because she'd already understudied it. I threw my arms around her excitedly.

"You looking for a summer job?" I asked.

"I sure am," she sighed.

"You've got one," I announced, and I pulled her off the stool, paid for her soda, and filled her in on the day's events as we bustled up Broadway and back to Papa Jules.

Within the week Mary Ellen was playing my role in the Bronx and I was sitting in the Lyceum watching my favorite playwright direct the road company in my favorite comedy. An experienced New York actress, Eleanor Lynn, was up there rehearsing the most coveted comedienne's role of the decade. She was good, too. My ears pricked up and my carrot hair stood on end every time Garson gave her any direction. Never have I listened and observed with such acute attention. The competition of superb comediennes who had played this role was fierce. What with Jean Arthur, Judy Holliday, and now Eleanor, I had plenty to live up to, if perchance I had to play it, or I would be out on my pricked-up ear.

On the weekend I stayed home in my dressing gown and did all the housewifing and mothering with Christopher in one hand and the play in the other, learning the lines. You'd have thought it was *my* opening night. And because I loved every word the character said, and the family was solidly behind me, I was able to memorize this very long part in three days. It went into my head like magic.

At the theater we understudies didn't get any rehearsals as the stage manager was too busy working with Gar for the opening in New Haven. This worried me. What if Eleanor sprained an ankle or something? There was one hell of a staircase that the character had to negotiate all through the play and it reminded me of the one the dancer had come tumbling down in *Rosalie.* I wanted to be prepared. So I persuaded the other understudies to rehearse with me in the foyer of the ladies' room.

"What's the fuss?" most of them grumbled. "You'll never play it anyway."

Exactly one week later, to that day, I was on the stage of the New Haven Theater playing the beloved Billie Dawn in a state of elated shock, to a packed audience and giving it my all, with my trouser fly open and my zippers undone.

It had all happened so quickly I hadn't had time to scare myself to death over it. Half an hour before the curtain went up I was told that Eleanor had had an attack of evening morning sickness. She was in her bed and I was in her dressing room, trying to get into her stage clothes, which were two sizes too small. The show was so new my understudy clothes hadn't arrived yet. Besides, nobody expects the understudy to go on in the first week.

Eleanor's dresser was cross because she had to send me onto the stage looking such a mess. "Why don't they choose the right-sized understudies?" she grumbled. I was too enraptured playing the role to care. Every time I came off for a quick change she kept nattering in my ear that I didn't know how to put my stockings on like the stars did. Curious lady. On the foot and up the leg like everybody else, I always thought.

After the first act Garson and his celebrated actress wife, Ruth Gordon, came around to the dressing room. They were beaming and almost as excited as I was. Gar grasped my hands.

"You've done it, Yolande," he enthused. "From now on you're a star."

"Gar's right," said Ruth, "it's all there."

I was in a daze and I think I said, "I hope it's all there in acts two and three." Nothing seemed real. Yes, I thought, it must be a daydream. We were all doing and saying things that happen in the movies. Not to real people. Was I a person? Not now. I was Billie Dawn. Everyone loved Billie. How good it felt to be loved. Even if it wasn't you.

They went out front again. The testy dresser poured me into the next unzippable costume and I sailed through the next two acts in a state of euphoria.

Everything about that day had been fortuitous, from Eleanor's sudden attack of the vapors, to Ruth and Gar's last minute decision to catch the new girl in the show instead of the train back to New York. Even Mother had arrived on a surprise visit to find her daughter on the stage. My only regret was that Philip missed it, but it was his turn to baby-sit.

On our next date, in Boston, Eleanor was back playing Billie Dawn and last week's "star" was back understudying and wondering if she would ever play it again. Then, suddenly, everything began popping at once. It started during a rehearsal, when Gar came over to sit next to me. He leaned over and whispered, "How would you like to play Billie Dawn in London?"

I was stunned. It came as a terrific shock. I had never thought of working anywhere but the States. My roots, my family, everything was here. But London? Over there in Europe somewhere? I couldn't come home on weekends. They couldn't visit me. It was crazy. But I couldn't say no. I might never get invited again. The urge to play Billie had become compulsive. I heard myself saying, "Oh, yes, Gar, I'd love to play her anywhere. Just anywhere in the world."

He smiled his leprechaun smile. "Well, I've written to Laurence Olivier about you. He's putting my play on in London and he can't find the right girl. I think you're the right girl."

"Oh, I hope so," I gasped.

The wheels started turning. Garson sent me to a Boston photographer to have pictures done as Billie Dawn, so Mr. Olivier could see what he was getting in case he took it. Within days Olivier cabled back he had taken it; rehearsals were due to start the following week in London, and he wanted "it" flown over as soon as possible.

I was breathless as the bigwigs began unraveling my contract with producer Max Gordon; hiring another understudy; getting a passport; ordering tickets from Boston to New York to London—everything seemed to be happening around me. And then came another shock. Max Gordon's manager traveled up to Boston.

"Why are you going to London?" he asked. "Mr. Gordon would like you to play Billie Dawn in Chicago."

"Chicago? But what about Eleanor?"

"She's pregnant."

"Well, what d'you know."

"Wants to leave before the show gets there. You can take over. What do you say?"

What could I say? I would love to have played it in Chicago. Philip and Christopher could be with me. Philip might find a play there. We had friends in Chicago. But the wheels had already turned. "You'll have to ask Gar," I said. "I'm afraid it's too late."

And when I spoke to Garson he confirmed it. "It's been settled with Max. You're definitely going to London."

"Whatever you say."

"Larry Olivier's a close friend. He accepted you. You agreed. His production has started and your work permit's been granted. We can't let him down now."

"No, of course not," I said, and knew there was no going back.

"You'll love it in London," Gar added cheerfully, "and they'll love you."

What he really meant was they would love Billie Dawn, as much as he and I did. It was strange to think only a few weeks ago I couldn't find my way in even to do a reading for her. And now people were telling me to play her everywhere. Somehow I felt she belonged to me now. I was Billie, and Garson's *Born Yesterday* had become part of the family.

He gave me photographs of the play to take to Laurence Olivier, also a typical gangster suit to fly over with me for the male star, Hartley Power, to wear in the show. It seems they didn't make gangster suits in London. At least, not American ones.

When I arrived home in New York with the news that I was definitely leaving for London at the end of the week, the boat started rocking. I was in fairyland, but Philip wasn't. He had uneasy worries of it breaking up the family.

"Don't be such a sourpuss," I said, trying to convince both him and me, "as soon as the play's a success in London I can afford to send for Mother and Christopher. She'll look after him while I'm doing the show, you'll be free from money worries and find a play, and I'll be back in six months with bags of dough."

"It sounds great," he agreed gloomily, "but it feels awful." It was a difficult position for any man to accept. Here he was, an experienced actor, out of work, and his newcomer wife was off to star in a London production. But at least it would keep us solvent for a while. "It's just that I hate to see you go away like this for so long," he added.

"How long in a lifetime is six months? Before you've had time to grow herbs on the terrace I'll be back with an all-walking, all-talking Christopher, savings in our bank, a hit role in my repertoire, and together we'll conquer New York."

It seemed so simple. And at the time I really believed that's how it would be. Philip didn't say much after that, but his glum silence penetrated even my euphoric enthusiasm.

Mother said, "You're so lucky, Yolande, to be able to take this marvelous opportunity and not have to worry about Christopher. I wish I'd had someone to look after you."

Ernie and Sylvia took us out to dinner and, although they

well understood the thrill of playing your first starring role in a first-class play, Ernie kept saying, "I know how you feel, Yo, but you're taking a risk with your marriage."

"No, Ernie," I pleaded. "Please. It's done. It's done." I pulled the shutters down. I didn't want to listen to anyone.

The morning I was due to fly, a freak snowstorm hit New York. I was frightened of flying, even without snowstorms. I had never been in a plane before and in those days, with stop-downs in Gander and Ireland, it was about a twenty-hour journey to London. Slightly less than it had taken Lindbergh. And now, nearly twenty years later, in November 1946, I knew exactly how he must have felt.

I loaded myself up with motion-sickness pills and several steadying brandies—and the flight was canceled. Every morning I got up, ready to go, and at the last minute I was always taken off the flight. It was right after the war when only priority business travelers were being given flights to Europe. And I wasn't priority enough. Laurence Olivier and Vivien Leigh kept going to London airport to meet the flights I wasn't on and cabling; WHERE IS SHE? The play was already in rehearsal and opening in Glasgow in two weeks.

With each new delay Philip was looking glummer but resigned. The atmosphere in our honeymoon apartment was getting prickly. I was already feeling the loss of the warmth of Christopher's hugs. The warmth of Philip's hugs had gone when I signed the British contract. What the hell was I doing anyway?

And suddenly the day came when I was up in the plane, in the air, over the clouds with all the problems hidden down there somewhere where I couldn't see them. There was only one worry now—how does this huge metal contraption stay up here, and can it last until London without falling down? I ordered a couple of dozen whiskies because they were free. I might as well go falling down drunk, I thought. By the third drink I steered my thoughts to pleasanter things. Like Laurence Olivier. Any moment now I was going to be working with the broodingly romantic Heathcliffe of *Wuthering Heights*. I conjured up the picture I remembered of him

213
☆

standing on the moors with the mist swirling around him.

Suddenly I realized it was swirling around me. Only it wasn't mist, it was smoke, and it was billowing up the aisle of the cabin. The other passengers began to cough and I began mumbling the last act of contrition prayer and getting it all mixed up in my head with Billie Dawn's dialogue. The captain spoke to us through the loudspeaker. He told us it was nothing to worry about. . . . Just a little fire. . . . We might have to return to New York. And he wished us a pleasant journey.

The fire was in the galley where our meals were being prepared. The stewards and stewardesses did a dignified trot up the aisle with fire extinguishers, pretending nothing was happening. Fortunately the flames were quelled and the event broke the ice among the passengers. We even began talking to each other. I shared a dining table with two American businessmen called Mike and Bill. In those days it was like dining on a train; we had table linens, china dinnerware, and real wine glasses for our champagne. While we were sipping our bubbles I asked if they were going to work in London.

"God forbid," said Mike, and Bill added, "I only hope we haven't missed our connection to Paris. I'd hate to have to spend even one night in London!"

I was surprised. I had thought it was a lively man's town with elegant lords in top hats and capes, luxurious supper clubs, the Cafe Royal, succulent roast beef and Yorkshire pudding, brightly lit theaters, sparkling, gay Piccadilly, and grand hotels with the finest service. . . . That was my London.

"Why God forbid?" I asked, frowning. "I'm going to work there for six months maybe."

"Oh, you poor kid," they sympathized, and between them they explained what had happened to London since Oscar Wilde had died. It was, they said, in almost as bad a state as during the Blitz. Because of electricity cuts it was freezing cold everywhere; the streets had so few lights you had to carry a flashlight; theater signs were out; Piccadilly

Circus unlit; the restaurant meals were inedible, and the nights dismal. There was nothing in the shops. Food and clothes strictly rationed and the weather unbearable.

Never mind, I told myself, Garson said I would love London and I had the play and my mink to keep me warm.

The sun was shining when the plane touched down. I remember it well because I didn't see it again for three months.

The Oliviers had stopped meeting planes because they both had matinees to do. So Mr. Olivier sent Anthony Bushell, a handsome blond British actor who hated acting and had become Laurence Olivier's company manager.

On the drive to London, Tony Bushell, who spoke like the Scarlet Pimpernel, brought me up to date on the Olivier productions. Larry, he said, was playing *King Lear* at the Old Vic and Vivien Leigh was starring in Thornton Wilder's *The Skin of Our Teeth* at the Piccadilly.

I kept my nose glued to the car window, capturing my first glimpse of London. We passed rows of disheveled semi-detached houses with their peeling paint and their trim, cared-for, boxed-in gardens, many of which still had their tin air-raid shelters. In the gaps between them, the shells of bombed out houses exposed their once private, varicolored rooms. I saw the huge flat squares of bombsites covered with rubble and bits of charred furniture, women wearing headscarves and carrying baskets, standing in lines outside the shops to collect their rations.

When we reached Mayfair the car turned into Carlos Place and pulled up in front of the Connaught Hotel, where Tony had booked a single room for me. The hotel was small, sedate, and silent. I was soon to find out that the only sound I was likely to hear at the Connaught was the kerplop of aristocratic monocles dropping as I wandered in my dressing gown, searching for the elusive, exclusive bathroom. But make no mistake, this hotel was no dump. When I told Tony the only hotel I'd heard of was the Savoy and I would like to have stayed there, he shuddered in horror.

"Dear girl," he said, "there's no comparison. The Connaught is where all the visiting nobility stays."

I wondered how long I was going to last there with my tarty, carrot hairdo. As it happened I was almost dispossessed after I had signed the noble register. I had suddenly remembered Garson's photographs and the gangster outfit in my suitcase, which I was supposed to hand over immediately. My case was so full of *Born Yesterday* scripts and American props there was hardly any room for personal clothes. They had been sent ahead by ship.

"Tony," I said, "I have some play things from New York for you. Would you come up with me and collect them?"

"Of course."

As we moved toward the elevator the graying receptionist called out in a loud, slightly tremulous whisper, "I'm sorry, madam, you cannot have a gentleman in your room."

I turned back to the immaculately groomed man, who looked not unlike Edward Everett Horton.

"But I just want to give him something," I pleaded.

"I'm sure you do, madam," he said. "However, those are the rules."

"It'll only take five minutes."

"I'm sorry but it's not allowed."

"But I hardly know him."

His gray eyebrows shot up. "Really, madam. . . ."

"I mean, he just picked me up at the airport."

The eyebrows came down again. "I don't doubt it, madam, but *not* at the Connaught."

It seemed the more I tried to explain the less he understood. The Connaught receptionist won. I had yet to discover the British always win in the end.

When I first met Laurence Olivier I didn't recognize him. He had long white hair and a longer beard. In fact I sat with him in his Old Vic dressing room for fifteen minutes waiting for him to come in. He had just finished the matinee performance of *King Lear* and until that moment I had only seen him looking beautiful on the screen as Heathcliffe and Henry V and on the New York stage as Oedi-pretty-puss Rex. You can imagine the shock of trying to recognize gorgeous Mr. Olivier hidden under the loony Lear's crinkled-up spook's garb. But once I got close enough I saw those beautiful steely eyes peeping through all that foliage. They had a dominant look of authority. In fact they were so dominant I started calling him sir long before he was knighted.

King Lear offered me a gin-and-orange, apologizing that it was the only drink he had. I had never before had orange squash in my drink and concluded it was an English kink. He explained that booze was still difficult to get and very expensive. He was so right; in those barely post-rationing days it was almost as expensive as it is now.

Then came the first hurdle. King Lear picked up a copy of *Variety* that was lying on the dressing room table and said, "I've just read this notice about you, Miss Donlan. It says you gave a creditable performance."

I gulped down my gin and the too-sweet orange. I knew that in Mr. Olivier's circles "creditable" just wasn't good enough. Damn it, I thought, I hadn't seen the little *Variety* spy's review. And what was he doing snooping around New Haven when I had to go on at half an hour's notice? Thanks to him, here was I having to prove it again to Laurence Olivier or get the sack.

"You see, Mr. Olivier," I choked out, "I hadn't rehearsed then and my flys and zippers kept opening because they weren't mine. But I'm sure the two weeks' rehearsal with you will make a great improvement."

The beard opened and a smile came through. "Yes, of course. And Vivien has selected some lovely clothes for you." He turned to his dresser, who was a lady, and asked her to bring Roger Furse in. "Roger has designed a magnificent set," he explained as a tall, dark-haired man with a black beard appeared. He looked like the laughing cavalier. And he was about to become one of my jolly playmates.

After Mr. Olivier had introduced us, he said, "Roger will be taking you for your costume fittings tomorrow after rehearsals."

"And I've booked a table at the Ivy tonight," smiled Roger, "if you'd care to dine there with Tony Bushell and me."

"It's the British Sardi's," explained Mr. Olivier.

"Oh, yes," I gasped, "that would be terrific." I was delighted I didn't have to dine alone in the hotel on my first night in London.

In contrast to the dark, bleak streets outside, the Ivy was brightly lit and bristling with activity. Most of the Who in the *Who's Who* of the British theater was there. Only I didn't know which was who except for my two escorts. I cased the French menu searching for my dreamed-of English roast beef and Yorkshire pudding. It wasn't there. Because of rationing, apologized Tony. So instead I ordered my first jugged hare. It tasted like my cocked-up *au vin.*

My escorts ordered plenty of wine, chatted and sparkled like perfect British hosts, and although until then I thought I spoke English, I only understood a third of what they said. It was the difference in terminology more than the accent that created the language barrier. In the beginning I found I could only understand one Englishman at a time. During the meal they pointed out the stage celebrities around us.

"That's Ivor Novello," said Roger, pointing to the handsome, middle-aged gentleman at the next table who had smiled so charmingly at me when my handbag almost knocked his wine into his lap as I sat down. "He's our foremost musical star. Writes and directs all his own shows."

"They're a bit sentimental," added Tony softly, "but the public adore him. Especially the ladies."

They didn't have to tell me who was scintillating at the table on our right. It was the inimitable Beatrice Lillie wearing one of her characteristic beany skull caps. I'd seen Bea perform in New York. Tony, who seemed to know more about everybody than anybody, told me her escort was the heir to a wealthy toilet-flush family. Later, the heir also turned out to be one of the understudies in *Born Yesterday.*

Directly opposite us was an animated, vivacious blonde lady whose gestures were as broad as her smile. I knew she must be somebody, even before she waved at us.

"Cicely Courtneidge," said Tony as they waved back. "One of our most popular comedy stars. In fact Hartley Power, who plays your Harry Brock, has just left her show to play opposite you."

"You mean a *British* actor is playing Harry Brock?" I asked with shock. The racketeer's role was so typically American.

"No, no," laughed Roger. "Hartley's American. He came over in a play twenty years ago and he's still here."

Twenty years! My God, I thought, it's a long time to stay away from home. I was blissfully unaware that I was destined to do the same.

That night I slept in my mink because it was so cold and fuel was rationed. And in the morning I ordered orange juice and got prunes because oranges were rationed.

I faced the first day's rehearsal with both excitement and apprehension. I felt a tremendous responsibility for Garson's hit play, and also the need to live up to his recommendation to Laurence Olivier.

Mr. Olivier introduced me to the cast who were huddled in groups around the large, freezing rehearsal hall in a drafty boys' club in Drury Lane. We all had our overcoats on, and kept them on. Hartley Power, who played the tough racketeer lead, turned out to be older and not as physically attractive as Paul Douglas, the original one. But he certainly talked like a genuine American racketeer and he was tough. Very. And a very experienced actor.

I was delighted to meet Bessie Love, who was playing the senator's wife. I remembered seeing her when she was a Hollywood movie star in *Broadway Melody*. Daddy Donlan had been a fan of hers. Told me she was great. She smiled warmly when I clasped her hand, and I thought, wouldn't my old man be surprised to see me acting in a real play with his favorite, Bessie Love.

My lover-tutor in the play was a tall, lanky Canadian boy, Bill Kemp, who had only been in one other show. But he played the piano beautifully; not in the play, though. After the show.

And then there was another Canadian, Stanley Maxted, who had been a much-decorated war correspondent. He had parachuted into Arnhem in the middle of battle to broadcast under fire. Stanley was playing his very first role, as a racketeer's crooked lawyer, and had a fight scene with Hartley which was normally faked. However, Stanley's inexperience worried Hartley who frequently let off steam by giving him an unfaked sock in the puss. Stanley wasn't too happy about this and after he'd played it for a while he said, "The battle in the theater is almost as rough as the battle was in Arnhem."

Michael Balfour, who played Harry Brock's bodyguard, was the only British actor who fooled all of us into thinking he was a genuine American. He had lied to get the role just as I had done with the French maid. So poor Michael had to keep up his American accent off stage as well as on. He was so good at it he even convinced me.

Although the cast had been rehearsing for a week, the atmosphere was still tense. Everyone, including the stage management, seemed to be in awe of Laurence Olivier; except Hartley Power. They spoke in hushed whispers whenever Olivier was around, like children in front of the headmaster. I would have been more nervous if I hadn't been so thoroughly familiar with the play. As it turned out I became less familiar with it as the day progressed.

The set was chalked out on the floor, and every single

piece of furniture was in an entirely different place from the American production. Furthermore, each of the moves Mr. Olivier had blocked out was also new. As a result I would start to sit down on what had always been a couch and the headmaster would say, "No, Yolande, you're sitting on the cocktail cabinet; the sofa is right of center."

At one point I had to be removed from inside the fireplace, where I went to sign letters, and led back to the desk which was now up on the entrance platform. I soon realized the only fixture that had remained in its original place was the staircase, and I hovered around it like an old friend. But I was determined to master this completely new and original production and by the end of the week I had been weaned off the old furniture positions and was no longer making exits through the sixteenth-story windows. I had also thrown caution to the wind, taken a deep breath, and called my headmaster Larry.

My next shock was the fountain. It was chalked out on the rehearsal room floor—a large circle with the word "Fountain" in it. There hadn't been one in the American production but as the decor was going to be different in London I didn't pay much attention to it. Until one night Roger Furse invited me to his home for dinner and showed me the model of his set. And there it was—the fountain.

"And it's practical," he said proudly. "Splashes all through the first act."

I remember saying, aghast, "But you can't do that!"

"Why not?"

When I explained to Roger and Tony Bushell that they should warn Olivier that a distracting fountain could kill the whole of act one, they fell about laughing.

"I think *you* better tell him," said Roger.

I had another worrisome night, and the following morning I cornered my boss before the others arrived. Larry listened most attentively.

"Well, we don't want to kill the *whole* of the first act, do we?" he said gravely. I wasn't sure whether he was being serious or trying to befool me, until a ghost of a smile flicked the corners of his mouth.

223
☆

The fountain stayed, but he did see that it only splashed for the opening effect. When I look back now I am more than a little astounded that anyone could get as obsessionally intent as I did about what, after all, was somebody else's play. Except that to me it was *my* play. And it *had* to be good, and I had to pass my own test.

Larry Olivier listened patiently to all my questing doubts. He was always completely charming, completely dedicated, and completely inscrutable. My insecure tummy rumbles got longer and louder. Apart from the new set, new moves, and new lines, which had been changed for British consumption, the rehearsals seemed to be so much more solemn than the American ones. I was beginning to doubt that anyone would laugh at anything when the play opened. Olivier's face was as long as our pauses as we struggled through rehearsals.

Mind you, it *was* his early sortie into theatrical management and it could be he was worried at the thought of losing all his dough on this foolproof comedy because he had cast it with fools like us who were not foolproof.

In the second act I had a crying scene in which Hartley Power had to slap me around. As he hadn't quite sorted out his technical business of hitting me, he kept going back over it slowly. So instead of crying each time, I just said, "Sob, sob, sob," figuring that as soon as we ran the play right through, the emotions would look after themselves. That's when Olivier stopped the rehearsal.

"Yolande, I don't like sob-sob-sob," he said. "From now on would you please do the scene as you're going to play it?"

"Okay," I said. "I just felt a bit of a nit making real crying while we're still flummoxing around."

"Never be afraid of making a fool of yourself," said Laurence Olivier. "I do it constantly. Even at home," he added and explained how his staff were quite used to him screaming and groaning away in his study and didn't bother to call the police.

One day during the rehearsals Larry told me he had organized seats for me to see Vivien in *The Skin of Our*

Teeth and that afterward they would like me to join them at their Chelsea home for a little supper party.

"Oh, yes please!" I accepted delightedly. I couldn't wait to dine with the actress who had finally landed Scarlett O'Hara. Except that I had every woman's problem—nothing to wear. But this time it was real. My trunkful of clothes, which had gone ahead of me by boat, was now held up by a dock strike. Aside from my slacks and skirts I had only one dress with me. It was the tarty audition one I had brought to impress Olivier that I was right for the role. Now I had to wear it everywhere. It was like going out dressed as a clown, and when it appeared on Park Lane the prostitutes kept snapping at me to get off their beat. I found I was also taboo in their other haunts, Curzon Street, and Shepherd's Market.

There was no question of buying another dress; I had already used up the clothes coupons, which Tony had given me, on a warm dressing gown for the icy hotel corridors. I wore my mink over the tart's dress at Vivien's play. It was just as well. None of the theaters was heated and the audiences all wore their overcoats, with hot water bottles under them and blankets wrapped around their feet. Such was the ardor of the London theatergoers in November 1946.

Vivien was ravishing in the play and as it was an American play and they all had American accents I could understand them for a change. I was glad Vivien was up there busily playing Sabrina or she might have been playing Billie Dawn. There had been rumors. She said Garson had coached her in her American accent.

Vivien and Larry's little supper party was nothing like I expected it to be. Neither was their Chelsea home. Unlike the stars' homes, Durham Cottage was a honeymooner's dream cottage. Small, delicately furnished with exquisite antiques, its cozy coal fires crackled their warm welcome as Vivien greeted Roger and me. She wore a minimum of makeup and a simple, beautifully cut black Balmain gown with regal bearing. Standing there in my tart's dress I felt like Sadie Thompson at the queen's garden party. Vivien, the perfect lady hostess, didn't blink an eye when she took me around to introduce me to her "little supper party" guests.

They were a collection of the kings and queens of theatrical history. Noël Coward, Judith Anderson, and Mary Martin to start with. I was surprised to see Noël Coward there. I had heard so much about him, seen all his plays, and he was so famous I'd always thought he must be dead. But there he was in his dinner jacket, standing by the fireplace, very much alive, sipping his champagne and punctuating his staccato speech with a flick of his cigarette holder.

Judith Anderson scared the hell out of me. I couldn't separate her from her screen performance as the evil Mrs. Danvers in Olivier's film *Rebecca*. She was also a highly esteemed classical actress whom I had recently seen on the New York stage playing Medea. This formidable Miss Anderson stopped me on her way to the buffet.

"I saw the show in New York," she said. "You're a lucky girl playing that marvelous part."

"Yes, I know I am," I answered. "But the production is so very different here. I'm confused, and not sure whether it will work."

"Nonsense," she laughed, "with Larry directing it's bound to be a success. The rest is up to you." And she swept away.

Had I put my foot in it? I wondered. They were all experienced stars on the same level in their profession. I was the new interloper. I suddenly felt homesick and wished I was in Chicago where everything was familiar, including the play. I took my dish of delicious food, which I could only pick at, and plunked down on the couch next to Mary Martin and her husband. At least they were familiar and we spoke the same language. Mary told me she had come over to star in the new Noël Coward musical *Pacific 1860*.

"Have you started?" I asked.

"Started worrying? Yes," she laughed. "I'm already wondering why I'm over here."

Her husband said, "It's just that all you American girls are too adventuresome."

I was comforted to hear that even a star of Mary Martin's

stature was having the doubting screaming-jeebies. I didn't tell her I felt that way too. Instead I said, "But, Mary, with your fantastic talent and name, combined with Noël Coward's, surely you can't miss."

"Oh, yes we can," sighed the experienced star. "You just never know." And she left to replenish her dish. At least she could still eat.

Noël Coward who, contrary to his razor-edged image, was kind to children, animals, and abandoned tarts, came over and sat next to Sadie Thompson.

"And how are you liking London?" he asked.

"I don't know," I said. "I haven't seen it yet. I think I should have done the play in Chicago."

"Chicago?" he clipped with horror. "Terrible place. They hated me in Chicago."

"You mean you played there?"

"Many times. And they never stopped hating me."

"I don't believe it," I laughed.

"My dear, we must all forget Chicago and rise above it. There is nothing like a London first night." He paused to light my thirty-fifth cigarette with his slim gold lighter. "I'm sure you'll be utterly enchanting," he continued, smiling his Mandarian smile and gently patting my hand. "Especially when you know I have a personal interest in Larry's play."

Oh dear, I thought, another genius to whom I am responsible. The gaggle of geniuses was becoming impressively oppressive. I felt a collection of champagne bubbles mustering together in my throat ready for action, a long loud burp. No, I told myself, one mustn't burp at the immaculate Mr. Coward in his dinner jacket. I excused myself, swallowed the bubbles and dashed upstairs to collect my mink from Vivien's dainty, Lady Hamilton bedroom. It was time for Cinderella Sadie to return to the monocled Connaught.

While I was thanking Vivien and Larry for having me at their party, Vivien said, "Would you like to come with us to Notley Abbey this weekend?"

I thought they were inviting me to go to church with them, and I said, "Of course, I'd love to." At least I knew all about churches, they were my old stomping ground. I found out later from Tony that Notley Abbey was their country home and I was to take a case for the weekend.

By the end of that week our rehearsals seemed to be gliding along smoothly and for the first time I sat back and really relaxed as Tony and Larry drove me through the English countryside, pointing out the beauty of every tree, bush and blade of grass with the inherent pride of all Britishers for their country. And when we arrived at Notley Abbey it was perched on a gently rolling hill and reminded me of a magnificent setting from *Henry V*, or was it *Wuthering Heights?* With infinite care they had converted this antiquated home for monks into a country abode fit for the royal family of the English theater. It even had a secret room where priests had hidden during the religious wars.

Vivien met us in the austere, high-ceilinged entrance hall. She was wearing purple Pucci slacks with a cashmere cardigan over her blue silk shirt. There was an instant scurrying of butlers and maids around our cases while she kissed everyone hello. I found the British were very affectionate, they had a habit of kissing everyone, especially if they didn't like them. One of the maids nipped upstairs with my suitcase and when I followed her up a few minutes later, she had already unpacked it. And there, hanging in the wardrobe all by itself, was that damn tart's dress.

The room was newly old and chintzy. It overlooked the gardens and had a live coal fire already burning in the fireplace. The wardrobe deserved at least a couple of Diors and a Balenciaga.

The other weekend guests were actor George Relph and his wife, the beautiful Mercia Swinburne, and Tony Bushell's fiancée, Annie. We had an elaborate tea in the large, elegant, m'lords-ladies-and-gentlemen drawing room and I wondered how I was ever going to get through the evening meal. My American stomach had great difficulty adjusting to the English habit of nibbling five times a day.

When the guests were sent upstairs to bathe and change for dinner I had another problem, a bathing dilemma. It seemed I was always taking my bath at the wrong time that weekend. I had been accustomed to bathing in the morning, and unless I had fallen into a coal bin or had been invited to the President's inaugural ball, that was the end of my major ablutions for the day. Nevertheless, in Notley, at around six in the evening an exuberant maid in a crisply starched apron arrived in my bedroom carrying a luxurious towel and hustled me down the Abbey corridor to the bath she had drawn. When I protested that I had already bathed and didn't want to repeat the experience in Britain's notoriously cold bathrooms, she explained that it was the custom of the landed gentry to always bathe in the evening before changing for dinner, and I succumbed.

Meticulously scrubbed and disinfected I came down to dinner in my tart's dress.

The dining room reminded me of a setting from *Citizen Kane*, with Larry at the head of a very long dining table and Vivien far away at the other end. I was seated on Larry's right. It was a very honorable seat and I knew I had to watch my knives and forks. In spite of rationing, Vivien's cook was able to produce a Cordon Bleu feast from the fruits of the Oliviers' farmland.

The chit-chat about the theater, war incidents and local politics bubbled gaily back and forth across the table. They all seemed upset that Winston Churchill had not been re-elected after the war. I asked why not?

Vivien elongated her swan's neck and widened her violet eyes. "I can never understand it," she blinked. "Never. Churchill was a brilliant leader. It was a dreadful shock. Frightful. Wasn't it, Larry?"

Larry was masticating his farm's produce and couldn't quite hear her from the goal post at his end, so he played safe and said, "Yes, Vivien."

Tony Bushell placed his Georgian silver knife resolutely on his flowered Capo di Monte dinner plate and leaned between the Battersea enamel candelabra, across the Brussels lace tablecloth toward me.

"Churchill was too successful," he explained, "and we British cannot tolerate success."

With every glass of wine the party grew merrier. And

then I did a silly thing. After my second glass of Dows' 1927 vintage port I passed the decanter to George Relph on my right. With a mischievous smile Larry deftly nipped it out of my hand and explained that port was always passed to the left. Oh dear, I thought, there were so many moves to learn, both on and off stage. My family hadn't worried about left or right, it just went straight down the gullet.

On Sunday Larry showed me around his estate with the love and enthusiasm of a gentleman farmer who had milked his first cow. In borrowed gumboots I trudged along the muddy road behind Henry V like an obedient lady-in-waiting. The mist was falling gently on the meadow. At least, he said it was mist; to a California girl it felt like rain. We came to a halt on the small humpback bridge where we basked in Larry's very own view of a real-life Constable painting. While the mist trickled down my nose I listened to Henry V's tale of the battles leading up to his conquest of Notley Abbey. He shuddered as he recalled the events.

"After Vivien's marvelous success in *Scarlett*," he said, "we both had an incredible streak of luck in Hollywood, and we put all our earnings into a new production of *Romeo and Juliet* in New York. My God, it was a disaster!"

"Really?" I puzzled. "I couldn't have thought of a safer bet." I meant it. At that period Vivien and Larry were not only two of the most famous super stars, but also the most publicized super lovers.

Larry shook his head. "We lost every penny," he sighed. "Your New York critics gave us absolute hell. When we came home to England we were cleaned out."

"With stars like you," I said, "no one knows about the down bits."

On our trek back to Henry V's castle he told me how much he relished working at the Old Vic, playing those classic roles.

"In spite of the lousy wages," he said giving me a pointed glance. This was because after one of the rehearsals I had asked him for a raise in salary, from £60 a week to £100, as living was so expensive in war-ravaged London.

"But a hundred is all I earn at the Old Vic," he said, horrified at my effrontery.

And I'd been horrified, too, that such an international star should earn so little. "You must have a lousy agent," I told him at the time. I didn't realize then that keeping the wages down was the only way the classics could survive in the theater.

However, *Born Yesterday* wasn't considered a classic and he eventually gave me a compromise salary of £80 per week—which was not much more than I had been earning as an understudy in the States. There was one certainty, the Oliviers couldn't have bought Notley Abbey with their theater earnings. Larry told me they had worked day and night on films, theater, radio, recordings, everything, until they had recouped their losses and his final thrill had been directing *Henry V.*

"I love directing films," he enthused. "It's the most stimulating activity of all." He took a deep breath of his Buckinghamshire mist and led me toward his Ancient Monument. "It may sound unbelievable," he said, "but I now have everything I have ever wanted."

Even that weekend he was preparing for his next directorial stint, *Hamlet,* in which he was to star as the droopy Dane.

After lunch, while we all sat around the fireplace reading the Sunday papers and Vivien did the *Times* crossword puzzle, Larry sat at his desk on the far side of the room working out camera angles on his model of the *Hamlet* set. The only dialogue I can recall from that afternoon was when Larry said, "Vivien, will you fix me a drink?" and Vivien, whose beautiful nose was still buried in the crossword, replied, "Get it yourself."

It sounded just like home.

The last week of rehearsal whizzed by with photo calls and last-minute costume fittings and almost before I knew it I was on the train to Glasgow, where we were to open our pre-London tour. Pre-London, that is, with two provisos. Firstly, that the play was a success and secondly that we could find a free West End theater to come back to.

Larry, Roger, Tony, and I had sleepers all in a row and before turning in we gathered in Roger's for a drink and a chat. With four of us in the tiny compartment there was so little room that Larry squatted on the floor in the corner. With a drink in his hand and a smile on his face he joked, laughed, and told wry stories, making fun of himself. It was the first time he had really seemed to relax. This was not at all the same Mr. Olivier of the somber countenance and piercing eyes who could suddenly encircle himself in an unapproachable aura. This was laughing Larry, the happy clown. Even Notley hadn't been like this.

I remember Roger and Tony teasing him about one very good notice that Donald Wolfit had received for his playing of King Lear. It had said Wolfit's Lear was better than Olivier's. Laughing Larry didn't give a hoot, especially when I asked, "Who's Donald Wolfit?" He giggled merrily into his Scotch while the rest of them explained to the new girl who Donald Wolfit was. Many years later I was to find out for myself when I played opposite Sir Donald. How I longed for Sir Laurence!

As a matter of fact, one evening during our rehearsal period Larry invited me to see his King Lear at the Old Vic. But I really couldn't have told you whose King Lear he was better than or worse than, because Olivier's Lear was the only one I'd ever seen. I was only puzzled that a very attractive man like him, loaded with sex appeal, wanted to camouflage himself as a nutty old King—and why wasn't he still playing Romeo?

For the next two days before the opening Mr. Olivier put on his inscrutable mask again and was back in business. He introduced me to the Glasgow press and handled them with the grace to which he was accustomed. Until I met the press I was worried the Scots only spoke Scottish and wouldn't understand the play, particularly as it was all in New York-Bronx-American. Mind you, I found the Scots even more difficult to understand than the English had been, even though Olivier kept telling me they were speaking English. But he understood them, and they were only interested in talking to him anyway. Me, too. But his fence was up again.

On the slightly fraught dress rehearsal day I lunched somewhere posh with Mr. Olivier, his entourage, and some of the press. I remember slurping down some Mulligatawny soup and the fish course and then starting to rise to go back to my hotel to shake in peace. I thought lunch was over. But Olivier gently pulled me back down into my seat whispering that the main course hadn't yet been served. So I sat and struggled through some sort of game-grouse something and couldn't even escape into my wine glass for fear of muzzing up my lines later.

At the dress rehearsal I was stunned to see the Washington hotel suite for the first time. It looked nothing like any American hotel suite I had seen. Instead of modern stream-lined furnishings it had ornate antique-style sofas and chairs. There was gilt everywhere, and that mad fountain was splashing away at the top of the stairs. However, it stopped splashing on cue and we maneuvered ourselves around the unfamiliar furniture and became acquainted with our props.

Now all we needed was an audience.

On the following night we got one. Before the curtain went up, while I was on the stage checking that my playing cards, drinks, books, and other props were all in their right places, I heard the growing murmuring of the customers as they took their seats. I wondered whether they would laugh in the same places as the Americans; or indeed at all. But somehow I wasn't nervous. Perhaps because I had such confidence in the play; I don't know. It was the first and last time I wasn't scared stiff before an opening.

When the curtain rose, the crazy set received a welcoming laugh and applause. But for the next twenty minutes there was almost no further reaction to Garson Kanin's *Born Yesterday*.

Then, suddenly, they began to warm up and laugh and enjoy themselves. By the second act they were rolling around in their seats. It was great to hear them react to the play with the same enthusiasm as people had in the States. The applause at the end was loud and strong. I was thrilled. So was

Larry. He came rushing back to my dressing room and gave me a great bear hug. There were tears of relief in his eyes.

"But you're so professional," he kept repeating. "Sooo professional. And your timing is quite incredible."

Across my mind flashed all those years of watching and listening to Daddy, Lloyd, Hope and Gallagher. Yes, they had finally paid off. I was pleased that Olivier's innovations had worked out, and he was pleased I hadn't messed them up.

It looked to us as if there was a chance for this strangely American play to transfer to London. All we needed now was a theater. Larry seemed very elated.

"Jack Buchanan owns the Garrick Theatre," he said. "He saw the show tonight and I'm bringing him back to meet you. You must be a good girl and charm the Garrick out of him." He started to dash out the door and suddenly turned back. "You were wearing the Buchanan tartan in the second act," he added. "Jack mentioned it. That was a stroke of good luck!" He hurried off to visit Hartley and the rest of the cast.

I found it puzzling that a man of Laurence Olivier's standing should have trouble finding a London theater. I didn't realize that it was mainly because he hadn't any names in the cast and it was a foreign play. That evening I gave Mr. Jack Buchanan my devoted attention. It wasn't difficult as he was an attractive, winning gentleman.

The Glasgow press gave it rave notices: "The smartest thing Broadway has exported." "Twenty minutes and she was a star." "Sharp, witty, and sophisticated, a hit." Even the crazy set was a smash: "Roger Furse has provided one of the most oppulent settings seen for a long time." It looked like we'd made it.

The only thing to mar our pleasure in the Glasgow open-ing were two letters I received from home. I gathered from Philip he was having mother-in-law trouble and I gathered from Mother she was having son-in-law trouble. There wasn't much I could do about it three thousand miles away. So in-stead of waiting until after the London opening to send for Mother and Chris, I organized tickets on the *Queen Eliza-*

beth for them to join me in Cardiff. They would be with me for Christmas and the last date of the tour.

The second night in Glasgow it was standing room only, and all us thespians, elated with our scintillating reviews, collected onstage prepared for our second performance. And just as the iron safety curtain was about to go up, it wouldn't go up. It stayed solidly and safely down to the floor and not a soul in Glasgow could move it. After a frantic forty-five-minute struggle with the stubborn curtain there was only one thing to do, and they did it—the audience and the actors were sent home.

After Glasgow the sweet smile of success was slowly wiped off our faces. With each new city the play was received with diminishing enthusiasm. On top of which my tour of the provinces was a series of frozen hotels, theaters, trains, and police stations. No, I wasn't arrested, but as an alien I had to report to the police in each new town. I guess in case I pinched something, if I could find anything.

Through the rain and fog and mist all these towns looked the same to me. After the show every restaurant, pub, or cafe was firmly shut and there was nowhere to go but back to the gray hotel. If I was lucky, a table would be kept for me in the corner of the empty dining room with one dismal light and a soup-stained waiter who would point out that everything on the menu was off it. Sometimes I would be joined by Bill Kemp, Stanley Maxted and his wife, Ronnie, and between us we'd manage to pilfer some edible tidbits and sit upstairs in my cold, gray bedroom pouring shillings into the gas fire, munching cream crackers, eating sardines out of a can and brewing powdered coffee in toothbrush tumblers. On one of these occasions I asked Stanley how the British had managed to win the war. The ex-war correspondent let out a hoot. "Hell," he chuckled, "they were too stubborn to know they had lost it. That's how."

I was lucky to spend most of my days with my dresser, Grace Russell, sharing her cozy living rooms. She was a warm-hearted Cockney blonde who looked after the show's wardrobe and me; and she always found the best places to live.

While I shivered in my expensive hotel room Grace was cosseted in theatrical boardinghouses with hot water bottles in her bed, coal fires in her sitting room, and three home-cooked meals a day. There was no hope of my booking one of these, they were as difficult to get into as Eton. You had to put your name down at birth.

Somewhere during this trans-Siberian theater trek Tony Bushell came back to my igloo dressing room.

"Yo, I have wonderful news for you," he beamed.

"You've found a pair of longjohns for me?" I asked eagerly.

"Sorry, no clothes coupons," he said, "but Larry has the Garrick Theatre and you open on January twenty-third."

By then I was almost too numb to care. I would have been much more excited with the longjohns, or a lamb chop.

Most of all I needed a flat to go to in London after we'd finished in Cardiff. Mother, Chris, and I couldn't live in the Garrick dressing room—it didn't have a kitchen for all that baby boiling. Olivier's agent, Cecil Tennant, had been searching for one ever since we left Glasgow, but the bomb damage had left London flatless. So when Bill Kemp said he had a friend who had found me a furnished flat I was in ecstasy. To make sure I wouldn't lose it I sent one hundred dollars to Bill's friend as a deposit. Silly me.

On the weekend before our Monday opening in Cardiff I took the eight-hour foodless, heatless train to London to pick up Mother and Chris. Fortunately, Grace, the touring connoisseur, sent me off with her thermos of tea, hot water bottle, blanket, and cheese sandwiches.

Mother, fresh from her luxury voyage on the *Queen Elizabeth,* was full of *joie de vivre* and caviar and thrilled to be in Europe again. She didn't know what she was in for. Ten-month-old Chris must have known because he bawled loud and clear all the way to Cardiff.

Mother saw the play that night while Grace looked after Chris in her wardrobe room and me backstage, for my changes. I shall never forget our Cardiff opening. The whole play was received in almost stony silence. Not a laugh anywhere, and the final curtain came down to listless handclaps.

I'm sure they were only trying to keep warm. Mother came to my dressing room all wide-eyed.

"They don't think it's funny," she said.

"Yeah. I heard them not thinking it's funny."

"And you're not nearly as good as you were in New Haven," she bubbled on. "Maybe you should have gone to Chicago."

Now she tells me, I thought.

After our icy Cardiff reception the actors began to wonder if it would survive even one week in London. On Tuesday night when they peeped through the curtains at the half-empty house they were all intoning, "Born yesterday—died last night."

On Christmas Eve our two damp hotel rooms were festooned with Christopher's damp baby clothes which refused to dry because of the damp hotel rooms. Christmas Day the three of us were in our beds with flu and dysentery, and between whooping and wheezing I read Philip's Christmas letter saying how I should be there instead of here and how good wives would be home with their husbands at Christmas. It made me feel guilty and I wished he were in Cardiff, but I couldn't afford him. And Mother kept recalling the warm rooms and succulent steaks we'd enjoyed in Chicago. Christopher just wailed.

When Laurence Olivier heard how well the show wasn't going he entrained to Cardiff, saw the play and came backstage and gave us hell. We were making funny faces that weren't funny, he scolded, playing "out front" and not doing the play as he had directed it. We had better pull ourselves together before London, he said, because it was his dough and he didn't want to lose it.

"Oh dear," I wailed to Grace. "Everyone is miserable, even Mr. Olivier, and it's all my fault."

"Not to worry," said Grace. "They all sound off like that before a London opening. What you need is the two weeks' rest in your new flat. You wait—it'll be all right on the night."

Grace was right—about me needing a rest, I mean. We had two weeks before we actually opened at the Garrick, and on the train journey back to London all I could think of was

237
☆

the joy of spending them in our own cozy flat where we could cook our own meals and Chris could be warm and happy and stop howling. No more frostbound corridors to the icicled bathroom, no more dank hotel rooms, no more tasteless, bellyaching meals. It wouldn't be long now.

The snow was falling when we pulled into Paddington Station. I could see Bill Kemp's friend, whose name was Allen, waiting for us on the platform. Graciously he helped us down with all our luggage before he broke the news.

"I'm afraid something's gone wrong with your flat," he said.

"Like what?" I asked tentatively.

"It's burned down," he said. "I'm dreadfully sorry."

"Burned down? . . . Burned down?" I kept repeating. I couldn't believe it. "Where are we going to live?" I knew no hotel would have room for us at this late notice.

By now the rest of the company had all waved good-bye. Mother, who had been busy unraveling Christopher from her makeup kit, chimed in.

"Did I hear him say your flat had burned down?"

"Yes, Mother."

"How did the flat burn down?" she asked.

"How the hell should I know?"

"Yolande, you're swearing just like your father."

"Oh, shit, Mother, I'm exhausted!"

"Not to worry," said Allen, "you can stay at my place."

We climbed into a taxi and drove through the blizzard to Allen's flat. On the way he said he had found another flat for us but it wouldn't be ready and furnished until the following week.

Allen's flat turned out to be in a basement, somewhere in London. He had a coal fire in the sitting room but the bedroom we had was colder than any hotel room, and the big shock was the bathroom. It was in a shed out in the garden somewhere in the Arctic. Every time we had to go we had to put on coat, gloves, mufflers, and boots and plough through the snow. Chris was lucky, he had a pot.

We shivered all night, and first thing in the morning I telephoned Grace to report our latest disaster.

"Not to worry," she chortled cheerfully, "you can stay with me."

Within a couple of hours she had collected the three of us and taxied us and all our luggage to her semidetached house in Wembley. The fires were burning, food was cooking, our beds were filled with hot water bottles, the bathroom was inside the house, and a hot cuppa tea was brewing. Christopher gurgled, Mother forgot about the comforts of the USA, and I thrived on Grace's loving hospitality.

Then came the day of the next new flat. Allen telephoned that it was ready. Happily we kissed Grace good-bye and trundled off to our new flat, at last. It was in Sussex Gardens off the Edgware Road, and the landlord, a dancer named Buddy Bradley, was there to greet us. It was on the first floor. It had been freshly painted in turquoise. There were two bedrooms and a kitchen with a cooker. But there was no furniture. Nothing but three iron beds and a charred saxophone and some crumpled drums in the living room, remnants of the Blitz.

"I was told it was furnished," I said to Mr. Bradley.

"It is," he said. "Only it hasn't arrived yet. I'm dreadfully sorry. But not to worry."

There was nothing to do but move into the empty flat. My strikebound trunk arrived just in time for us to use it as our dining table. When our preopening rehearsals started and I gave my new address to Tony Bushell he hooted with Scarlet Pimpernel laughter.

"You can't live in Sussex Gardens," he said. "It's the tarts' district."

"Just as well," I said. "If this play isn't a hit I may have to join them."

Until then I had more than overspent my wages on hotels, and Mother and Christopher's return trips on the *Elizabeth*. This venture which had started out hopefully to become a capital gain was becoming a great fat capital loss.

"Not to worry," I told myself. The English phrase was catching.

At the theater Grace bustled around my first London star dressing room making it snug and pretty. It even had its own john—indoors. Until this play I had always shared rooms with another actress. In a way I missed the companionship. Strangely, it turned out to be the same dressing room Ernie Truex had used nineteen years earlier, in 1928, in the play *Call Me George*.

The day before the opening the stage doorman arrived with a huge bunch of roses. Grace squealed, "Cor, look at them!" They had arrived a day early. Excitedly I tore open the card. It said: "We are all so very happy for you. This is *It!* All good wishes, Fredric March."

"Fredric March!" gasped Grace.

"Yeah," I sighed, "all the way from New York."

He was doing Ruth Gordon's play *Years Ago* and must have heard of our opening from her. It was nice of him to think of someone he hardly knew.

"He was smashing in *Doctor Jekyll and Mr. Hyde*," recalled Grace. As I was admitting I had had a childhood crush on him, Larry Olivier suddenly appeared at the door and we both stopped gushing over Fredric March and stood to attention. Two photographers followed him in and took pictures of him and me looking happy. Then he clasped my hand and we hurried off to sign some papers or something at his agent's office. As his car wasn't there and there were no taxis he pulled me on to a red London bus.

Olivier knew his way around on all the public transportation. He often bused me about, to and from rehearsals, and I was always surprised that such a well-known star was able to hop on and off unrecognized. As Mr. Olivier was usually wearing a trilby hat, hornrimmed spectacles, dark blue overcoat, and carrying an umbrella, he resembled a city stockbroker more than one of the world's greatest classical actors. Maybe that was why our fellow commuters never blinked an eye.

After our rehearsal that day, when one of the world's greatest classical actors had put the play back the way he had left it in Glasgow, I took Fredric March's roses to our empty flat and placed them in front of the charred saxophone and crumpled drum set. They didn't quite hide them, but anything was an improvement.

"Oh, look at the lovely roses," said Mother as she came out of the kitchen with our weekly ration of one boiled egg each and a piece of Cheddar cheese.

"Yeah," I said, "too bad they're not dandelions. We could make a French salad and eat them."

Chris was gurgling on the iron bed in front of the trunk and I sat exhausted beside him to eat my egg and contemplate. Was this what Daddy had meant when he said, "Third time lucky. She'll be the star"?

On the morning before our last dress rehearsal Olivier was putting the finishing touches to the lighting. For one of the scenes I remember finding myself sitting on the arm of a very bony couch on my even bonier behind. He had placed me in this position and I hadn't liked it since the first rehearsal. Now was my last chance to change it.

"Please, Larry," I pleaded, "I've been so uncomfortable in this position for the whole eight weeks. Couldn't you move me now?"

Mr. Olivier's voice echoed from the stalls of the Garrick Theatre. "No, Yo," it said in soft, iron, resonant tones. "You look lovely. Never in your life will you be lit so beautifully as you are in that position."

Then we all had a nice cuppa tea.

Our last dress rehearsal was in the afternoon of the day we were opening. In the empty, silent Garrick Theatre it plodded on with clockwork precision. Larry, Vivien, Tony, and Roger were our only audience. Nothing feels quite so desolate as playing a comedy to an empty house. It's like telling jokes in a graveyard.

A couple of times I saw Vivien waving her arms trying to catch Larry's attention. But he was moving around the house from stalls to gallery to check that everything could be seen and heard from every seat.

When the final curtain came down for the last time before it was to go up again on the opening that evening, Larry gathered the cast onto the stage and gave us all the finest advice any comedy player could receive.

"Whatever you do," he said, "please do not try to do anything to make the audience laugh. I don't care if there is not one laugh in the show. Just play it for the play, as you do at rehearsal."

It helped to relax some of the tension. Countdown had started. Liftoff was in two hours.

Larry and Vivien went home to change into their evening clothes and we performers returned to our dressing rooms to sort out our telegrams and flowers which began to arrive in droves. As I had never been a leading lady before I wasn't prepared with a well-stocked bar for aftershow visitors and vases for all the bouquets of flowers. Since then I have found these items indispensable for both postoperative hospital rooms and postoperative first night dressing rooms.

Like magic, Grace produced dozens of vases for the flowers and a most welcome first night gift—a woolen vest and long woolen drawers. Grace called them knickers. We immediately put them on me to see if they could be hidden under the sexy white negligee I wore at the end of act one. With a bit of rolling up past the knees, the long knickers worked. Grace was hysterical.

"Just fancy," she giggled, "if the posh first-nighters knew you was sitting on stage all over glamorous with your long-johns on."

A telegram arrived from Ruth and Gar: WE ARE THINKING OF YOU AND WISHING YOU ALL THE LUCK YOU NEED WHICH ISN'T MUCH.

"Crumbs," said Grace, "it's from Miami."

"Our author's no fool. He's staying where it's warm."

I began wishing I was there. Anywhere but here. The butterflies were collecting in my stomach. We actors began darting in and out of each other's dressing rooms saying, "Good luck." We were all keyed up and had to keep moving. Fantastic flowers arrived from Vivien and Larry, cheering cables from Philip and the Truex family, a warming telegram from Noël Coward, and a fun cable from the Harold Lloyds saying, REMEMBER WE KNEW YOU WHEN. It was all too much. The callboy knocked on the door.

"Half hour, Miss Donlan."

Larry and Vivien popped in to wish me luck. They were both looking fabulous. He in his tails and Vivien in a jewel-encrusted Cleopatra-style evening gown. I paced up and down the dressing room like a demented cat.

"Why do we do this?" I mumbled. "What makes us want to be actors? It's crazy."

At that moment I felt a bond with these two superb artists who had had to pass this test many times before and knew exactly how it felt. They made consoling noises and as they left I remember saying to Larry, "Not to worry. It's up to us now. We won't let you down."

Mother breezed in wearing a black chiffon evening gown and a feather boa. Her deep brown eyes were sparkling with excitement.

"Now don't worry, baby girl," she smiled. "It will all be over in a couple of hours and you can have a good supper. You're getting too thin. The Maxteds have invited us to the Café de Paris. You'll enjoy that."

I didn't feel I could enjoy anything except maybe throwing up. She gave me a good luck hug before she went out front and I thought, I'm doing what she never had a chance to do, and I wondered if she would have changed places now, jitters and all.

"Quarter of an hour, Miss Donlan," the callboy knocked.

"Put your fox on," said Grace. "And here's your mink to carry. Now off you go." Grace kissed me on the cheek. "Go on. You'll be lovely."

I went on to the stage to check my props. Yes, the playing cards were in the drawer. The whisky bottle on the bar. The papers, the books, the pen. . . . Will that curtain never go up? Maybe the iron curtain will stick and we can all go home.

The audience was talking very loudly; they were first-nighters and knew each other. I could hear the programs rustling. We actors peeped through the side curtain; the theater was packed and everyone was in full evening dress.

Every star in the British theater seemed to be there. I didn't know them but Bessie Love and Michael Balfour told me who was whom. Vivien and Larry were seated in the stage box on the left. Photographers were hurrying up and down the aisles taking flash photos of the celebrities.

Backstage the stage manager was checking his lighting and curtain cues and counting all of us who were due on first in case any of us had defected.

Suddenly, the curtain was up and just as we starters walked onto the stage there was a hoot of chaotic laughter from the audience. We were surprised, no one had laughed there before. As I had no lines on my entrance I was able to glance out front and see what caused this unexpected eruption. A photographer, who had perched on the rail of the orchestra pit to photograph the Oliviers in their box, had fallen backward into the pitful of palms. And as I started up the stage staircase, the photographer's befuddled head popped up out of the palms and there was another great hoot. Hurriedly he scrambled back over the rail and the play went on.

This curtain raiser must have put them in a merry mood. From then on they rocked with glee in all the right places and didn't miss the tiniest nuance. The contact between audience and players was electric and the applause after each act was deafening.

Every time Grace zipped me into a new costume she said, "See? I told you it would be smashing in the West End."

The final curtain came down to the loudest roar of applause I have ever heard. The "Bravo!" shouts came clear through the heavy curtain, and when it went up again the audience were on their feet cheering and shouting.

As one by one we took our curtain calls I was amazed to see all those stiff-upper-lip Britishers throwing their programs in the air and shouting, "Bravo!" and yelling, "Well done!" as they stamped their feet and banged anything that would make a louder noise than clapping.

Then we all held hands together while the curtain went up and down and we listened to that rapturous noise of appreciation. I thought of Gar Kanin in Miami. If only he had been here to see how warmly his play was being received. The reception was much hotter than any sunshine could be. There was no one out there I knew except Mother. The curtain came down, then up again. The noise became louder. They were shouting something. It couldn't be "Author, Author," as they knew he wasn't there. Then I heard, "Larry! Larry! Bravo! Good show!"

Laurence Olivier walked onto the stage. He had told me that if the play went well he was going to come on and make a speech. But he didn't tell me that after he had praised and thanked all of us and the audience he was going to take my hand and lead me down to the footlights to face all these happy strangers.

I stood there, my hand in his, trying to take it all in. As though in a dream I heard continuing applause and shouts, saw the misty shimmer of the white shirts and evening dresses of the still standing audience. . . . Olivier was saying something. . . .

". . . brought her from the United States. . . . my new star. . . . enchanting. . . . memorable night. . . ."

I can only recollect snatches of what he said because my thoughts were wandering. Was this it? Shouldn't I feel elated or something?

Olivier's speech was over, and after they'd thrown more programs in the air I stood beside him and felt nothing again. It was like being alone at a football match with the crowd cheering, and suddenly you don't care which team wins because Daddy wasn't there to see it happen at last.

Where are you, James Donlan?

"Third time lucky," you said. "She'll be the star of the Donlans." Remember?

Did you hear what the man said, Daddy? I'm a star. I made it finally, Daddy, you darling old soak. All for you. And you're not there to see it. Or are you?

By God, it's lonely up here on this damn Garrick stage, in London, England. . . .

245
☆